COOL *Women,* HOT *Jobs*

...and how you can go for it, too!

Tina Schwager & Michele Schuerger

free spirit PUBLISHING®

Works for kids®

Library of Congress Cataloging-in-Publication Data

Schwager, Tina, 1964–

    Cool women, hot jobs—and how you can go for it, too! / Tina Schwager and Michele Schuerger.

      p. cm.

    Includes index.

    Summary: Profiles twenty-two women and the jobs they do, from choreographer to FBI agent, describing their education, duties, personality traits, and other factors in their career success, and gives specific ways to determine one's own future work.

    ISBN 1-57542-109-7

    1. Vocational guidance for women—United States—Juvenile literature. 2. Women—Employment—United States—Juvenile literature. 3. Young women—Case studies—Juvenile literature. 4. Achievement motivation in women—Juvenile literature. [1. Vocational guidance for women. 2. Vocational guidance. 3. Women—Employment. 4. Occupations.] I. Schuerger, Michele, 1961– II. Title.

HF5382.65 .S39 2002

650.14'082—dc21

                                                        2001040908

At the time of this book's publication, all facts and figures cited are the most current available; all telephone numbers, addresses, and Web site URLs are accurate and active; all publications, organizations, Web sites, and other resources exist as described in this book; and all have been verified. The authors and Free Spirit Publishing make no warranty or guarantee concerning the information and materials given out by organizations or content found at Web sites, and we are not responsible for any changes that occur after this book's publication. If you find an error or believe that a resource listed here is not as described, please contact Free Spirit Publishing. Parents, teachers, and other adults: We strongly urge you to monitor children's use of the Internet.

The photos of Tina Landon on pages 8 and 13 appear courtesy of GILLESTOUCAS.com; the photo of Jennifer Wegner on page 19 appears copyright Tom Jenkins, Dallas, Texas; the photo of Courtney Macavinta on page 51 appears courtesy of Snowball.com and her photo on page 55 is used courtesy of Natalie Lyon; the photo of Carol Marino on page 74 is produced by Robert Isacson/Isacson Studio and her photo on page 81 is produced by Marge Thornburgh/Creation Waits Photography; the photos of Lucy Spelman on pages 85 and 92 are used courtesy of Jessie Cohen/Smithsonian National Zoo; the photo of Maureen Holohan on page 96 appears copyright Evanston Photographic Studios; the photo of Betty Lennox on page 106 copyright 2001 NBA Entertainment, photo by Barry Gossage. Her photo on page 110 is copyright 2001 NBA Entertainment, photo by David Sherman; the photos of Kathy Mangum on pages 117 and 119 are by Jess Allen, copyright Disney Images; the photo of Maria Fernandez on page 128 appears courtesy of the FBI; the photos of Rebecca Taylor on pages 139 and 142 appear courtesy of Kaija Berzins Braus; the photos of the Ahn Trio on pages 172 and 177 appear courtesy of Arthur Elgort; the photo of Terri Cadiente on page 182 is used copyright MarkHussman.com and her photo on page 185 appears copyright 2001 Columbia TriStar Television Distribution, All Rights Reserved; and the photo of Dawn Turner Trice on page 205 is by Janet M. Sheard.

Editors: Elizabeth Verdick and KaTrina Wentzel • Assistant Editor: Douglas Fehlen • Index by Randl Ockey

Cover photo of the Ahn Trio by Arthur Elgort

10 9 8 7 6 5 4 3 2

Printed in the United States of America

Free Spirit Publishing Inc.

217 Fifth Avenue North, Suite 200

Minneapolis, MN 55401-1299

(612) 338-2068

help4kids@freespirit.com

www.freespirit.com

Dedication

For Joan,
Our loss was heaven's gain.
We hope you're proud of the newest flower in your garden.
We miss you.

Acknowledgments

We are so honored to have the opportunity to once again reach out to teenage girls with our message of believing in yourself and going after your dreams. Writing this book, like our two previous ones, has truly been a dream come true. As always, we want to thank our family and friends for hanging in there with us during the hibernation needed to finish this manuscript. Especially Grace . . . for being so patient and a constant source of inspiration. We love you Scootie.

Assembling a group of women as amazing as these isn't an easy task. It's like a treasure hunt, and each discovery is a precious jewel. But you definitely need help, and we would like to extend our heartfelt thanks to the following people who assisted us in our quest:

Darcy Winslow—NIKE; Sally Sparks, Ernest Porter, and Gwen Hubbard—FBI; Mark Pray—WNBA; Pam Healy—NBA; Stockey Clarke—Outward Bound; James Rose and Aimee Whalen—JPL; Chuck Davis, Lt. Lars Anderson, Lt. Paula Kurtz, Cpt. Ron Watrous, Lt. Eric Cox, Aaron Reed, and Chief Master Sgt. Stanley—USAF; Amy Suter—HealthSouth, Miami; Dena Hoagland—Island Dolphin Care; Michelle Bender; Ann Kaup—Anthropology Outreach Office at the Smithsonian; Joanne Rile—Joanne Rile Artists Management; Jessica Galvin; LaTanya Marble—Envy Public Relations; Miguel Melendez—Melendez Management Group; Donna Freed—Terry Hines and Associates; Carolyn Frye—ChickClick; Roger Padilla—MAO Public Relations; Elizabeth Bugdaycay; Tom Looby—the Walt Disney Company; Robert Hoage and Mike Moran—Smithsonian Institution National Zoo; and Jennifer Jones.

And, of course, many thanks to the remarkable women whose passion for their work is captured on these pages. Your enthusiasm for this project has meant a lot to us.

Contents

Introduction

If you could be anything in the whole world, what would you be?

- A fashion designer setting trends with your latest creations?

- A fighter pilot willing to protect and fight for your country?

- A professional basketball player dazzling fans with your power and grace?

If you could spend your life doing the one thing that speaks to your heart, what would you do?

- Strive to bring a sense of hope and a smile to the face of a critically ill child?

- Make a monumental scientific discovery?

- Produce a film with an important message?

The good news is that you can do any one of these things. There are thousands of job options available to young women today and many more that exist in the creative minds of entrepreneurs and visionaries. With so many amazing and wonderful careers to aspire to, the possibilities that exist for your future are endless. The sky's the limit! Nobody expects you to make such a big decision today, but there's no better time than now to start exploring your options.

Thinking about career options now will allow you to:

- **Chart Your Own Destiny.** Your future should be just that—yours! While you can get valuable input from family, friends, teachers, and others, *you* should be the one to decide what you want to do with your life. It's up to you to figure out what kind of career you'd like to have, and it's up to you to go for it! When you take responsibility for your future by researching different career options and mapping out a plan to reach your destination, you put the wheels in motion to get where *you* want to go. The more informed you are about a career, the better your chance for success.

1

- **Have Fun.** It's exciting to daydream about your future and how you'll contribute to society. Do you see yourself as a chef? A news reporter? The first female President of the United States? There's no pressure and there aren't any rules, so you're free to visualize yourself being anything you can possibly imagine. Be as silly or serious as you desire and know that no matter what your aspirations are, you won't know what's possible if you don't let yourself dream. Dreams have helped many people achieve feats that were at one time unthinkable, so stretch your imagination as far as you can!

- **Learn About Yourself.** Now is a great time to get to know yourself and think about what moves you, what's important to you, and what interests you. Spending time figuring out your likes and dislikes, as well as what your natural talents and skills are, will make it easier to determine what kind of careers match your unique attributes (skills and abilities). If you love to travel, becoming a flight attendant or a tour guide might be a fit. If you're drawn to social studies and the plight of people, becoming a lawyer or an urban planner might be worth researching. And if you're drawn to the arts, you might explore the idea of becoming a photographer, an animator, or a museum curator.

- **Discover New Possibilities.** Once you begin researching careers you think you might like to pursue, there's no telling where the journey will lead you. For instance, you may dream of becoming a basketball player with the WNBA, only to discover that the competition, travel, and intense training and dedication aren't what you had in mind. But that doesn't mean you can't have a career in sports. A little research will open up possibilities you may never have thought about, such as becoming a sports agent, a sports publicist, an athletic trainer, a sports psychologist, a coach, an orthopedic surgeon, or an exercise physiologist. New worlds will open up to you once you start looking into different career options.

- **Develop a Plan.** The sooner you start thinking about career choices, the sooner you can begin working on a plan to achieve your goals. Once you know where your interests lie, you can start investigating colleges, universities, or vocational schools (including admissions requirements and financial aid programs) that offer the type of education or training you'll need. Having an idea of what you want to do will allow you to think about the things you can do *right now*. You can apply for internships, volunteer, or go to informational interviews.

You can take electives or community courses that relate to your field of interest. Or you might even be able to land a part-time position related to a career you're interested in. Doing these things now will not only give you an edge when it's time to fill out college applications or apply for a job, they'll also help you determine if your chosen career path is *really* the path you want to follow. Whatever your goals in life may be, having a plan of action will help you reach them.

What Do You Want to Be When You Grow Up?

The question, "What do you want to be when you grow up?" is one of the oldest in the book. When you hear it, does something pop into your head? Do you know immediately what you want to do and can't imagine doing anything else? Or do you cringe, with a big "Ugh," because you haven't got the slightest clue? Relax. At this point in your life no one expects you to have your future career plans set in stone. All you need to be doing now is starting to think about the different options you might enjoy once you graduate from high school or college. You don't have to commit to anything, just consider the many different careers you might like to pursue.

You have the potential to do something great with your life—to make a difference in the world somehow. It could be through entertaining, caretaking, leading, or fixing. It could be through researching, managing, or creating. One contribution isn't better than another, they're just different. That's the great thing about discovering and pursuing a job that interests you, it's meant to fit *your* personality and *your* special talents and skills, not those of your family or friends, and not what society says. There's an exciting career out there with your name on it, something that will give you the chance to express who you are, something that's right for *you*.

Thinking about a career—let alone researching one—may seem overwhelming when you're unaware of all the amazing jobs that are available, especially if you're not sure what your interests and talents are. What can make it easier is hearing firsthand from women already working in cool fields. Finding out about the journeys they took, their on-the-job experiences, and the education and skills needed for their professions will give you the inside scoop about their particular careers. You might become motivated to pursue something similar or inspired to discover your own dreams. You might feel that extra push to take a step toward your career goals. Or you might become excited about all the doors that are open to you. Regardless, figuring out which "hot job" might be worth pursuing becomes a lot more fun!

About This Book

Part 1 of *Cool Women, Hot Jobs* introduces you to 22 women who have jobs that they love. All of them have interesting and challenging careers that they're incredibly passionate about. The fields they work in are just as varied and diverse as the women themselves. Some are famous for their accomplishments, like Tina Landon, who choreographs the latest and greatest dance moves for recording artists like Janet Jackson, Christina Aguilera, and Ricky Martin. Some are making important contributions that are less visible to the world, like Laura Hogg, who works for the Starlight Children's Foundation, granting once-in-a-lifetime wishes to seriously ill children. And others have careers that you may never have thought about, like Outward Bound instructor Robyn Reed, who planned and carried out a cross-country bike ride to celebrate girls and women and raise their self-esteem. The achievements of these women demonstrate the unlimited potential that exists for girls like you to become anything you desire.

When you read about the talented women in this book, you'll get a feel for their jobs and experiences. You'll learn that hot jobs can be hard jobs, that dream jobs aren't always "dreamy," and that the bottom line is feeling that you've chosen a career that's right for you. You'll have the opportunity to learn about these women as individuals—who each one is, why she chose her profession, and why she loves it so much. And at the end of every story, you'll also discover more about each job including:

- good and not-so-good aspects

- dress code

- how many hours a week it takes to get the job done

- what the work environment is like

- education and skills needed to get hired

- personality traits best suited for the position

- perks and rewards of the job

- list of things you can do right now to explore the field yourself

Each story is wrapped up with a few words of heartfelt wisdom followed by some resources to help you continue to learn more about each career.

But then what? Exactly how *does* a girl figure out what she wants to be when she grows up? Or for that matter, what she wants to do in her life at this very moment? Part 2 of *Cool Women, Hot Jobs* will help you learn about yourself so you can define your dreams and set goals to achieve them. Whether you decide you want to try a new sport, improve your grades, or someday add the letters M.D. after your name, Part 2 will help you learn how to reach those goals. Whatever your aspirations may be—now or in the future—they can be achieved if you know how to go about them. Part 2 gives you fun projects and tips that will help you get on your way, including:

- developing the qualities and skills that provide you with the keys to success

- how to keep a journal and why it's important to get to know who you are

- how to figure out what you might want to do

- the importance of setting goals and how to come up with a simple plan you can follow to reach your goals

- information about internships, volunteer activities, and other foot-in-the-door opportunities

- what it takes to reach for the stars

Part 2 also will provide you with additional resources to help you get where you want to go. Organizations, books, and Web sites are included so you can find information on careers, improving your study habits, reaching goals, getting an internship, or taking an extracurricular class about something that excites you.

* * * * *

Cool Women, Hot Jobs is written just for you. You'll find inspiration, information, and some of the tools you'll need to figure out what you want to do with your life. It's meant to pump you up, help you explore your interests and talents, and pique your curiosity about the endless career options that are available to you. It's easier to shut the door on doubt and uncertainty and believe in your amazing potential when you have a cheering section shouting "You can do it!" or "Don't give up," instead of, "That'll take years," or "You'll never be able to do that." This book, the amazing women highlighted, and we (the authors!) are that cheering section. We're rooting for you all the way!

Going after your dreams can give you a real sense of power, so get ready to uncover the possibilities. Our hope is that *Cool Women, Hot Jobs* will convince you that your dreams are reachable, your interests are commendable, and your future holds no limits!

We'd love to hear about your career aspirations and the steps you're taking to reach them. Write to us at:

Tina and Michele
c/o Free Spirit Publishing Inc.
217 Fifth Avenue North, Suite 200
Minneapolis, MN 55401-1299

Or send an email to:
help4kids@freespirit.com

Every girl has a dream or two tucked away in her heart. No matter how grand your dreams may be, you have the ability to make them come true!

Tina and Michele

PART 1

COOL *Women,* HOT *Jobs*

HOT *Job…*

Choreographer

As a choreographer, I've helped create the "signature grooves" for many famous recording artists, including Janet Jackson, Jennifer Lopez, Ricky Martin, Christina Aguilera, Britney Spears, and Marc Anthony.

Home Base: Los Angeles, California

Number of Years in the Field: 10

Personal Philosophy: "Learn as much as you can. Try to take in everything around you. But most importantly, be true to yourself."

I've been dancing my whole life, so dancing for a living has always felt like something I was meant to do. For me, it's as natural as getting dressed in the morning. There was a time when I thought I wanted to be an architect or a flight attendant, but what I realized is that dancing is in my soul. I love being able to tell a story through dance and really, that's what choreography is all about. There are many times an audience can't understand all the lyrics to a song and I feel like it's my job to make sure they understand its meaning through the movements I create.

My parents started sending me to dance lessons when I was three and I loved it. I was the kind of kid who wanted to try anything that came along; I took jazz, tap, and ballet lessons—anything that was offered at the studio I attended. I also wanted to enter every talent show there was (I guess you could say I've always been a performer!). It's my natural personality to be a leader so I often would gather a group of friends— whoever wanted to dance with me—and just take charge. It wasn't even anything I thought twice about. If we were listening to the latest hit song and somebody said, "Hey, let's come up with a dance . . . who wants to make it up?" I was always the first one to pipe in, "I will!"

Even though my heart was set on dancing professionally, it wasn't easy to get started. After graduating from high school I started going to auditions, but it took almost two years before I landed my first big job— dancing in Michael Jackson's video for the song "Smooth Criminal." While auditioning and hoping for a big break, I still needed to support myself, and my experience as a cheerleader (from seventh to eleventh grade) ended up paying off. In 1984, I survived two days of tough auditions and hundreds of cuts to land a gig (job) as a Laker Girl, the cheerleading squad that performs during games and at halftime for the NBA's (National Basketball Association) Los Angeles Lakers. Being a Laker Girl turned out to be much more valuable than I ever could have imagined. It got my dancing career moving in a new and exciting direction.

One of the women on the squad was an up-and-coming choreographer named Paula Abdul. Paula was working on a music video for the song "What Have You Done for Me Lately" by Janet Jackson, and she asked me to be one of her dancers. Even though I had already danced with Michael Jackson, I still had to go through several auditions before I was hired for the Janet Jackson video. At the time, Janet was just starting to become popular as a recording artist, so the thrill of working with her came more from the fact that she was Michael's sister than anything else. That video was the first time Janet and I worked together, and we hit it off really well. Over the next few years, I auditioned for and danced in several of Janet's other videos, which helped her get to know me and my style.

But just because I was in a few videos didn't mean I had it made. In between dance jobs I worked at a retail store five days a week and at a restaurant two nights a week. I also managed a dance studio for my sister and cleaned her house for 25 dollars just to have extra money. I had all these jobs at the same time as I was auditioning and performing in videos! In 1989, Janet asked me to join her on her "Rhythm Nation" tour. Most of the other performers on the tour were men; I was one of only two female dancers. While we were on the road, Janet told me she wanted to incorporate newer moves and a more feminine image into her upcoming video "Love Will Never Do," and she asked for my help. Of course I was glad to.

I ended up becoming Janet's choreographer for the "Love Will Never Do" project as well as several more after that, including her next two world tours. For me, the choreography side of it came hand-in-hand with performing. It's not like that for everybody. Some people make a conscious decision to stop dancing and start choreographing. But for me, they were one and the same. Once I started working with Janet Jackson, both as a dancer and a choreographer, my career took off.

Dancing from the Heart

A lot of my dance moves come from figuring out what the song's lyrics mean to me, and then trying to tell the story through movement. I talk to the artist about it, too, but when I'm working things out, it's always crucial that I have the lyric sheet in front of me to help me find meaning in the words. Then I imagine the audience and try to create moves that will help them actually "see" this meaning. Whether it's a video or a live performance, it can sometimes be difficult to understand the words of a song. For example, if someone is sitting far from the stage at a concert, they may only hear music (not necessarily all of the words) and see movement. It's my job to help the audience understand the songs they hear through the dancing they see.

I also think it's important to have a lot of versatility as a dancer, and the way to get that is by experiencing a lot of different styles. Over the years I've taken classes in jazz, tap, ballet, and Polynesian dance, in addition to studying Flamenco and other dance styles. At one point in my career I felt myself starting to get stale, so I decided to take some African dance classes. For the first time in my life I knew what it felt like to be completely lost in a classroom. African dancing is much looser and wilder than the "controlled" style of dance I've always done, especially jazz and ballet. It was a scary place for me to be, but it actually helped me gain a better understanding of why people are sometimes afraid to let go, why they feel insecure or nervous about moving their bodies.

Making Music Videos

Choreographing music videos is a demanding but rewarding part of my job. While some things like schedules are pretty similar, each video is a completely different piece of work. Sometimes an artist or director will have an idea about the direction they want the video to take. If that's the case, then my job is about making their vision a reality. But on most projects, I'm given almost total creative freedom, which is great. It allows me to come up with an interpretation and a vision of my own for the song.

When I start a new project I like to get the music early on. Not too early, though, because then I'll just procrastinate . . . three to four days before rehearsal starts is perfect. Then, when it's time for me to buckle down and really get serious about creating, I have to literally leave my house. At home there are too many distractions—I'll end up playing with my dog or doing chores like washing dishes. So what I usually do is take the music and go to the gym.

While I work out on some type of cardio machine (like a bike, treadmill, or stair climber), I'll put on my headphones and listen to that one song over and over and over. I'm sure it looks like I'm having an attack or something, because I'll be dancing on the treadmill and tripping over myself, or sitting on the bike with my arms flying all over the place! Once I've listened to the song enough times, I'll get a flood of ideas, sometimes so many that I don't know which direction to take. As I listen more, certain movements, feelings, and ideas continue to repeat themselves, and I start to decide what movements to keep. It's kind of like I'm creating a basic shell or an outline for the story I'll end up telling through my dance moves. Then, once I figure out what my body physically wants to do with the music, I'll ask myself, "What's the song about?" I already have the physical aspect of the song going, so I start to figure out how to get the words out through my body.

Usually, at some point during this process, I'll get to a plateau when the music's playing but my mind starts to wander and I start thinking about what I want to eat for lunch or something. So rather than get frustrated, I'll just stop. I leave it alone and go do something completely different. After a break, I'll listen again, and typically this is when things really start to stick out: one guitar lick (a catchy guitar part or solo), one part of the music, or even a single word will inspire me. And that's the part of the song where I'll start creating something solid. Sometimes it's the beginning of the song, sometimes it's the middle or the end. But wherever it is, that's where I begin putting movement to it. After I've got the first couple of steps—which are always the hardest—the rest just flows.

On the first day of rehearsal I usually sit down with the artist and go over the ideas I have, as well as where I see the choreography going (the director will come in on the second or third day so he or she can see more of the finished product; directors often get inspiration from seeing exactly what they will be shooting). As rehearsals continue, the routine evolves and changes because I get new inspiration by watching the dancers. I'm the type of person who likes to conserve my energy, so I don't like to spend a lot of time and effort creating a new dance, only to get to rehearsal and find that it doesn't look right on a particular person. So what I do is start with a chunk, teach that to everyone, then decide from there what is and isn't working. While this process is going on, the music plays through the parts I don't have figured out, which is how things start to flow for me. While this might sound a bit risky, it's pretty common for choreographers to start a project with an unfinished routine and piece it together as they go along.

We generally have three to five days of rehearsals and then we have to shoot. Personally, I like five days better, because that leaves more room for unexpected things that might crop up, for example, problems with the clothing the dancers are wearing. A lot of times the females are dressed in tight clothing or high heels, both of which can make certain dance moves more challenging. Another potential problem is that the stage we use to shoot or do a live performance on is usually not the same as what we rehearse on. In a dance studio, where most rehearsals take place, the floor is wooden and smooth. For a video or when we're on tour, you never know what surface you're going to end up with. When we did the video for Janet Jackson's song "Together Again," the ground was supposed to resemble ruins in a desert, so the floor that was built for the video shoot was extremely uneven. It had grooves between the tiles and sand covering it, so it would blend in with the "desert" surroundings. Our shoes kept getting caught between the grooves and we were slipping on the sand. This was a very difficult shoot and completely unexpected. You can't rehearse for stuff like that.

Touring with Janet Jackson

Two experiences come to mind when I think of how amazing it is to do what I do, and both of them happened while touring with Janet Jackson. One was during her "Janet" tour in 1994. We were in Manila, the capital of the Philippines, to perform a concert. I'd never been there, so I didn't know anything about the country or its economy. I discovered that 50 percent of the population lives in poverty, and years of conflict between the government and communist rebels had resulted in a constant military presence.

I got my first glimpse of Manila's living conditions as we drove to our hotel from the airport. On one side of the street were million dollar homes. On the other side, people were living in shacks, side-by-side in very crowded conditions. Some were actually living on the ground with tin coverings for roofs.

Once we arrived at the hotel, we weren't allowed to leave because it wasn't considered safe. There were even guards with machine guns at the fast-food restaurants. At first I was a little freaked out by all of this, because it wasn't something I was used to. But the people who lived there seemed to take it in stride. That's the way they lived . . . it was a fact of life for them.

The place where we were performing wasn't very nice, either. For starters, there wasn't any air conditioning and we were all sweating like crazy just getting dressed. Sometimes we had to wear three outfits at a time (called underdressing) for when we perform three numbers in a row without time in between to do a full costume change. It was incredibly hot—close to one hundred degrees—and we all had three layers of clothing on. To top it off, bats were flying around the so-called arena. Believe me, a lot of groaning and complaining was going on back-stage about how uncomfortable we were, all the clothes we had on, and how the sweat was pouring off of us.

But once we got onstage, none of that mattered. There were all these kids in the audi-ence, and when I looked into their eyes, it was important to me that the next two hours be a great experience for them. Performing for them made me want to cry. Seeing

Tina shows her dancers the moves.

how other people lived, especially when they had so little compared to what we have in the United States, made me feel lucky for what I had, where I lived, and who I was. I realized that what I did for a living had the poten-tial to bring a lot of joy to others, and it didn't feel like a job anymore.

Another experience that had a strong effect on me happened on Janet's "Velvet Rope" tour in 1998. It was a very grueling tour; we trav-eled for about ten months with very little downtime. Our very last show was in Hawaii. We were on this open-air stage in a not-so-fancy venue, and at one point I looked out and it was pouring rain. Through the down-pour it looked like every single person in the audience had turned on a lighter. Some actually had lighters and some had glow sticks that they had purchased at the concert. Stage lights can be so bright that it makes it hard to see the audience, especially at night. Sometimes when we look out at a stadium, all we see is darkness. But at this concert, with everyone holding so many lights, it was possible to see just how many people were actually there. The combination of that and the fact that it was raining made it seem like the audience was literally glowing with appreciation!

We were dancing and Janet was singing and the rain was coming down hard. Not one person got up to leave. I almost started sobbing right in the middle of the number. To do what I do because I love it is a wonderful feeling. But it takes everything up a notch to know that other people get enjoyment from what I do as a performer. The fact that those fans stayed in spite of the rain showed how much they appreciated us. It made it worth every ache and pain and stress it took to get through that tour.

A Passion from Within

You wouldn't believe how many people come up to me and say, "Oh, your moves are great. You taught me everything I know." When I quizzically ask them "When?" they respond by telling me that they learned moves from my videos. I find it interesting that a lot of people think they can learn choreography from watching videos. I'm not opposed to learning moves on TV, but when that's the *only way* somebody's learning, he or she is missing out on the discipline that's taught in a dance class. In a class, dancers experience what it means to dance with others and how to learn a routine quickly. When you're rehearsing for a video or show you don't get to rewind and take your time to learn a move or a routine. You have to pick it up on the spot, very quickly. Being in an actual dance environment, as opposed to imitating dancers in a video, is the best way to develop that skill.

Another thing that someone misses out on when picking up moves from TV is the explanation behind those moves. Understanding the motivation behind a movement is a pretty big deal. My dancers laugh at me all the time because I'm always giving them verbal examples of dance moves that are aggressive: "I want you to push your arm out like you just socked it through a wall." It's true that my expressions are extreme, but it's the only way I can explain exactly what I want them to do. And when they get it, they dance like it's in their soul because they know *why* they're doing it. It's very important to understand the motivation behind your movements, and you can't get that from watching a video. It comes from studying dance with teachers who know how to draw out what's already inside of you.

Dancing is a tough business, and the more training you have, the better your chances are of success. Years of professional training as well as my stubbornness are part of what's made me successful in my career. Anytime you go to an audition or do something creative, you're putting yourself on the line. And if you're too sensitive, you'll endure a lot of heartache. I don't listen when people tell me I can't do something. I think I'm still sensitive to what people say, but because my family is strong and I was raised to be strong, I've learned to roll with the punches.

To me, having the career I have is a true blessing. It's very difficult to explain the power of performing, to be able to express yourself and feel really good about it. Anytime you can pursue something that you enjoy and that makes you feel good is a gift. But being able to do the thing that you *love* and extending that feeling to others magnifies the significance by a thousand percent.

A Behind-the-Scenes Look at the Job

Favorite Part: The freedom to create is the coolest part of my job. Being able to see my creation come to life, like a seed that has bloomed, is a wonderful experience. I start with this tiny idea, and after a lot of work and practice, I'm onstage and hundreds of thousands of people all over the world are watching it come to life. It's amazing that a little idea that flickered to life inside of me created fireworks in thousands of other people.

Least Favorite Part: The hours and traveling in this business can be really, really grueling. For example, when I was Jennifer Lopez's choreographer for her 2000 tour promoting her new single and album, we first flew from Los Angeles to New York for a radio show (which is a concert promoted by a radio station), then got on a plane at 11 P.M. and flew to Europe. When we arrived, we went straight from the airport to a television station where we were appearing later—without stopping for any food or anything—and basically sat there for about six hours. Then we had a half hour to go to our hotel, shower, eat, and return to the TV station for the show where Jennifer and the dancers performed the song. This went on for the next six days in *five* different countries. To top it off, I had a horrible head cold the entire time! But even at times like that, I'm still so thankful, because no matter how bad things get, there isn't anything else I'd rather be doing.

Hours: Rehearsals for a live show are usually six to eight hours long. I prefer six—and since I make the schedule, that's usually what we do. You can rehearse for 12 hours, but I've found that you're only going to get six quality hours out of people, so it's better to just work six and make everybody happy. But on tours, as we get closer to opening night, rehearsals tend to get longer because we're in "full production," meaning the sound, lighting, and stage cues all have to be right. It's much more than just rehearsing the dance, and all those things take time to perfect. It's part of my job to be involved with that process.

Video shoots, depending on the director, typically range from 12 to 18 hours a day. The start time depends on whether we're indoors or outdoors, but it's usually around 7 A.M. and we can go until around 3 A.M. the next day. There is generally a turnaround time of 10 hours, which means you get at least 10 hours between the time you leave and the time you have to come back, but this doesn't always happen. So we shoot 12 to 18 hours, go home, rest, then come back. This can typically go on for up to five days.

Dress Code: This is one of the great things about my job. As far as rehearsals go, dancers can wear whatever they want, whatever's comfortable. I usually wear sweats, as big and baggy as I can get them. But for me, the most important thing is to wear proper shoes. I wear tennis shoes in rehearsals, something that's going to get me through the day. I got tired of wearing "fashionable" shoes that weren't necessarily comfortable (like high heels) and then being in pain or ruining my knees because I wasn't wearing the right shoes to rehearsal.

On video shoots or in a show, a wardrobe department decides what we wear. Sometimes we underdress, which means wearing as many as three outfits at once. If we're doing three numbers in a row and there isn't time to change, we just pull off one outfit and the next one is underneath. But as far as the clothing itself, you usually get stuck having to put on something you'd never wear in a million years and try to dance in it. The clothes are always too tight and too short, and the shoes' heels are always too high. Always.

Work Environment: I prefer to rehearse in a studio that's designed for dancing (meaning it has a wooden floor and mirrors), but sometimes the production company has us rehearse with the band. Even if I'm not going to be at a dance studio, I still demand wooden floors and mirrors because they're crucial for dancers. Wooden floors have a "spring" to them, which lessens the chance of injury. Of course, when you're performing you're not always going to be on the ideal floor, but you're also not pounding away for eight hours a day. And mirrors are a must no matter how great a dancer is. The entire choreographing process goes more smoothly and is more unified when people can watch themselves perform.

On tour, all of the stages are generally the same. We stay in hotels but the stage is most like "home" because it's where we are every day and it's the one place that looks familiar no matter what city we're in.

Education/Skills: It's not necessary to have a formal education in dance to get into this field, but you definitely have to take classes, preferably as many different ones as you can. Versatility is extremely important. People ask me, "How do you always make things look so different?" If I only studied one style, that would be the only thing to come out of me. I hated ballet, but I still did it, and I'm thankful I stuck with it. Ballet really is the foundation; it's like the weight lifting of dance. It may not be the most fun part, but it's the part that builds the strength you need to excel at everything else.

Personal Qualities: As a choreographer you're in charge, so leadership is an important quality to have. I consider myself the mother of everybody; it's my responsibility to make sure all of the dancers have what they need, stand up for them, and help them grow in their profession. They're the ones I have to nurture and also keep in check. If somebody messes up, it always reflects back on the leader.

I've also found it beneficial to be willing to collaborate and compromise. You have to be open and able to work with people because there are so many different personalities and creative minds that choreographers and dancers deal with. When I work on a video, I'm not only working for the artist (who has particular ideas) but also with the director of the video, who has his or her own ideas, too.

Professionalism is another important quality, both in terms of style and attitude. If you have the right attitude—you're friendly and willing to work hard—the rest comes pretty naturally (like being on time, being polite, and learning quickly). Sometimes professionalism actually has more to do with getting hired for a job than dancing ability.

Perks and Rewards: You get to see some really incredible places in this line of work. On the "Velvet Rope" tour I flew to Brunei, a tiny country in Southeast Asia, and performed for the Sultan's niece. I got to see the royal grounds and learn about Brunei culture. It was incredible. And another perk, we sometimes get to keep the clothes we wear in a video shoot!

HOT TIPS

- Expose yourself to as many different types of dancing as possible such as jazz, ballet, salsa, hip hop, modern, tap, and Hawaiian by taking classes, going to dance performances, or watching videos.

- Get whatever training you can, either formal schooling, studio classes, community education classes, or seminars. If dancing is your passion, you can never learn enough!

- Try several different teachers. Each one will have something to offer you and you may find someone who's truly inspiring.

- Go to a club (if you're under 18 or 21, check the phone book for under-age clubs in your area) and learn the latest dance moves. A lot of ideas are out there; sometimes you can gather them from people who aren't formally trained.

Take care of your body by exercising regularly, eating right, and getting plenty of rest. As a dancer, your body is your tool, and you have to treat it right in order to get the best from it.

WORDS OF WISDOM

If choreography is something that you're interested in as a career, first ask yourself why you want to do it. Is it because you've seen it on TV and it looks like fun? Or is it because it's in your heart and it would be the right path for you to follow? There's a big difference. It isn't about the fame and it isn't about doing the video, it's about doing what truly inspires you. And if dance is something that truly, truly inspires you, then you need to go for it 100 percent. It isn't easy. The hours are long; you work before the dancers arrive and after they leave. It's your responsibility to find the right dancers for the job, the ones that can execute the choreography and get along with others. And if one of them isn't working out, you're the one that has to fire them. You have to be involved with every aspect of what's going on, even with wardrobe; the stylist has to know what you need and what is going to work for the particular number. The overall concept of the song is basically your design and you have to make sure it comes out the way you want it to. This is a really tough business and you can't do it halfway.

Find Out More!

Conversations with Choreographers by Svetlana McLee Grody and Dorothy Daniels Lister (Portsmouth, NH: Heinemann Publishing, 1996). This book offers interviews with the best choreographers of Broadway, film, and television. Read about how the most successful dancers and choreographers in the business got started.

Dance Magazine
111 Myrtle Street, Suite 203 • Oakland, CA 94607 • (510) 839-6060
www.dancemagazine.com
Discover features, interviews and profiles, and informative articles about shows and performances.

Tina Landon's Web site
www.tinalandononline.com
Tina's Web site details her latest accomplishments and upcoming auditions. Read her biography and several interviews.

Egyptologist

At the University of Pennsylvania Museum, I'm a research specialist in the Egyptian Section, meaning I do research on our collection, teach classes, plan exhibits, and maintain an inventory of all the pieces in the Egyptian Section, making sure things are numbered and safely stored. I also participate in digs at various sites in Egypt.

Home Base: Philadelphia, Pennsylvania

Number of Years in the Field: 13

Personal Philosophy: "If you love something and set your heart on it, you can make it happen."

I think a lot of people have a fascination with Egypt. They don't seem to know why, but so many people I talk to say, "Oh, when I was little I loved mummies, and I used to read all these books about ancient Egypt." For some reason, this middle eastern country has a way of capturing the imagination . . . maybe it's the mystery of it.

I consider myself fortunate because my work revolves around unraveling, understanding, and appreciating this mystery. As an Egyptologist I get to literally dig up Egypt's history when I'm doing fieldwork and then immerse myself in the findings back at the University of Pennsylvania Museum. I love that my career allows me to become involved with such an amazing civilization.

Part of my work as an Egyptologist is being a keeper. A keeper, at least at our museum, is someone who works in a particular section or with a particular collection. I work in the Egyptian Section and part of my job as a keeper is doing curatorial responsibilities, such as researching the material in the collection, answering questions and assisting researchers, writing labels for objects on display, and planning exhibits. I also work with our exhibits department to ensure that the objects on display in our galleries are in good condition.

Another aspect of my job is collection management, which means I monitor our inventory. I keep track of any objects that travel inside the building (for exhibitions, photography, or research) or out of the building (if an object is loaned out) and maintain records of all of the pieces in the collection. We have more than 40,000 Egyptian objects at the museum, and less than 5,000 of them are on display. The rest are in our storage areas. Knowing where all of our Egyptian items are located is important because researchers may contact our museum for help with a project (for example, they may want to see all of our mummified cats), and it's my responsibility to know where to find what they need and determine what information is available for them.

In July 2000, I was given the new responsibility of a Research Specialist in the Egyptian Section. Now, in addition to my responsibilities as a keeper, I'm also doing a lot of research and planning for the reinstallation of our Egyptian exhibit that's currently underway. Our existing Egyptian galleries were installed in 1926 and haven't been changed significantly since 1956! The expansion we're working on will increase the number of artifacts on display and present the ones we already exhibit in a new, dynamic, interactive way. In order for this to happen, a lot of research needs to take place; we have to decide what the story line of the exhibit will be (or the context in which everything will be displayed), select the artifacts to be included, and research the chosen pieces so we can write label copy, text panels, teacher's guides, and other material for the new displays.

Keeping a Record of Egyptian Artifacts

One of the museum's primary goals is to educate the public about world cultures, art, and history; the objects in our museum make it possible for people to experience things they ordinarily wouldn't be able to see. The museum also serves the academic world. Researchers from around the world visit our collections on a daily basis. Students at the University of Pennsylvania use the collections for research and class work. In fact, many classes are taught right in the museum. The museum also is responsible for the objects it houses. Conservators are people at the museum who carefully monitor the conditions of the objects to make sure that they're safe and not deteriorating. If we don't take care of the objects, we'll lose them. These objects are part of history, and once they're gone, we can never replace them.

This is especially true in the Egyptian collection because obtaining new objects is very rare. When there's an excavation in Egypt, none of the things we discover can be taken out of the country; according to Egyptian law everything has to remain there. It used to be that when you excavated in

Egypt, there was a division of finds. The foreign mission and the Egyptian government would split up the objects that were found during an excavation. Some objects would leave the country while others remained in Egypt. Now everything remains in Egypt. The Egyptians are very interested in preserving and protecting their cultural heritage and we, as foreigners working in Egypt, are very fortunate to be able to go there and do excavations.

Today, if our section of the museum gets new material, it's generally an item that's been donated to the museum from, say, someone whose aunt went to Egypt back when it was possible to buy antiquities. And occasionally, under certain circumstances, the museum will purchase an object. Any new object that arrives has to be accessioned, meaning that specific information is recorded in our computerized inventory such as the type of artifact it is, where it came from (its provenance), what it's made out of (its material), measurements, and a general description. As the keeper, compiling the accession records is my responsibility.

Once all that's done, research on the piece begins. First we compare the item to similar pieces that might be in our collection or other collections around the world. Then, any inscriptions or text on it are translated, which is my area of expertise. Right now, along with a colleague, I'm researching a papyrus (a written scroll made from a papyrus plant) housed in our collection that contains a previously unknown mythological story about the goddess Anat. Using resources in our museum library and on my computer, I look up each symbol to figure out what it means, then search for similar stories that were written in the same language that might be preserved on other papyri. The whole process is kind of like being a detective, tracking down the missing pieces of an ancient puzzle.

I find ancient Egyptian languages to be fascinating, and it's really exciting to be able to read and write hieroglyphics (the picture-language everyone thinks of as typical "ancient Egyptian writing"). The language classes I took in college were among the most challenging of all my courses—there are several hundred hieroglyphs that you have to memorize and that's just the beginning! There are also several different languages (such as Coptic, which mixes Greek and Egyptian scripts), different phases of languages (for example, Middle Egyptian hieroglyphs, considered the classical phase), and different scripts (such as hieratic and Demotic, which is like a shorthand version of hieroglyphs) used in those languages that were adapted and modified throughout the ancient Egyptian era. The language classes were also enjoyable. I especially enjoyed learning the Demotic script (which everyone says looks like chicken scratches); literature written in that script became my passion and I eventually wrote my dissertation on a Demotic topic. Deciphering and working with ancient Egyptian languages is incredible, a specialty I'm so happy I've worked to develop.

Digging Up the Past

Going on digs is a really fun aspect of being an Egyptologist, but it's physically grueling; the days are long, it's terribly hot, and you're standing, squatting, or walking the whole time. Depending on where you're working, it can also be a challenge just getting to the site. For example, the first dig I ever went on was at a site called Bersheh, and we had to climb up and down a cliff for half an hour at the beginning and end of every day just to get to and from the site.

I've worked on field projects at three different sites in Egypt, and each one is a little different.

Inside the burial chamber of the tomb of Ihy at Saqqara.

The team I was on in Bersheh stayed on one side of the Nile River in a hotel in the small village of Mallawi. Sounds pretty snazzy, except that the "hotel" didn't have plumbing and rarely had electricity! Each day we took a ferryboat across the Nile and piled into a pickup truck that drove us out to the low desert and dropped us off at the base of a steep hill leading up to the high desert. At this level, a relatively flat terrace housed a number of large tombs that were built for provincial governors almost 4,000 years ago. The site's amazing because the tombs are literally cut into the cliffs. At some point in time, a terrible earthquake collapsed many of the tombs. Because of this, we sometimes only had enough room to crawl into the tombs on our bellies! The tombs originally were beautifully decorated with carved and painted scenes and texts, which was why we were there—to copy the decorations.

Another site I've been to (about five or six times) is Saqqara. Our accommodations for this dig are like night and day compared to Bersheh; we stay at the Saqqara Palm Club. But the best part is that it's just a 10-minute walk to the dig site. If we didn't stay there, we'd have to stay in

Cairo and drive 90 minutes there and back every day . . . so we make the sacrifice and stay at a fancy hotel instead!

The other project I've worked on is more typical of what excavation life is *really* like. It's at a site called Abydos, located in the southern part of Egypt. As a foreign investigator, you need a concession (permission) granted by the Supreme Council of Antiquities (part of the Egyptian government) to work at a particular site, and the University of Pennsylvania (Penn) has had a concession at Abydos since 1966.

In the late 1960s, Penn built a dig house at Abydos, a relatively small U-shaped compound constructed in the same traditional mud-brick style of architecture as most of the village houses. The bricks are made of mud and are dried in the sun, then whitewashed with a sort of plaster to protect them from melting or eroding. Along one arm of the "U" compound are the sleeping areas, which are a series of domed rooms. The idea is that the high, concave ceilings create natural air conditioning, drawing the heat inside the dome to cool off the room. It doesn't work, though. I was there in June and it was horribly hot! We sleep on jariid beds, which are like primitive wicker cots covered by bug-ridden mattresses (the first time I was there, the whole field team wore flea collars on their ankles). And there's more: the toilet is a bucket and the shower is a metal drum mounted up high with a pipe sticking out of it where the water streams out.

The back part of the "U" consists of the kitchen, eating area, and a small sitting room where people can relax after work. A house staff of local people cooks our meals and manages the place. The food isn't bad, but variety isn't something you enjoy while you're there. Basically, we eat combinations of boiled chicken, potatoes, and tomatoes.

The rest of the compound consists of work and storage rooms, where artifacts such as pottery, statuary, jewelry, and amulets (inscribed charms) are processed as they come out of the field. Whatever is found is brought to the house, sorted, drawn or photographed, and then stored. Some items are not fully processed within one season, so people will do further study on them when they return the next season.

There's usually a fairly large team in the field, consisting of different specialists. The excavators or site supervisors oversee the workmen and do some of the actual digging, while a photographer takes pictures of the excavation for the record, as well as of each artifact that is discovered. Surveyors map out the entire dig site ahead of time and, as we work, they constantly revise their plans of the area. The other team members at the site take care of the artifacts that are discovered in their area of expertise. Pottery specialists process the sherds, which are broken pieces of pottery.

They can tell what the original vessel looked like, what material it is, and what time period it came from, just from a single bit of broken pottery! Faunal specialists take care of any animal bones that come up. From these remains they determine what kind of animals were eaten or left as offerings in the temples. Archaeobotanists evaluate any plant remains. And finally, epigraphers and artists draw and record all the objects and inscriptions found at the site (both scenes and texts). Using an enormous piece of tracing paper, everything on the walls of the tomb is copied, including hieroglyphic text, decorations, and any damage that may have occurred. For our project at Saqqara, I'm the chief epigrapher, and at Abydos I work as an epigrapher and artist.

As an epigrapher and an artist, I draw artifacts and inscriptions that are found during excavations of tombs and temples, anything from beads to statuary to pottery. It is important to make an accurate drawing of these objects (and take photographs) since we can't bring them back to the States. Sometimes the walls of temples have been destroyed and all we have left to work with are blocks of stone from the walls or small fragments with pieces of decorations on them. Trying to reconstruct how the walls originally looked becomes like a jigsaw puzzle.

One of the greatest field experiences I ever had involved climbing the Great Pyramid, which is the original burial place and tomb of King Khufu (sometimes he is called Cheops). Khufu came to the throne around 2551 B.C. and reigned for about 30 years. The Great Pyramid is the largest of the three big pyramids built at the site of Giza, near modern Cairo. This pyramid was originally 481 feet tall, contains more than 2,300,000 blocks of stone, and is one of the seven ancient wonders of the world. The inside of the pyramid contains several chambers and sloping passageways. The inside is not decorated and was robbed of its contents in antiquity.

Climbing the Great Pyramid used to be something tourists would do all the time. I remember seeing old Victorian etchings of women in their giant skirts being helped up to the top of the huge structure by Egyptian guides and thinking how incredible it would be to do that. Today, though, because of safety issues and concern about the wear and tear on the monuments, it is strongly discouraged. But in 1995, with a handful of classmates, I was thrilled and honored to get special permission to make the climb.

I was an undergraduate at the time, and had traveled to Egypt for a field project with a group from the University of Pennsylvania. While we were there, we paid a visit to Dr. Zahi Hawass, who was the General Director of the Giza Plateau, Saqqara, and the Baharia Oasis, and also happened to be a Penn graduate. He asked if there was anything special we wanted to do while we were at Giza, so I said, "Yes, I'd really like to climb the Great Pyramid." He said, "Well, when do you want to do it?" Figuring if I replied, "Oh, some day," my request would be pushed off indefinitely, I said, "Right now."

An inspector who worked for Dr. Hawass escorted our group of six to the base of the Pyramid, looked at us, and said, "Go ahead." Just like that! The monstrous structure loomed before me, and I could hardly believe I was about to do something I had dreamed of since sixth grade—the year we studied Ancient Greece, Rome, Mesopotamia, and Egypt in school. I had the most amazing teacher. You always hear stories about teachers who change people's lives, and for me, Mr. Farrell made the ancient civilizations come alive. Our class had a medieval banquet, made stone tools, and created a giant, room-size diorama (a big mural) of the Giza plateau.

So up we went. Some of the blocks are massive, about three and a half feet high—they're huge—and since I'm not very tall, it was quite a climb. I basically hauled myself up, reaching with my arms then crawling onto each block, one by one. Physically, it was exhausting, and it seemed like the climb was never going to end. Looking up, all you faced were more and more pyramid blocks. When I was about a quarter of the way up I turned and looked down, and I could see all these policemen approaching the poor inspector. I guess he had to explain why he had given a bunch of Americans permission to climb.

It took about 45 minutes to reach the top. The original pyramidion (the cap stone that would have been the point) is no longer there, so the area on top is basically flat. The view looks down on the entire Giza cemetery, the two other main pyramids, all of the Queen's pyramids, and the entire area around it, which is filled with tombs of nobles and officials who were associated with the rulers buried within the monuments. You can see for miles and miles. It was awe-inspiring!

Going down was much more precarious; you see how high up you are, which is kind of scary. I'm not much of a rock climber, and even though our fieldwork is physical, it's nothing compared to the physical strain we experienced on that climb. I don't quite know how to describe the way I walked in the days that followed, but my legs were shot for about a week and a half! I realized there aren't many people who get the chance to do what I had done. And now, every time I look at a picture of the Great Pyramid, I can say, "I was up there!"

I've wanted to be an Egyptologist since I was 12 years old; it's all I've ever been interested in. When I was in the eighth grade, one of my graduation presents was a summer class about archeology and Egypt at the University of Pennsylvania Museum. I was so excited to come to the museum every Saturday to take this class. Now, I work in that same museum! I can visit the Egyptian galleries anytime I want and go into our storerooms and look at the Egyptian artifacts whenever I'm feeling curious. It's like a dream come true! But the best part of my job is when I am on an expedition. It's what makes me the happiest. There's nothing like the feeling of being a keeper of the past.

A Behind-the-Scenes Look at the Job

Favorite Part: I love traveling to Egypt (I've been there about 10 times) and going out into the field. Being able to stand in ancient spaces, places where people lived and were buried thousands of years ago . . . it's really unbelievable. There are times when I've gone into a tomb that was excavated 100 years ago by early archaeologists, and have almost been brought to tears. To see how vibrant the colors are on the walls, how beautiful the scenes are, is a really emotional experience. And it's amazing that they've lasted this long.

Least Favorite Part: The only thing I can think of is the general office politics, the day-to-day grind you experience no matter what job you're doing. Even though fieldwork is hard and sometimes the living conditions are difficult, I can't say that I mind it. I can't imagine doing anything else but this.

Hours: In the office, I work a regular 9-to-5 day. But on a dig, we're generally up around 4:30 or 5 in the morning. We'll work until around 1 or 2 in the afternoon, take a break at the dig house, and then work there from around 3 to 6 in the evening. We're usually in bed by 8 P.M.

Dress Code: For the museum work, I can more or less wear whatever I want. When scholars, researchers, or important visitors come—or if I'm giving a tour of the galleries or storage—I like to look more "business-like." A lot of times I have to work in our storeroom, which is a fairly large warehouse-type space full of wooden shelving covered floor to ceiling with pottery, mummies, and other artifacts. It's pretty dusty, so I wear clothes that I don't mind getting grubby like jeans and a sweater.

Egypt is a Muslim country, so when I'm in the field, I dress conservatively and keep as much covered as possible; you invite fewer problems for yourself that way. I also think the people appreciate it when we show respect for their culture and belief system. However, our excavations are often in the late spring or early summer, and it can be well over 100 degrees, so layers work best—long pants and a T-shirt under a work shirt. Most people wear work boots, but I usually wear sandals because I like having less on my feet.

Work Environment: I have an office at the museum, which is actually a lab space that I share with another person. There's an area where pottery drawing is done, and a few tables that are used by different people who are working on sherds or other artifacts. The rest is just your typical office setup: desks and a computer area. We also have an Egyptological library with a pretty good collection of books that we use for research. I also work in the galleries (when a new display is set up or an existing one is removed) and in the storeroom.

Education/Skills: If you want to become a curator (oversees collections in museums, zoos, botanical gardens, aquariums, or historical sites), an archivist (maintains records), a museum director (formulates budgets and policies), or a conservator (manages and cares for the artifacts), most employers require a bachelor's degree as well as a master's degree. You can earn your degrees from almost any background, but it helps if you've studied a related field, like anthropology, archaeology, ancient history, art history, or religious studies—something that helps familiarize you with ancient Egypt, the ancient Near East, or the ancient Mediterranean world.

If you want to become an Egyptologist or a professor, plan on earning your doctorate. I majored in Egyptology and received my undergraduate degree from the University of Pennsylvania, then did three years of graduate-level coursework at Yale University where I earned my Ph.D. in Egyptology in May 2001.

Personal Qualities: First and foremost, you need a real love for ancient Egypt. This isn't the type of field where you're going to become rich; you've got to do it because you have a passion to learn about what life was like thousands of years ago and are inquisitive enough to look at an object and wonder, "Who made this? Who used it? How did it get where it is now?"

Patience is very important, too, and you need a lot of it because the work doesn't move quickly. When you're excavating, it takes a long time to uncover things. And if you're translating text, it's not like picking up a newspaper and being able to read it fluently. You have to work through it piece by piece, like a puzzle.

Perks and Rewards: Being able to travel is a big perk. The position I have and my association with different field projects means that all my travel accommodations are covered by the project. Many of the Egyptological conferences I attend are held in places I've never been, and I sometimes try to stay a little bit longer. It's great to go and present a paper on Egyptology as part of my job, and see Paris at the same time.

HOT TIPS

🔥 Volunteer for a museum summer program so you can see if you like working in that environment. The earlier you get a feel for what it's like, the sooner you will know if this is an area of study you would like to pursue.

🔥 Learn a second language. In Egyptology you need to decipher ancient writings. Familiarity with other languages—no matter what they are—can help you have an appreciation for the work. Plus, it's always good to have another language under your belt—in the archeological sciences you never know who you'll meet or where you'll travel!

🔥 Focus on getting good grades in school so you will have a better chance of getting into the college of your choice. You'll need a college degree as well as advanced graduate level work to get hired in this field.

🔥 If you're curious about ancient Egypt, read books on the subject. There should be many to choose from at your local library and they'll help you learn about this fascinating time in history.

🔥 Find out what kind of museums are in your area. Call, visit them in person, or look on the Internet (if they have a Web site) to see what exhibits they'll be hosting. Select the ones that interest you and set up a time to see them. You'll see amazing works of art and pieces of history.

🔥 Explore the history of your own neighborhood, community, or state. The skills you learn and observations you make will transfer to archeological sciences—even Egyptology!

WORDS OF WISDOM

If there's a particular area of study that you're interested in, find out as much as you can about the opportunities that are available to you now. You don't have to wait until you're in college to get involved in Egyptology or anthropology. It's also important to find a mentor. I've been very fortunate to have had a number of people take me under their wing and give me opportunities I probably wouldn't have had without that connection. It may not be easy to find that person but so worth it to try!

Find Out More!

Ancient Egypt: The Great Discoveries by Nicholas Reeves (London: Thames and Hudson, 2000). From the Rosetta Stone to the Valley of the Golden Mummies, this book highlights the important discoveries that brought Ancient Egypt to life for the world to see. The beautiful photographs capture the excitement of these major archaeological finds.

Ancient Egypt Magazine
Empire House • 1 Newton Street • Manchester M1 1HW, England
www.ancientegyptmagazine.com
This magazine was created by experts in the field of Egyptology for anyone interested in ancient Egyptian civilization. Whether new to or familiar with archaeology, this magazine is interesting with monthly visits to museums and academic reviews.

The Ancient Egypt Site
www.geocities.com/amenhotep.geo
Discover 3,000 years of Ancient Egyptian history. A great resource with lots of useful information, this site offers research help for all imaginable aspects of Ancient Egypt.

Nancy Parker HOT *Job...*

Dolphin Trainer

I love dolphins, and I can't think of any better way to spend my days than working with them. As a dolphin trainer, I teach these amazing animals to develop different skills, and help the guests of our Dolphins Plus facility appreciate them.

Home Base: Key Largo, Florida

Number of Years in the Field: 3

Personal Philosophy: "Never give up. When it comes to fulfilling your dreams, determination is probably the most important thing."

My parents instilled in me a love for animals. When I was growing up, they would stop at the side of the road if we saw an injured bird, put it in a shoebox, and take it to the vet. And we always had several pets—dogs, cats, turtles, hamsters, hermit crabs, you name it—scurrying around the house. A lot of them just wandered onto our front doorstep and we would take them in and make them part of the family.

As a child, I spent more time with animals than I did with people—they were the focal point of my life. I had a dachshund that was a year younger than me and when I was 12, she died. To me, it felt like losing a little sister. She had grown up with me and it was really hard to say good-bye. My love of animals was true and intense, and I knew even then that somehow animals were going to be a big part of my life.

All through high school and college, my biggest dream was to work with dolphins. I graduated from Emory University with a double major in biology and ecology. Biology is a great major if you're interested in working with marine animals, because it gives you a broad, encompassing education in science. Majoring in marine biology may seem like the obvious choice if you want to work with dolphins, but it may limit your future options. In fact, very few marine biologists actually work with dolphins; most end up working in a laboratory. If I could do it over again, I would have studied psychology as well, because animal behavior is a major part of what we do at Dolphins Plus. A psychology background gives you an understanding of the learning process as well as concepts such as "positive reinforcement," which is quite helpful.

Many of my teachers and counselors in college discouraged me from pursuing a career as a dolphin trainer. They told me how competitive the field was and that only a small percentage of people find jobs working with dolphins. Basically, they said I should expect to fail and be ready for disappointment if I chose to go after my dream. But I wasn't going to give up without trying.

I wanted to get all the experience I could working around animals and spent four years as a technician in an emergency veterinary hospital. When I graduated from college, I also did as much volunteer work with animals as I could, including working for a horse vet and the Dolphin Project, which was a 10-year survey to study and count the Atlantic bottlenose dolphins. While I was working at related jobs and gaining experience as a volunteer, I kept applying for jobs that would allow me to work with dolphins and get paid. Again and again, I was turned down, usually because there were no positions available. Since most people who work with dolphins love their jobs so much, they tend to keep them, which means there aren't many openings for newcomers. Although discouraged, I wasn't ready to give up.

Dolphins Plus

My determination and persistence finally paid off, and I landed a job at Dolphins Plus Research and Education Center. It was the first facility in the world to offer a program where the public could put on a snorkel, mask, and fins and swim with the dolphins. The center specializes in dolphin-human interaction and provides a unique way to teach guests about these amazing creatures. The focus at Dolphins Plus is to educate people about dolphins and their environment and give them the opportunity to interact with these playful marine mammals up close.

Dolphins Plus has three programs: structured swim, natural swim, and a not-for-profit therapy program for children, which is run through Island Dolphin Care. This last program uses dolphin-assisted therapy to help children (and their families) who are coping with various physical, emotional, and developmental difficulties, including chronic and terminal illnesses. It's an amazing program that has a lot of wonderful results, but it isn't the area I specialize in. My primary job is to train dolphins and then assist while our guests swim with them in the structured and natural swim sessions.

During the structured program, our guests get in the water and the trainers lead the dolphins through all kinds of fun behaviors. We may have the dolphins "shake hands"—they'll come face-to-face with you and lift themselves up vertically so you can lightly hold on to their pec fins and shake. Another cool thing is we have the guests float on their backs, and the dolphins push them through the water by their feet. We also have water fights; you splash a little water at the dolphins and they'll splash you back with their mouth—that seems to be everyone's favorite.

The nice thing about our "swim with the dolphins" program (natural swim) is that for many of our visitors, the experience becomes more "What can I do for the dolphins?" instead of "What can they do for me?" Our guests find themselves making cool noises, seeing how fast they can swim, or turning upside down in the water to entertain the dolphins. Once they've interacted with these guys, they realize there is so much more to them than jumping through hoops or bouncing balls. I believe that the next time our guests see these incredible animals, whether in captivity or the wild, they'll have a new appreciation for dolphins' grace, beauty, and intelligence. They'll come away with a better understanding of these creatures and want to help them any way they can.

Educating People About Dolphins

One of my responsibilities working at Dolphins Plus is to educate our guests. Our goal is to change the way they perceive animals and to improve the health of dolphins in the wild. We emphasize that as friendly as dolphins seem, they are still wild animals and people shouldn't swim with or feed them in the ocean because the animals could become seriously ill. I hope the more knowledge I can share about them, the more people will be concerned about polluting our oceans and infringing on the natural environment of these animals.

Before our guests (adults and children) can join the dolphins in the water, we conduct a 45-minute educational briefing to teach them about dolphins, including their anatomy, their intelligence, how they communicate, their social structure, and the environmental issues surrounding dolphins. During the structured program briefing, the most important rule we stress is that they must never touch the dolphins on any part of their face because we don't want them poked in the eye, mouth, or blowhole. We ask our guests not to reach out to touch the animals until we tell them it's okay. Although the dolphins are trained, if they're not expecting hands to be placed on them, they may get scared or shy away.

The briefings are an important part of the program because we want to make sure everyone understands the rules before they get into the water. Our guests learn that their behavior in the water is serious business. This isn't an amusement park where they're sitting on the sidelines watching a show; they're actually participating with the dolphins and could harm them if they don't follow our instructions. We do have the right to pull people out of the water if we feel they're a threat to the dolphins. If someone is thrashing around or reaching to touch the animals when they're not supposed to, I'll ask them to leave because I won't put the dolphins in harm's way.

Bonding with Isla and Fonzie

We have twelve dolphins at our center and each trainer is assigned to work with a pair of dolphins. It works out great because it gives us a chance to bond with them and get to know their personalities. The pair I currently work with is Isla and Fonzie. Isla is approximately 8.5-feet long, weighs about 550–600 pounds, and is very wise. Fonzie's a complete ham, full of charm and personality—he's a real dolphin Casanova! He's about 10.5-feet long and weighs 700 pounds. The relationship I've developed with them during our time together is unlike any other I've had. They're very trusting, very complex, and very intelligent. They depend on me to make sure everything's okay and they should— my job is to make sure they're happy and healthy. I feel so connected to them it's like they're my kids.

Nancy with Isla and Fonzie.

As smart as Isla and Fonzie are, it took a lot of time to teach them new behaviors. We use positive reinforcement and food to train the dolphins and it requires a series of baby steps. For example, imagine that I wanted to train Fonzie to jump high in the air. I would wear a whistle around my neck and when he jumped out of the water exactly the way I asked him to, I'd blow the whistle, toss him a fish, and tell him what a great job he did. The key is that the animals are reinforced immediately, meaning they have to be rewarded right after they've performed a behavior so they associate the treat with the behavior. If there's the slightest delay, they may not realize what they're being rewarded for and get confused.

Since it's not always possible to reward them immediately, like when Fonzie's high up in the air, the whistle acts as a "bridge." What this means is that every time Fonzie hears the whistle, he knows a reward will follow for performing the behavior correctly. The signal "bridges" the behavior (for example, jumping high in the air and swimming back to me) with the reward (getting food and praise). On the flip side, if I don't blow the whistle, he knows he hasn't done what I asked him to, so he won't get a reward.

Once you teach dolphins a simple behavior, you can graduate to more complex ones. For instance, when I (and her trainers before me) wanted to teach Isla to push me through the water by my feet, I didn't just jump in the water, stick my foot in the air, and hope she would push me. I had to break it down into small steps, teaching her very specifically what I wanted her to do.

The first thing I did was give her a target, my hand. I would stand on the platform, hold my hand out, and wait for her to lift her head out of the water and touch it. As soon as she did, I'd blow the whistle, get all excited and yell "Whoo-hoo!" and give her a big fish. What this taught her was that every time she lifted her head out of the water and touched my hand, she received something positive in return. Not only would she get food, she'd see me jumping up and down, shouting "Whoo-hoo!" letting her know she had done a good job.

As soon as Isla mastered this behavior, I moved to the next step. Instead of using my hand as a target, I used my foot. When she'd lift her head out of the water and touch my foot, I'd blow the whistle, give her a herring and a big round of applause. Then came getting in the water with Isla. I'd lift my foot up, have her touch it, blow the whistle, toss her a fish and give her lots of praise. She was still doing exactly what I'd been asking her to do; the only thing that changed was the environment.

Next, I wanted her to actually push my foot, so if she only touched it, I wouldn't blow the whistle. When she'd come back, I'd try to get her to push it a little bit, and when she did, I'd blow the whistle and reward her with a big fish. I kept leading her step by step, giving her lots of positive reinforcement when she did a good job, until she learned to push me through the water by my feet. With love, respect, and positive reinforcement, it's possible to teach dolphins all kinds of new behaviors.

The dolphins need a lot of attention from their trainers, but they need down time, too. Just like us, they have days when they don't feel like performing or swimming with the public. They need time off to play or simply relax. There are moments when they'll look at you with an "I don't feel like doing this today" kind of expression, and that's okay; we expect that occasionally. When this happens, we give them a break, and when they're ready, we try again. The dolphins' happiness is our top priority; we do everything we can to make performing and learning new behaviors so exciting they don't want to stay away from all the fun.

When I start a session, Isla and Fonzie are usually totally excited. They'll start jumping out of the water, making noises as if to say, "I can't wait to get started!" They're really enthusiastic. I attribute this to the fact that they're having a good time. As a thank you to them for doing really well in session, sometimes I'll grab my mask and fins and get in the water to swim with them. It's my way of saying, "Thanks guys, you're amazing."

In addition to making sure Isla and Fonzie are happy, it's my responsibility to make sure they're healthy. If, for example, they develop a new mark on their body or their mood or personality changes and I overlook it, it would be my fault if they became sick. To make sure this doesn't happen, I regularly check their bodies and their mouths for any abnormalities, and I log what and how much they eat. If there is ever a problem, I report to my supervisor immediately.

The animals at Dolphins Plus get the best care available. The dolphins live in a natural ocean environment in a canal off the Atlantic Ocean. There's coral, algae, and rocks at the bottom of their pens, and fences (instead of concrete tanks) are used to separate the pens so that the animals can still talk to each other. If they don't want to perform a behavior, they don't have to—it's completely up to them. We don't force or starve them so they'll be more likely to perform tricks for food. The dolphins are fed the best quality fish from the clean waters of Nova Scotia (herring), Iceland (capland), and Venezuela (sardines). The mercury, metal, and other pollution in these waters has been all but eliminated, so the fish are safe and healthy for the dolphins.

Amazing Moments on the Job

Watching the birth of a healthy baby calf is the most incredible thing I've seen since I've been a trainer at Dolphins Plus. Seeing a dolphin burst through a cloud of bubbles and sea foam as he or she is pushed up for a first breath is a vision to which none can compare. Even though I've witnessed several babies being born at our facility, watching a birth and seeing a baby bond with its mother are such miraculous events for me that I can't contain myself and cry practically every time. After the birth of one particular calf, Cosmo, I looked at my coworker and said, "Can you believe how lucky we are to work here and see things like this?"

With his wobbly dorsal fin, pec fins, and tail, Cosmo couldn't move through the water very well, but he was strong. We named him "Cosmo" because his endearing clumsiness reminded us of the character "Cosmo Kramer" on the TV show *Seinfeld.* The little guy kept surfacing for tiny breaths of air. He was just so small and was the most amazing thing I'd ever seen. He was less than 3 feet long, and at most he weighed between 30 and 50 pounds. The actual gestation period for a dolphin is 12 months, but Cosmo went 14. To see this perfect little creature after 14 long months of anxious anticipation made my heart sing.

We call Cosmo's mom Ding-a-ling—Dinghy for short. She's not a ding-a-ling at all, she's actually unbelievably smart; she was given her name as a little joke because it means the opposite of who she really is! She's probably about 24 years old and she's what is called an alpha (first or dominant) female, which means she's quite intelligent. She's the most dominant female in our facility. She can yell at another dolphin across the canal and they'll go cower in a corner because she admonished them. Cosmo's father is L.B., which stands for Lil' Bit. He used to be small, but now he's the largest dolphin here, so we had to shorten his name to L.B. What's exceptional about L.B. is that he is one of the first males ever to be left in a pen while a baby is being born. Usually, when a calf is about to be born, the mom and dad are separated due to concern about the dad harming the calf.

The theory that males may harm a calf came from the fact that in the wild, males are not monogamous, meaning they don't stay with one partner. Instead, they go off in search of other females. They'll hang out with a pod of dolphins, mate with a female, then leave to find another pod and mate with a different female. Typically, researchers have found that in the wild, if an adult male encounters an adult female who he wants to mate with and she is either pregnant or is nursing, she won't be receptive to the male. The male knows when the baby is not his and he'll sometimes kill it so the female will stop producing milk and be receptive to him.

It was assumed, then, that in captivity males shouldn't be left in the pen with their newborn calves. But we've found this isn't always the case. Dinghy is a strong female and L.B. has a good temperament—"laid back" is a good term to describe him. Some males are naturally aggressive, but L.B. is not aggressive toward Dinghy in any way. And even if he were, Dinghy wouldn't put up with any hostile behavior toward her baby. So he was allowed to stay in the pen with them. We figured it was his baby and he'd be okay with it. Sure enough, he did great.

When Cosmo was first born, Dinghy would swim right by the trainers with the baby at her side. It was as if she was saying, "Look what I did!" L.B. would cruise alongside, too, sometimes taking Cosmo and swimming with him. This is a lot different from females who go hide with their calves because they don't want to show them off and want to keep their babies away from people to protect them.

Dinghy was so bonded with the trainers at our facility that a couple of days after Cosmo was born, she allowed the trainer who works with her the most, Nicki, to swim with them. About a week later, I had the opportunity to swim with the new family and it was unbelievable. I got into the water and was immediately welcomed. The mom and dad were on either side of me and the baby was right in front of me. I couldn't believe it. While I was swimming with them, I kept popping my head up out of the water to look over at the other trainers standing on the platform. All I could say was, "I can't believe this is happening! It's so incredible!" I was as emotional as I've ever been, alternating between crying and laughing. To be in their presence was truly a gift.

In fact, most days I look at my job as a gift. I feel so lucky to be here. The relationship I have with these animals is one I cannot compare with any other. I feel my purpose in life is to do this job and help educate the public about dolphins and help preserve their place on earth. I just can't believe I'm doing it!

A Behind-the-Scenes Look at the Job

Favorite Part: Getting in the water and swimming with the dolphins is the best part of my job. I love that they know who I am. They'll actually show me they're happy to have me in the water with them and welcome me like I'm part of their family. They do this by surrounding me, one on each side, or one on top and one in front, making direct eye contact and swimming right next to me the entire time I'm in the water.

Least Favorite Part: Seeing a baby born that doesn't live is a really sad event. In the wild, the mortality rate for a dolphin's first calf is as high as 80 percent, and in captivity, the rate is about the same. We've had really good luck here, though. I've only seen two calves not make it; one had a heart defect and the other had complications related to the birth. But that's when you have to remember this is nature; it's something that happens in the wild all the time and there's nothing you can do during the birthing process to help them along. You just have to wait and see if the calf is going to be okay. The dolphins usually know before you do, and they'll try to put the baby out of its misery by killing it (sometimes they'll chase the calf and the stress from the chase will kill it or they may swat at it with their tail or bite it) if they know it's not going to make it, which is kind of rough to see.

Hours: I get to work a little before 7:30 A.M. and usually end up leaving around 5:30 or 6 P.M. We're open 364 days a year, so we work most holidays. Holiday time is always busy, so we don't get to go home that often to visit our families (unless they live nearby). And since the animals become bonded with the trainers, we like to stay around as much as we can because it's hard on them when we leave; they actually can become depressed.

Dress Code: I wear a uniform, which is a one-piece black bathing suit with the words, "Dolphins Plus" written in royal blue letters on the front. I also wear black shorts and if I give a briefing or speak to the public, I'll put on a T-shirt that also says "Dolphins Plus." Since I'm in the sun most of the day, I wear a baseball hat or sun visor, sunglasses, and flip-flops. When I'm standing on the platform working with the dolphins, I always have a whistle around my neck.

Work Environment: Unlike most dolphin pens, we don't have concrete pools. We're outdoors, actually on a canal in Key Largo, Florida, which is open to the ocean at both ends, so we've got natural ocean water for these guys that flows in and out of the fences around their pens. We stand on platforms made of Styrofoam and wood (built by us!) that are attached inside their pens.

Education/Skills: In high school, take as many math and science classes as you can. Taking biology, chemistry, and physics classes will give you a foundation to study these subjects further in college. You need good grades to get into college, so study hard! Most marine mammal jobs require a Bachelor of Science degree, with a major in biology, psychology, or animal sciences. College and university undergraduate programs don't usually offer specialized programs to work with specific animals, but you can get that training through hands-on work experience, volunteering, or going to a graduate school with a specialized program.

As for skills, depending on where you interview, most marine mammal facilities require you to take a rigorous swimming test. When I interviewed at Sea World, for example, I was asked to dive down 26 feet without fins and pick up a 10-pound weight, then do 25 push-ups, pull myself onto a seawall, and swim 110 feet while holding my breath. I can't guarantee exactly what kind of swim test you'll be given, but you will need to demonstrate that you're an excellent swimmer.

At Dolphins Plus, we do a lot of underwater construction and repair, so SCUBA certification is a major bonus, and believe it or not, so are any kind of carpentry skills!

Personal Qualities: First and foremost, you've got to be an animal lover. You also need to be very silly when you work with dolphins; the goofier the better. The dolphins love that!

Second, you definitely need to be outgoing and comfortable speaking in front of large groups of people. We do briefings for groups of up to 60 people at a time, educating them about dolphins, our facility, and what they can and cannot do while they're in the water with our animals.

Perks and Rewards: I get to work with dolphins. I would have moved to the moon for this job.

HOT TIPS

δ Join a swim team or take swimming lessons to improve your skills as a swimmer. You can't get a job as a dolphin trainer unless you're an excellent swimmer.

δ If you have the opportunity, learn to scuba dive. SCUBA certification can give you an edge when interviewing to work with marine mammals, since you'll probably have to get in the water with the animals. You don't need to be near the ocean to get certified, many local pools offer certification.

δ Get as much experience working with animals as you can. You might want to consider volunteering at a zoo, museum, aquarium, veterinary hospital, the Humane Society, or a state park; many places like these have volunteer programs. No matter what kind of animals you want to work with, any experience will be valuable.

WORDS OF WISDOM

Never accept the word "no" for an answer. So what if it takes 10 years to achieve a goal. The important thing is to hang in there and keep trying. The bottom line is you can't listen to negativity; you've got to follow what's in your heart and you will get there. It took me a long time to reach my goal of working as a dolphin trainer, but my persistence and determination to get here were worth the effort. I feel completely fulfilled and happy in my job!

Find Out More!

Dolphins by Tim Cahill (Washington, DC: National Geographic Society, 2000). Three scientists researching dolphin behavior lead readers on a fascinating underwater fantasy as they explore these mysterious animals in their natural environment. The book is a companion to the IMAX film *Dolphins (dolphinsfilm.com)* and is filled with more than 125 photographs.

In the Wild: Dolphins with Robin Williams (Video) (PBS Home Video, 1995). Williams, whose adventure takes him to the Bahamas and Hawaii, talks with research experts and attempts to communicate with dolphins in captivity. In the wild, he frolics with 60 spotted dolphins and forms a special kinship with an older dolphin. To order this video, call PBS at 1-877-727-7467, or check out their Web site at *www.pbs.org.*

Sea World
www.seaworld.org
This is a great site to learn about all kinds of animals including killer whales, dolphins, polar bears, and sea turtles. Also find information about animal training, adventure camps with animals, the environment, and career opportunities.

Dolphins Plus Inc.
P.O. Box 2728 • Key Largo, FL 33037 • 1-866-860-7946
www.dolphinsplus.com
Learn more about the Dolphins Plus facility and the opportunity to swim with the dolphins. Information is also available about marine mammalogy courses and internship opportunities.

Laura Hogg

HOT *Job...*

Executive Director

of the Starlight Children's Foundation

As the Executive Director of Starlight, I try to bring a smile to the face of seriously ill children by granting them wishes. I also get to brainstorm new and creative ideas for providing support to the children and families that we work with. On a management level, I'm responsible for the day-to-day operations of the foundation. I make sure we're within budget, that the children's programs are running smoothly, and that we're continuing to raise the necessary funds to support these programs.

Home Base: Toronto, Ontario, Canada

Number of Years in the Field: 10

Personal Philosophy: "Don't let the things you can't do stop you from enjoying the things you can."

The summer after tenth grade was just like any other for me, but when school began in the fall, everything changed. A close friend of mine, Jessica, had spent that summer with her family in New York. No one heard from her the entire time. When school started back up in September, she wasn't there. One of our friends called her family and found out that Jessica had died over the summer. In February, she had been diagnosed with a fairly rare brain tumor, one that progressed very quickly. By the time school was out in May, she was just starting to show signs of being ill, but nothing so obvious that we were alerted to the fact that something was seriously wrong with her health.

When I heard the news of her death, I had so many conflicting feelings. For starters, I was devastated. I felt cheated because Jessica was a friend and I never got the chance to say good-bye. I was also angry with her for not telling me she was sick and with her family for taking her away for the summer. But among all the other feelings, I also felt isolated. At school, none of the kids talked about her death. The news that she had died traveled quickly through the grapevine, so everyone knew. But no one ever mentioned it or brought up her name and it bothered me. She may have died, but to me she was still a part of our lives and I wanted to talk about what had happened. Losing Jessica had a profound effect on me. Even though I was only 17 years old, I came to realize that each of us has to deal with death at some point in our lives. All I wanted was to find something I could do so that the pain and confusion I felt wouldn't happen to anybody else.

After high school, I investigated careers that focused on the process of death and dying. I thought about becoming a nurse, but was more interested in learning about the emotional side of losing a loved one. I stumbled onto some classes about grief counseling, where I learned about different techniques for handling grief and traumatic loss. It was exactly what I had been searching for. I earned my degree and worked for a while as a grief counselor, but after about four months I started to feel like I wasn't ready for the undertaking. I was only 21 years old—what did I know about helping parents cope with the loss of a child? Then I heard about the Starlight Children's Foundation, a nonprofit group that helps grant wishes to seriously ill children. I applied for a "Wish Coordinator" position in hopes that it would give me the experience I needed. After working at Starlight for about two years, the workload of the foundation dramatically increased and a new position was created, Director of Children's Services. I was promoted to that position and promoted again a few years later to my current job as Executive Director.

Joining the Starlight Children's Foundation

Starlight believes that every child should be free to wish and dream. My job is to grant wishes for seriously ill children and plan fun activities to make their days more cheery. It's kind of like playing Santa Claus except I get to work all year long and get paid for it!

Through word of mouth—or possibly from a physician, social worker, or nurse—families find out about Starlight Children's Foundation and what we offer. When they first come in, I have an initial conversation with them to make sure they meet the basic eligibility requirements for the wish-granting program. The child must be between the ages of 4 and 18, be critically, chronically, or seriously ill, and have the cognitive level of at least a 4-year-old. Some of the kids I work with have had traumatic injuries such as diving accidents. Others live with illnesses like cancer, cystic fibrosis, AIDS, or heart disease. The final stipulation for our wish-granting program is that the child hasn't had a wish granted by another organization. Unfortunately, because of all the children who are ill in this world, we need to spread out our resources and we can only allow one wish per child.

Next, I set up a meeting with the entire family. This could include the mom, dad, or other adults who care for the child. It also includes the ill child and any siblings. Illnesses often cause people to focus on the one who's sick, so we try really hard to include the healthy children in the family who may feel left out. We listen to their feelings, offer support, and encourage them to get involved in a variety of ways. For the first meeting with a family, we try to create an element of fun and surprise by bringing little presents such as coloring books and crayons, funky nail polishes, soccer balls, or dolls. It's kind of a fairy-godmother approach, which is really exciting. Some kids will meet me at the door and know exactly what wish they want granted. Others don't have a clue, so I have to work harder to help them determine what they might like. The possibilities can be a little overwhelming and it's my job and the job of volunteers to ensure that children make wishes for things that they really want, things that are true to their hearts.

Laura and a coworker bring a child some cheer.

We're very whimsical at Starlight and have granted all types of wishes. What children choose to request is as unique as the children themselves. Wishes we've granted have included camcorders, trips to Disney World, shopping sprees, meetings with famous people like sports stars or actors, and redecorating bedrooms. There was one young lady, Anna (some names have been changed due to confidentiality), who even wanted to be a princess for a day. To grant her wish, we had a limousine pick up her and her mother in the morning and take them to a salon where Anna had her hair washed and styled, her nails manicured, and makeup applied (age appropriate of course!). Then we presented her with jewelry becoming of a princess and a pretty, pink, to-the-floor dress (with matching shoes, naturally). The crowning touch was a beautiful tiara—essential to every princess's regal ensemble.

Once Anna was all dressed up, we got in the limousine and headed to her favorite restaurant for lunch, where a special table had been set up in her honor with balloons and a "Welcome Princess Anna" sign. Anna's family was there as well as a few of her closest friends. There happened to be a parade in town that day and we had prearranged for Anna to be a participant in the festivities. So after lunch, Anna got to ride in the last float of the parade as the Paradise Princess. After the parade, as Anna stepped back into the limousine for her ride home, we handed her a bouquet of beautiful roses. Granting wishes always takes a lot of thought about what's important to the child. Anna's "princess for a day" wish is just one example of how we can make a child's dream come true.

While it's fun, granting wishes is a lot of work. Even helping a child come up with the perfect wish takes a little bit of research and investigation. You have to begin by spending time getting to know the family so that you can develop a relationship with them. I do everything possible to make sure the child's wish is a once-in-a-lifetime kind of event, too, by embellishing upon their request. For example, if a child says he or she wants a fire truck, it's up to me to expand on that idea. Maybe that child will end up being a "firefighter for a day" or get a shopping spree at a toy store where he or she can pick out a fire truck and all kinds of other cool toys.

As Executive Director of the foundation, however, my job is much more than helping with wish granting. I'm in charge of keeping our foundation running smoothly. A big part of my day-to-day responsibilities is helping with fund development, which means brainstorming creative ways to raise the money needed to keep the children's programs running, making sure we stay within our budget, and ensuring that we're honoring the trust placed upon us by our donors. Another aspect of my role is the management of the office, which includes hiring and training the staff and volunteers and making sure that everybody's doing their job effectively. I also work with a team to think of new ideas for wishes and plan how they'll be fulfilled, arranging everything from airline tickets and hotels to providing any type of medical support a child may need, such as oxygen or wheelchairs. While it's not the exciting part of the job, it's a necessary part. Without all the details being taken care of, the amazing wish granting that we do wouldn't be a reality.

Inspiration

All the children that come to Starlight are special in their own way, and I've learned something from each of them. But there was one little boy who truly is my inspiration. I have a picture of him in my office and when I'm having a rough day or can't figure out what to do about something, I find myself looking at his photo and asking for a hand. I'm sure he's up there helping me somehow.

Matthew was a 4-year-old (4 going on 40, actually) diagnosed with HIV (the virus that causes AIDS) and by the time he came to Starlight he was in the advanced stages of the disease. He initially made three wishes; one was to get well, two was to go to Disney World, and three was to grow up and get big. While we couldn't meet his first wish, we dealt with it by explaining that everybody was doing what he or she could to help him. Our job was to focus on something we *could* do for him, so we set up a trip to Disney World to make his second wish come true.

But about a week or two before he was supposed to leave, Matthew took a bad turn and was hospitalized. His doctors felt the trip to Florida would be too much of a strain, so the trip was canceled. We tried to make it up to him by throwing a Disney-themed party, but I felt like it just wasn't enough—it wasn't his wish. And Matthew's third wish, to grow up and get big . . . well, let's just say he didn't have much time left. How could I go back to a 4-year-old and say, "Hey, sorry we can't do your first three wishes, can you give us three more?" Somebody at work overheard me discussing this dilemma and said, "You know what, you're too close, you're not being objective. What do you do when you grow up and get big?" "You get a job and go to work," I said. "Exactly!" he replied.

So I asked Matthew what he thought about growing up and getting big in the next couple of weeks. He loved the idea. A tailor measured him for a little suit, I gave him a briefcase, and we set up an office for him at Starlight. I even hung a plaque on the door with his name on it. Every Friday for about four weeks, Matthew came into the office to work. We had a staff meeting with him and gave him specific jobs to do, like sorting all the colored paper into separate piles and coloring important pictures for us. He worked very hard, and we gave him a paycheck, too.

Matthew also enjoyed looking around the office at all the pictures of kids who had been touched by Starlight. He'd point to one and ask, "Who was this child? What was his wish? Is he in heaven now?" He was particularly fascinated by a picture of a young girl named Sally who had gone to Disney World for her wish. She had systemic juvenile rheumatoid arthritis, a chronic illness that causes inflammation of one or more joints as well as many internal organs. But because of all the medication she was taking her immune system was unable to function. About two weeks after returning from her trip, she came down with a cold on a Friday, and by Sunday she had died. Since it happened so quickly, it was especially hard on her family—they didn't have time to prepare.

About two months later, Sally's dad stopped by the office and Matthew happened to be working that day. I told him there was someone special I wanted him to meet. Matthew looked at him and asked, "Is Sally in heaven?" When her dad replied that she was, Matthew came at him with another question: "Do you miss her?" "Yes, I do, very much. She went to heaven very quickly and I didn't get a chance to give her a hug good-bye." We were all getting a bit teary at this point, and it was clear that Sally's dad just wanted to turn away and go into another room where he could have some space.

But then Matthew said, "Hold on just one second." None of us were sure what he was going to do. Sally's dad turned around and Matthew said, "You know what, I'm going to go to heaven soon, and if you want, you can give me a hug and I'll bring it to Sally for you."

Her father replied, "You know what, I would be very honored to do that," and he walked over to give Matthew a hug. But Matthew put one hand up and said, "Now hold on. First I have to tell you, I have AIDS." (This was quite a while ago, when AIDS and how it's contracted wasn't as well understood as it is now.) Sally's dad said, "It's okay," and gave him a great big hug. Then Matthew went right back to work and we were all left in my office crying.

Matthew passed away several weeks later. I phoned Sally's dad to let him know and when he called me back he said, "I have to tell you, for whatever it's worth, I know he went to heaven and gave my daughter a hug. For the first time, I have peace." Those words and the emotion behind them have stayed with me, and I'll always remember Matthew and the impact he had on so many.

What I Get Back from My Work at Starlight

Working at Starlight has helped me to realize that you have to be grateful for the small things in life, because you never know what might happen tomorrow. I've seen so many families whose lives have been changed in an instant as a result of having a child diagnosed with a serious illness. One day life is fine, and the next they're going back to the doctor for more tests because their child is having recurring flu symptoms. And then they hear it's not the flu, but a form of cancer or lupus or another serious illness.

It's taken me a long time to realize that it's okay to put importance on my own problems, even though they might seem small in comparison to the issues facing the families I work with. I learned this from them. Many have said to me that even though what I'm going through may seem small compared to what they're facing, my problems are important, too.

But when I find myself getting too wrapped up in the smaller, more trivial things that annoy me—like not getting around to cleaning out the garage—I don't have to look very far to get a reality check. I just glance at the photos of children I've worked with on my bookshelf and notes from them tacked on my bulletin board thanking me for doing my job. I meet a lot of wonderful people, including children whom I admire beyond words. I get a lot of courage from them; if they can brave the difficulties that they face, then I should be able to get up and tackle my challenges, too.

I once read an anonymous poem that said: "A hundred years from now it won't matter what kind of car I drove, what kind of house I lived in, or what my bank account said. All that will matter is that I was important in the life of a child." It's a poem that has stuck with me, in part because I believe in it so completely. When I'm asked what *my* wish would be, what I would ask for, I think of this verse. Because if I really had to pick a wish, it would be that an organization like the Starlight Children's Foundation didn't have to exist.

A Behind-the-Scenes Look at the Job

Favorite Part: Getting to know the families and being able to make a child's wish come true. I also like that this job has helped me find joy in simple things, like laughter and playing cards with a child.

Least Favorite Part: A child's death is never easy, but I try to focus on the positive. I know I can't affect the outcome of what's going to happen medically, but I can affect the time they have with us and make it the best I possibly can. I keep a journal of all the kids I've come to know at Starlight and write down one or two things I've learned from each one of them. When it gets really hard, I look through it and see all the wonderful things these children have given me.

Hours: My day typically starts around 7 A.M. and I try to leave by 5:30 or 6 P.M. But even after I get home I usually spend a few hours on the phone calling families to see how they're doing. And it doesn't stop there. If I'm at a store, I might see a toy or something and think, "Hey, so-and-so would like that," so I'll show the manager my business card and ask if I can get the item for cost or free.

Beyond this, I'm always networking, trying to meet people who might be helpful to the foundation. Networking is a big part of nonprofit work. You are always looking to get connected to a new individual, corporation, or group who might be able to help raise funds, donate goods or services, raise awareness, or connect you to someone else who could be helpful. I even work some weekends, attending Starlight events. But I love what I do so much it doesn't seem like work. What I do is more than a job, it's a lifestyle, a big part of my life.

Dress Code: My work attire varies depending on what I'm doing on a particular day. On the days that I'm in the office or if I have a donor meeting, I wear business attire. When I'm out visiting kids or granting a wish, I wear fun clothes—jeans so we can play, and a sweatshirt or T-shirt with a Disney character on it.

Work Environment: The Starlight Children's Foundation is located on the eleventh floor of an office building centrally located in the city of Toronto. My personal office is filled with photos of families enjoying their wish process and mementos that my coworkers or I have received from the kids with whom we've worked, such as key chains, beaded necklaces, mugs, and drawings. My job also takes me outside the office. I end up everywhere from visiting children in their homes and in the hospital, to fundraising events such as our annual Gala, and Starlight family activities, like carnivals.

Education/Skills: On the administrative and fundraising side of things, a lot of nonprofit organizations look for people with a university or college degree. Good majors to consider are fund development, business administration, social work, or humanities. You might also want to consider courses in fundraising that are available at many community colleges and universities. On the program side, a college degree may not matter. I hired most of my staff because they had volunteer experience or a passion for helping kids.

Personal Qualities: You'll never get rich doing nonprofit work, so you need to have a strong desire to give back. Nonprofits aren't usually able to pay what a corporate business would because there isn't a lot of money left over each year to go toward paying salaries (a nonprofit can receive money by selling its goods or services as well as receiving donations, but any money left over after all the expenses are paid has to go back into running the organization and fulfilling its mission). The funds raised basically equal the funds spent, and you're accountable to each and every donor to spend as much as you possibly can on the programs you provide—after all, that's what they're donating for. Although people who give money to nonprofit organizations realize there is a need to spend some of the funds on salaries and administrative costs, they donate with the assumption that those costs will be minimal so the majority of the monies will be spent on making seriously ill children and their families very happy. But even though you may not get paid much, you'll get rewards that no dollar amount can match.

Perks and Rewards: I know a number of wonderful people I would never have met were it not for my work at Starlight—the people I work with, all the volunteers, and of course, the amazing families. I get back things like knowing my priorities and keeping myself on track. This job has helped me stay focused and clear about what I want to happen in my life and where I want to go.

HOT TIPS

- 🔥 Get involved in volunteering, community service, or service learning. Not only does this build good experience (and a nice résumé), but you'll also be helping others—and feeling good about yourself.

- 🔥 Help plan a fundraising event at school or for a local charity. You'll get a taste of the amount of organization, public relations, and communication that is necessary in working in a nonprofit organization.

- 🔥 If you want to work with children specifically, work on having more inter-actions and experience with them. This can be anything from working as a part-time baby-sitter to volunteering for Special Olympics to reading to children at a local hospital. Perhaps you can help with childcare at your place of worship or volunteer at your neighborhood elementary school.

WORDS OF WISDOM

Believe in yourself and your dreams. Together, they're an unstoppable combination and the result is simple . . . anything is possible! If you're interested in pursuing a career in an organization like Starlight, I can offer you two pieces of advice: first, finish school. You need to show that you have the courage, determination, and ability to do that to earn the respect and confidence of the people who'll be looking to hire you. Second, spend some time volunteering with children in hospitals to see if there's a good fit. You may discover that it's not the right direction for you and that's okay. You'll gain the benefit of the experience and the children who you touch will receive the benefits of your time, comfort, and dedication.

Find Out More!

The Kid's Guide to Service Projects: Over 500 Service Ideas for Young People Who Want to Make a Difference by Barbara A. Lewis (Minneapolis: Free Spirit Publishing, 1995). From simple projects to large-scale commitments, this guide has something for anyone who wants to make a difference. Kids can choose projects involving animals, crime prevention, the environment, hunger, politics, and many other areas.

Teens with the Courage to Give: Young People Who Triumphed Over Tragedy and Volunteered to Make a Difference by Jackie Waldman (Berkeley: Conari Press, 2000). Profiled in this book are 30 amazing young people who have overcome great personal odds and put their own pain aside to reach out and help others. Stories include that of the son of a cancer patient who created a support group for other kids with sick parents. Also read about a young girl who helped her mother and sister as they died from AIDS, later becoming an AIDS awareness and prevention volunteer.

America's Promise—The Alliance for Youth
909 N. Washington Street, Suite 400 • Alexandria, VA 22314 •
1-888-559-6884
www.americaspromise.org
A diverse and growing alliance of nearly 500 national organizations, this federally created and sponsored organization offers kids and teens the opportunity to participate in activities that strengthen communities across the nation.

Starlight Children's Foundation International Headquarters
5900 Wilshire Boulevard, Suite 2530 • Los Angeles, CA 90036 • (323) 634-0080
www.starlight.org
Starlight Children's Foundation is an international nonprofit organization dedicated to improving the quality of life for seriously ill children and their families. At their Web site, find information on the many programs that Starlight provides and ways to get involved.

Youth Service America
1101 15th Street NW, Suite 200 • Washington, DC 20005 • (202) 296-2992
www.ysa.org
A resource center and an alliance of organizations committed to increasing the opportunities for young Americans to volunteer locally, nationally, and globally. A powerful network of organizations makes it easy for young Americans to help create healthy communities while experiencing personal development.

HOT *Job...*

Editorial and Co-Network Director

for the Web site for girls and young women 13–30, ChickClick.com

As Editorial Director for ChickClick.com I oversee the work of 12 different editors and interns, each of whom writes or runs a different section or "channel" of the Web site. It's also part of my job to work on ways to increase the size of our audience. But keeping tabs on our editorial vision—to make sure that things are current, relevant, and meaningful—is what I really enjoy. I love being part of something that gives girls and women information that isn't focused on their looks or how they can attract men, but instead gives them a platform to be themselves. ChickClick is for girls and women who are sassy and smart.

Home Base: San Francisco, California

Number of Years in the Field: 6

Personal Philosophy: "My job is my cause."

Most of my career has been working with—and on—the Web. I started in 1995 with an internship at *Wired* magazine, and in 1996, I took a job as one of the founding editors of the *Sacramento Bee* Web site. Later that year I made another move, becoming a reporter and eventually a senior writer for CNET's News.com, a Web site that provides extensive information about computers, technology, and the Internet. I had one of the best beats—civil liberties and online policy—and I covered politics, online culture, and everything else related to the world of high tech. Rules were being made that would affect free speech and privacy, rules that would have an impact on people who weren't even online yet. It was really exciting following the development of a new industry, and watching everything unfold as the Web grew into the phenomenon that it is now.

After about five years in the online industry, though, the Internet "firsts" were beginning to fade and, for me, the excitement and newness started to wane a bit. I began to realize that I had been involved in so many different things, including reporting, concepting, strategizing, and Web design, and I was ready for a change. I knew that I wanted to stay involved in technology and the Internet, but my heart was really with girls and young women. I believed there was so much information that teenage girls needed and thought that I—and the Internet—could help them get it. Through my previous experiences, I had gained a lot of business knowledge by watching companies that had succeeded as well as those that had made mistakes. I was ready to take what I had learned and share it, to help build on an idea from more of a grassroots level. I wanted to work on something that I could in part call my own.

As part of my beat at CNET, I covered sites and issues pertaining to women, so I decided to look a little closer at the companies that targeted women with their products and services. After researching a lot of these companies, I discovered that ChickClick appealed the most to me—and not just because I knew people who worked there (I went to high school with the company's founders, Heidi and Heather Swanson). What I liked was that ChickClick served teenage girls, a group I care deeply about. Their tag line "Girl sites that don't fake it" spoke to my heart as did the core concept of the site—giving users a voice and a safe place to talk by fostering an online community.

As I was researching how to make this shift in my career focus, ChickClick was in the process of changing its format to build on its success. It was looking to expand its original editorial content. As luck would have it, the woman hired to lead that drive was someone I knew from my days as a political reporter at CNET. We had met in Washington, D.C., when we were both covering stories as competing reporters. I was ready to roll up my sleeves and ChickClick was looking to revamp the look, feel, and editorial offering of the site. The timing couldn't have been better.

Working on the World Wide Web

In early 2000, I made the move to ChickClick.com and became a part of the technological movement aimed at empowering girls and young women with information and advice to help them make smart decisions, realize their limitless potential, and become a powerful political force. At ChickClick we encourage girls to speak up, use their voices, and not lose the opportunity to be heard. At the core, we're radically changing the way the media speaks to women. We give teens and young women the real deal about their bodies, relationships, self-esteem, money, power, and the world.

ChickClick started out as a "tool and community site," meaning it offered things like free email, homepages, and instant messaging while also featuring ChickShops (boutique shopping) and message boards (online communities). But over the last year and a half, more content (such as articles and quizzes) has been added. Girls and young women had issues and concerns that they were talking about on the site—growing pains, so to speak, about coming of age in today's world—and we realized that we could provide our users with information that would supplement what they were already talking about. We try to "connect the dots" for our users by recognizing their experiences, offering advice on what they're going through, and pointing out the next step for them to take. For instance, if there are a lot of girls on the ChickBoards complaining about how fat they are, we don't offer them a diet. Instead, we'll run an article on body image or the power of advertising and guide them toward getting to the root of their bad-body thoughts: are they really unhealthy and overweight or are they just buying into society's unhealthy expectations? We don't preach or repeat the same line girls have heard before. We take things in a new direction, starting at the point at which their conversation began, moving on to how their thought process got them there, and ending by showing them different ways they can go in order to lead a more empowered life.

Our users are on the message boards at all hours of the day talking about issues, posing questions, and sharing whatever is on their minds, and our staff of expert columnists helps them find answers. For example, we have a column called "Barely Relating," in which a teen and parent each state their side of an argument and a team of therapists chimes in to help them sort it out. Other columns on ChickClick have included "For the Record," news young women can use; "Friendship 101" for teens; "Out of the Closet," for users who have questions about their sexuality; and "Wander Women," which is all about travel.

In addition to the free services (tools) and message boards, there are currently 11 ChickChannels (everything on the site is "chick-something;" for instance, email is ChickMail and homepages are ChickPages). The ChickChannels are Body+Soul, College, Home+Craft, Relating, Society+Politics, Sports+Fitness, Stars+Style, Work+Money, ChickRadio (an online player with songs programmed by us), MissClick (relationships, friends, family, and other informative topics aimed at teens), and EstroClick (topics for young women, such as sex and relationships, travel, and personal stories slanted to an older audience).

We want our users to know that their voice is as important as ours as an editorial publisher. On every single channel, the right-hand side is dedicated to quotes from our community users. We also have "My" features—"My Body," "My Play," "My Life," "My Voice"—which are personal stories or rants shared by our users relating to a channel's topics.

The biggest difference between ChickClick and other Web sites targeted at girls and women is that we don't have a beauty channel. We want to integrate a sense of equality into our content and not talk outright about beauty. Users can get that somewhere else if it's an important topic to them. We even very consciously put the word "sports" before "fitness" on that channel because our goal is to teach girls how to be athletes, try new things, and have courage. ChickClick would rather give messages about building self-esteem and confidence and being intelligent. We're basically telling everyone out there that *that's* what we think is beautiful.

Life as a Tech-Savvy Editorial Director

My role at ChickClick is twofold. As editorial director I supervise our 12 editors and interns and help to maintain our content strategy. This includes everything from helping choose article topics to managing and training the editorial team. When it comes to working in an Internet-related field, I come from the school of thought that you pretty much learn by doing. Of course, we have Web designers and creative people who have extensive training specifically for what they do, such as designing our illustrations and handling complicated programming issues. But from an editor/Web producer standpoint, being tech savvy is really a trade; the skills you need can be improved upon with practice. That's definitely how I learned. When I went to the *Sacramento Bee,* my job was to help put the newspaper online, and I had no experience whatsoever in doing something like that. I had to get very technical very quickly.

All of the editors at ChickClick have journalism training but for a lot of them, this is their first Web job. Whenever there's something technical that has to be done, ChickClick editors learn as they go along. I figure, if they had taken a big instructional class ahead of time but there was no practical use for what they were taught, they probably wouldn't remember it, and I would end up having to show them again anyway.

During weekly editorial meetings we go over the specific stories and original content that will appear on the site in the coming week. I'm always on the lookout to make sure we don't fall into the typical "mainstream" women's magazine fare, and address any problems I see with what is being planned. I remember one editorial meeting where a new editor pitched a story on what kind of hairstyle you should wear to a job interview. My response? "Scratch that!" We just don't do superficial advice on style; we're smarter than that. We're not going to talk to you about your hair; we're going to talk to you about how to get a raise, earn respect, and be heard.

Whatever appears on ChickClick also needs to fit our content strategy, which is very simple and based on three things: what our users *need* to know about, what they *want* to know about, and how their needs fit our business goals of being profitable and staying in business. Everything we spend money on, from paying freelance writers to updating our technology, is very simply focused on serving our users, serving our mission statement, and serving our business.

My other title, co-network director, means I'm essentially a co-CEO (Chief Executive Officer) of an independent unit (ChickClick.com) at Snowball.com, which is our parent company. Along with the other co-network director, it's my responsibility to do things like write the budget, track where the money is being spent, deal with invoices, and handle human resource issues. A big piece of this aspect of my job is dealing with technology issues, which is

Courtney backstage interviewing the band Fenix∗TX.

where an Internet site like ours really differs from a print magazine. Anything new we want to do with the site always ties back to technology: Do we have the necessary tools to do what we are planning? Will our publishing system support our efforts or does it need to be enhanced? It's my job to work with the engineers and producers to help figure out things like that.

Teens and Technology

Teens face a lot of intense pressure. There's the pressure to succeed academically and excel on standardized tests. There's pressure to have sex, to be consumers, to stay constantly busy and productive, you name it. Some teens have to worry about who may be bringing a gun to algebra class. And then there's the issue of self-esteem. Many studies have shown that girls' self-esteem may start to plummet when they enter high school, which changes their entire outlook about themselves and what they can achieve in their lives.

In many high schools you're categorized based on how you look, how much money you have, or what you're interested in. And that's what carries you through those four years. It can be a really great experience for some people and really horrifying for others. But in college or in the working world, there's so much more freedom. You get to decide what interests you and then pursue it. It seems easier to find people who are like you with whom to build a community of friends. For many young women it's a time when they can empower themselves with information and start to question certain systems.

All the things that I love about life after high school is what ChickClick is all about: empowering the younger generation to question certain beliefs and systems, realize there aren't any limitations, and use their voices to make a difference. We empower girls and young women with the fact that they can negotiate with their parents, teachers, friends, and bosses; empower them with the knowledge that they can be anything they want to be.

One of the advantages of the Internet is that it gives young women a place where they can talk to other teens outside of their own high school, anonymously and safely. When I was in high school, it was this insulated little universe unto itself. But the Internet provides a way to learn about other people's experiences and different ways of life. We find that girls go onto the ChickBoards and talk for hours about something that's going on in their lives. And what's great is that they're getting all these different perspectives; they're not limited to a few friends at school. I think this type of interaction is really going to make a difference for girls, helping them become critical thinkers at an earlier age and question what's really going on in the world.

There's a lot of intellectual conversation going on, too, not just discussions about favorite bands or popular actors. For example, I was really surprised to discover that one of our most popular boards is our poetry and prose board. It just confirms how diverse teen girls' interests are!

Understanding the Digital Divide

It's no secret that technology is a part of many aspects of our world. It plays a very practical role in education as well as in the workforce. Today's Internet generation is obviously really tech savvy; one of the primary ways they communicate with friends and acquaintances is by email, chat rooms, and "instant messaging." And because of this technical know-how they wield a lot of power—which is a good thing because that's the direction in which their world is heading.

When I was a reporter, one of the things I covered extensively was technology and education. The federal government and many large corporations are trying to bring technology to more people by donating computer equipment to schools. It's a great idea, yet at the end of the day, a lot of people still don't have access to the Internet and everything that computers offer. No doubt the Internet is creating a global community, but a segment of the population is being left behind—some because of their own conscious decisions, but others because of cultural or socioeconomic circumstances.

This very real phenomenon that exists in our society, the so-called digital divide, means that the people in this country and around the world who don't have access to the Internet or computers are at a disadvantage when entering the workforce or are in need of critical information. Being tech savvy is a practical tool in most jobs these days, especially those that can really differentiate economic status. Without that knowledge, it's not only difficult to get a job, it may also limit a person's ability to advance in their chosen field. When I was applying for the job at CNET, having Internet experience surely gave me an advantage over the other applicants who actually had more journalistic experience but no tech experience.

My own family is an example of the digital divide. While I am immersed in computers and the Internet and technology, my cousins, who live in a rural area, have very limited online access. This means they can't quickly search for better prices on items they want to purchase, get information for school reports or about topics of interest, communicate long distance in an easy and inexpensive manner, and see all the great things that sites like ChickClick have to offer, such as information about going to college. ChickClick shows users that not only can they *go* to college, but also *how* they can do it—scholarships to apply for, and all the tools they need to fill out an application. There's advice on how to choose a career that fits your interests—either as a high school student or a college graduate—how to make money, get ahead of the game, be smart in relationships, be confident and think for yourself, and solve problems. People without Internet access are missing out on so much valuable information and perspectives from people around the world.

The staff of ChickClick tries to stay involved in the community, reaching out to girls who may not be online but who could benefit from what our site and others like it have to offer. Our editors volunteer for girl-focused organizations, like the Bay Area Girls Center, which provides wilderness programs to empower adolescent girls to develop and express their strengths. We also go to high schools and conduct journalism workshops. One of the events we attended was a teen health fair held in San Francisco in October 2000. More than 1,000 girls were there, and we discovered many of them didn't have a home computer or know how to use the computers at school. There was also a definite division along racial and economic lines in terms of this technical gap. Add to this studies showing that Latina girls like myself have a very low entry rate into college, and the digital divide gets even bigger. Since I'm part of this statistic and have overcome the technology gap, I want to help others to do the same.

For ethnic minorities like me, "making it," so to speak, means you can go on to become a mentor for someone else, which can help close the class gap and narrow the scope of the digital divide, even if it is one step at a time. Because of the position I'm in, "making it" has also come to mean that I can use my own cultural values to affect technological and online content development to insure that services and products are designed for all kinds of people, not just educated white males.

Making a Difference

My career has given me so many opportunities to learn and grow, to make a difference in girls' lives, and to be a role model. There was the time I got to cover the Supreme Court hearing on the Communication Decency Act, a 1996 landmark case about online free speech. I was 22, and it was only the second time I'd been on an airplane. I was nervous, lost in a big city, and excited all at the same time. Then there was the time I met the feminist icon Gloria Steinem. We interviewed her for ChickClick in October 2000, right before the Presidential election. It was incredibly exciting to connect how the progressive work we are doing is a direct result of the trailblazing she and her generation started years ago.

Then there's the daily stuff. Every day we get letters from girls who are in trouble or are confused and have found a light at the end of the tunnel thanks to ChickClick's online community and content. I'll never forget one letter we received from a teen whose parents were alcoholics, and she was always left to care for her little brother. For some reason it struck a chord with us. We knew we could help her by writing an article about where girls like her could get help and connecting her with other girls on the boards who were going through the same thing. It made me realize we have the power to validate the experiences of young women and girls and help them get through difficult times with solid information.

Every day I feel pride in what we do. It's a tremendous motivating factor and is truly what makes this a great job. There's definitely pressure; I'm responsible for everyone who works for me, keeping us on budget, and helping to drive this business to success. But everyone here is so passionate and sisterly that it gives me the energy to push forward during hard times and keep serving our audience. And that's what it's all about—the chicks!

A Behind-the-Scenes Look at the Job

Favorite Part: Having the freedom to talk straight to young women and teen girls is the best part of what I do. Not a lot of people in the media can say that. We don't write about beauty tips, publish diets, or talk about how to get a boyfriend. We're teaching our subscribers that being beautiful is about being smart, tolerant, outspoken, passionate, unique, honest, caring, and both mentally and physically healthy.

Least Favorite Part: Administrative and budget meetings are the worst. Part of my role at ChickClick is to work with the executive staff to guide us toward being profitable while still meeting the goals of growing our audience and keeping costs down. Many of the meetings I attend have to do with examining our budget to assess what we need in order to achieve our growth goals versus what the company can actually afford. We have to spend money on top-notch staff and invest in technology in order to enhance what we're capable of doing, so it's a tough balance to achieve. Meetings like this are obviously necessary, but they make my head hurt.

Hours: I generally work about 50 to 60 hours a week. During relaunches, when we've overhauled the site and worked like crazy to get everything done, our days have been as long as 14 hours. I usually put in a few hours on Sundays, too, doing administrative tasks, reports, and answering back-logged emails.

Dress Code: One thing I love about my job at ChickClick is I can wear absolutely anything! Leather skirt and boots one day, jeans and sneakers the next. If I have a meeting with the executive staff, I'll go more conservative; I want them to focus on my ideas, not my outfit.

Work Environment: My entire staff and I sit in what we call the "hub," a fairly open space with cubicle-like dividers between some of us. Each work space has several shelves and push-pin boards, where we hang all sorts of things—inspiring reader letters, funny heart-throb pin-ups from old teen magazines, pictures of friends, ChickClick stickers. I sit in one of the darker areas in the office, away from the windows, but I don't mind because I'm at meetings most of the time.

Education/Skills: You have to be a great communicator, both written and verbal, in order to edit and write for the Web and other media. Having basic Web design skills is a plus, as is experience building Net communities or moderating them, which are crucial aspects of running a site that has so much user-generated content and interaction. It also helps if you're already an active participant on the Net. Web production skills can be learned on the job, but you definitely need traditional journalistic training, which you can get either in a work situation or through college experience.

I went to a community college and became hooked on journalism after joining the school paper. I love to tell people that I went to community college first and then transferred to San Francisco State University; you don't have to go to a fancy four-year university right away or get an advanced degree to get somewhere in this world!

Personal Qualities: Flexibility is a good trait to have in this line of work. You must adapt quickly to changes in the marketplace that trickle down to our daily operation. Yet at the same time I would say it helps to be a bit on the "type-A" side. "Type-A" people have tremendous energy, tend to be very organized, and are good at getting their tasks done each day. There are so many daily deadlines, technical procedures, and other systems we have in place, so you constantly have to pay attention to detail.

You also have to love brainstorming! We put stop times on our meetings because we all have so many awesome ideas. But the staff must also be able to see the big picture of our business—we've got to succeed financially in the end to keep doing what we love—so you have to be a smart businesswoman, too. And you have to be able to surrender; many aspects of our business are controlled by the parent company. We have to focus our energies where we *can* make change.

Perks and Rewards: Tapping into more than two million teen girls and young women every day for their opinions, stories, and triumphs makes everything I do worthwhile. Our community is really huge and thriving, not to mention honest and smart. I have so much respect for all of our users. Having personal passions that are fulfilled by your work is also a major perk.

HOT TIPS

🔥 Join the school paper, write for a community paper, or find another avenue to work on your writing skills.

🔥 Design your own Web site. Plenty of community colleges have basic HTML classes that will show you what it takes to get one started. Developing this skill will help you understand how to get a site up and running, as well as keep it growing.

🔥 Email women who are working on the Web and ask for their advice or mentoring. A good way to track someone down is to surf the Net and explore sites for girls and young women. Most have a page with contact information.

🔥 Find an internship in a related field, like journalism, Web design, or information technology.

🔥 Network—cultivate relationships with people who are doing the things you're interested in. They may be able to offer some help.

WORDS OF WISDOM

When I was starting out in reporting, I didn't know all the rules, protocol, and "etiquette" that you were supposed to follow in pursuing a story. So I had a tendency to go after my stories in rather unconventional ways; I didn't box myself in or set up boundaries for how far I could go to get the information I needed. That often meant I got stories faster and from a fresher angle than seasoned reporters who were following more of a "formula." I feel like I've done some of my best, most exciting work when I was new at a job. Sometimes when you don't know the rules, you are more creative and take more risks. Don't be afraid when you're the new kid on the block—you may have the best ideas and the zest to go after them!

Find Out More!

 Career Opportunities in Computers and Cyberspace by Harry Henderson (New York: Checkmark Books, 1999). This comprehensive guide offers information on more than 80 jobs in technology and Internet industries, including salary information, necessary skills, advancement prospects, and tips for getting hired.

 ChickClick.com
www.chickclick.com
The Web site where Courtney works is a one-stop shop for news, health information, and advice. A network of teens and women discuss college, society and politics, stars and style, and physical and emotional health issues.

WebGrrls
www.webgrrls.com
The mission of Webgrrls is to inspire women toward tech careers. Through articles and advice, tips and tutorials on job-related topics, and quizzes pertaining to the business world, learn about new media and technology careers.

 Association for Women in Communications
780 Ritchie Highway, Suite 28-S • Severna Park, MD 21146 • (410) 544-7442
www.womcom.org
This professional organization champions the advancement of women across all media by recognizing excellence and promoting leadership. Read up on industry news, network, or seek employment at this site for women on the cutting edge of communications.

Captain Esther Obert   HOT *Job...*

U.S. Air Force Fighter Pilot

I pilot the F-16, an extremely fast and sophisticated plane, in simulated missions and, if it arises, in combat. In my squadron at Shaw Air Force Base, I'm the ECP, or electronic combat pilot, which means I'm the "go to war" expert in the area of electronic signals that may be emitted by the enemy and considered threats to U.S. safety.

Home Base: Shaw Air Force Base, Sumter, South Carolina

Number of Years in the Field: 5

Personal Philosophy: "Go for it! Women can do anything in the Air Force a man can do, including being a fighter pilot."

I became interested in the military after my older brother went to West Point (the academy for the Army) and I saw all of the opportunities he had. I decided the military was a good option for me, because I wanted to major in engineering. With a six-year Air Force commitment, my education would be free. The Air Force also presented opportunities to do a lot of things that the average college student doesn't get to do, like jump out of airplanes, ride in helicopters, and travel.

In 1996, I graduated from the Air Force Academy as a second lieutenant with a degree in engineering science, and that's when I first decided I wanted to be a pilot. I just thought, "You know what? That sounds pretty adventurous. I think I'll try it." Believe it or not, the majority of the Air Force isn't made up of pilots. They're a small percentage of the personnel and the rest of the Air Force supports their missions. I wasn't dead set on being a fighter pilot—to be honest, I didn't even know if it was something women were allowed to do—but I wanted to fly and applied to go through training. I was chosen for the program after passing the medical exam and doing really well in the first phase of training. I figured, "Hey, I have the opportunity to become not just a pilot, but a *fighter pilot* and that's really cool." So I decided to go for it.

63

There are four different Air Force bases in the United States where pilots are trained, and the training process lasts a little over a year. Once you finish, depending on how you perform and what you're interested in doing, you can either fly tankers (big planes that refuel precision attack aircrafts called F-16s while they're in flight), transports (big planes that carry people and supplies to wherever we deploy), cargo planes (which carry supplies), or go on for additional training to fly fighter or bomber attack planes, which is what I did.

I've never worked as hard in my life as I did during pilot training. For every flight, I was graded and ranked, which determined my overall ranking. At the end of training, everyone gathers in a small room with a projector screen that shows a list of all the planes available to fly at that time. Each person is called to the front of the room in the order that he or she ranked at the end of training to choose the type of plane he or she wants to fly. It's a pretty big deal; you're there with your family and your peers, basically deciding what you're going to do for the rest of your life. I did well enough in training that I was able to choose a fighter plane, and I chose the F-16.

For me, the allure of flying fighter planes didn't have to do with their weapons or power, it had to do with the personal challenge. In addition to flying from point A to B, fighter pilots are also responsible for employing all kinds of weapons and the hand-eye coordination is more difficult because tactical (combat) maneuvering is involved. Fighter pilots also fly in a single-seat jet, so there's no crew to help out.

For my specialized fighter pilot training, I spent eight months at a school called Introduction to Fighter Fundamentals. I took an F-16 training course, where I learned the basics of being a fighter pilot. Because this schooling happens after general piloting training, it took about two years for me to become an operational fighter pilot.

Reporting for Duty

The cockpit of the F-16 is designed to fit around your body and is very ergonomic, meaning all the controls (there are about 100 little switches and knobs) are right there so you don't have to turn or reach. Most U.S. fighter planes are designed this way, which makes it easy for pilots to perform switch actuations (turning switches and knobs on or off) without having to look down while flying. This way the pilot can concentrate on a task, whatever it may be.

Panels, switches, and instruments are all around you, in front of your face and alongside your legs. There's also the throttle and stick, which are like the gas pedal and steering wheel in a car. The throttle is on the left side of the cockpit and controls how much fuel you're giving the engine. The stick is on the right side. It takes very little movement to control the plane because the F-16 is a "fly-by-wire" aircraft (meaning it's flown by electronic rather than mechanical signals). Once you're strapped in, you've got fairly good range of motion with your upper body, but your lower body is stationary. The cramped quarters are pretty tolerable for someone my size, but some pilots are 6'2" and 6'3", and they can't move at all in there.

The F-16 can go up to 800 knots (1,500 mph)—which is really, really fast. This speed produces a huge force of acceleration on your body, which is called "G" force. Sitting on earth, we're at 1 G, and the F-16 can pull 9 Gs. The way the Gs affect the body is a serious deal for pilots. As the amount of Gs increase, blood is basically pulled from your brain because the force of gravity is pulling it down. As a result, your brain loses oxygen and you can actually fall asleep—this is called "G-LOC" (G-induced Loss of Consciousness) and a lot of people have died from it. To prevent G-LOC, pilots learn to perform what's called an "anti-G strain maneuver."

Our flight gear also helps prevent G-LOC. In addition to a helmet with a visor and a mask, pilots also wear an "anti-G" suit, which covers the legs and stomach. The suit is filled with air bladders that expand with oxygen. The suit connects to the aircraft's oxygen system, and the more Gs a pilot pulls, the more air gets pumped into the suit, which puts pressure on the legs and stomach. This pressure keeps the blood from rushing to our extremities and out of our brains. As we pull more Gs, we also squeeze our lower bodies and breathe in short, quick breaths (this is the anti-G maneuver), which combined with the inflated suit, maintains our blood pressure and keeps us alert under the G-forces.

During training to become an F-16 pilot, students also condition their bodies to handle the pull of Gs at the Holloman centrifuge, located at Holloman Air Force Base in New Mexico. The centrifuge is a huge spinning chamber that can simulate up to 9 Gs (the limit for F-16s). The idea is to build up a tolerance to the Gs, and it also gives you a chance to practice the anti-G maneuvers in a safe setting.

Physically, G force is probably the hardest part of flying the F-16. When you're in an air-to-air engagement and want to turn as fast as you can, you're going to pull 8 to 9 Gs, and you have to be ready or you'll just nod off. It's also important to drink plenty of water before flying, because being dehydrated affects the fluid levels in your body, which makes it easier for G-LOC to occur. You have to be mentally *and* physically prepared for every mission.

Esther ready to take to the air in her F-16.

A large part of my job is piloting the F-16, but an actual sortie (daily flight or mission) involves much more than just flying the plane. The first order of the day is to attend a pre-flight briefing. The entire flight squadron (30 pilots, of which I'm the only woman, and about 150 maintenance and support people) meets for about an hour in a small room to find out what we'll be doing that day. We're told what our tactical mission will be and how we're going to do it. It could be an air-to-air (for example, four F-16s against four F-15s—we use simulated air-to-air missiles that cover a large distance) or air-to-ground mission (we fly out, drop practice bombs, and shoot the 20-millimeter machine gun at targets—every F-16 plane is equipped with a machine gun). During these missions, we train like we're in a real combat situation except that we use computerized weapons simulations instead of real weapons. (While most of our trainings use simulated weapons, I've also dropped live bombs twice in training. This usually occurs in the desert or ranges in unpopulated areas.) We also discuss what we're simulating, for example, which type of bomb we're dropping, and things like that. Then we go out and fly. A typical sortie lasts about an hour and a half. When the flight is over, we meet again for debriefing to review everything that happened while we were in the air.

In the F-16, an 8-millimeter tape is used to record the different screens in the plane and the HUD (or Heads-up Display, a projection of the flight data on the windshield that enables us to read the display and look forward at the same time). At the debriefing, the tapes from each plane in the mission are played back. We hear our own voices as well as the radio transmissions, and see exactly what was done throughout the flight.

Whether we used live or simulated weapons, the squadron critiques how each pilot performed—whether their bombs were effective, how they did in air-to-air engagement, and how they functioned in other parts of the flight. If things went wrong, we try to figure out why. All this information helps us pick apart each mission in great detail and that's where most of the learning takes place. The goal is to come up with a lesson learned, so the next time a pilot can avoid the same mistake. A typical debriefing session can last up to three or four hours.

Because we discuss our mistakes, debriefing sessions require a thick skin. The Air Force has three core values: integrity first, service before self, and excellence in all we do. These principles guide us through our training and into our military careers. The most important value to me is integrity. One of the great things about the Air Force, or the military in general, is that when you ask someone a question and look them in the eye, you know you're going to get an honest answer. It's a bond that's especially important between fellow pilots. You need to know that everything said to you is the truth; that you can count on everyone in your squadron to always be honest and give 110 percent. You're out there putting yourself on the line, and protecting your buddy, too. We're not afraid to be blunt with each other either: "Hey, you messed this up. Why?" We bring up all the bad stuff, learn from our mistakes, and move on.

After the debriefing, only a couple of hours are left in the day, and this is when we perform our other duties. At Shaw, our mission is SEAD—Suppression of Enemy Air Defense. Essentially, this means that we deter our enemies from targeting any United States or coalition aircraft (any aircraft sponsored by the United Nations such as the United States, United Kingdom, or France) with their radar. Using the sophisticated technology in the F-16, we can do a lot to prevent that from happening. As the ECP (electronic combat pilot), I need to have a detailed knowledge of the systems and weapons that we use and carry. This involves a lot of studying as well as having practical knowledge of the systems themselves. I also train the squadron so that *they* learn what our capabilities are, too.

Danger in the Line of Duty

In February 1999, I was undergoing training to become an operational F-16 pilot at Luke Air Force Base in the Arizona desert. (I was already an official pilot, but training to become a fully trained *fighter* pilot.) It was a typical desert morning—60 degrees, clear blue skies, you could see for at least 50 miles—and we were on a simulated mission. I was doing a type of bombing attack where we fly very low and fast, and then pop up at the last second and roll in on the target. We do this so the enemy can't see us from the ground and we can surprise them. My airspeed was about 500 knots and I was flying at an altitude of 500 feet. I tried to switch my engine over to afterburner (the rear section of the turbofan engine, which makes the plane go super fast by dumping fuel into the combustion chamber) to achieve the high speed I needed, but it didn't work. Instead, I felt this big clunk and I knew something was wrong. At first I thought, "Oh, my engine must have stalled." We never fly alone, always in groups of two or four planes. The guy who was flying next to my plane looked over and radioed, "Hey . . . you're missing the back of your engine." As it turns out, 4 feet of my engine (the entire afterburner section) had disconnected and fallen off.

I had read about this happening a couple of times in the history of the F-16, but with this type of plane, you can't just land anywhere you find level ground; you need a long runway because the plane comes in at such a high speed. In both the instances I had read about, the pilots were able to make it to a suitable runway and bring the plane down safely.

I tried to climb away from the ground to get to the nearest airfield, which was about 20 miles away, with the intention of trying to land. Whenever a pilot has a problem with a plane and he or she is close to the ground, the first reaction is to climb. We're trained to do this because the ground will kill you if you hit it, so it's safer to climb. My instructor and I were working together; I was piloting and making the decisions, but he was helping me via radio because he had a lot more experience than I did. We have a button in the F-16 called "the emergency jettison button" and when you push it, all of your external stores (such as tanks and bombs) fall off the aircraft to make it lighter and more maneuverable. I had to jettison my fuel tanks, which allowed me to climb about 2,000 feet higher.

I was now at 3,000 feet and wanted to go higher but my engine wouldn't let me. I was moving very slowly and my thrust (the amount of power the engine is putting out) was extremely reduced, making it difficult to maintain level flight. I pushed the power forward as far as possible and focused my effort on getting into a landable position. I could tell that the engine was trying as hard as it could to keep me level at 3,000 feet off the ground. The problem was I had too far to go.

About 5 miles from where I planned to bring the plane down the engine started to eat itself apart; a turbine blade went through a fuel cell and caught on fire. It was high-pressure fuel that ignited, so it was actually a pretty big fire. At that point I didn't have too many options. The only thing I could do was eject. So I reached down, pulled the yellow handle between my legs, and the next thing I knew I was underneath a parachute. The parachute automatically deploys once the seat is far enough away from the airplane. A rocket motor inside the seat pushes you straight up. The ejection seat actually knows how fast you're going and how high up in the air you are, so if you're close to the ground, it puts the parachute out fast and if you are in higher altitude, it waits awhile to deploy it. Since I was close to the ground, it all happened in 1.3 seconds. I landed in the Arizona desert in a dried up creek bed. I steered it there to avoid the cacti!

When I listened to the radio transmission of the incident afterwards, it amazed me how calm I was the entire time. It all happened pretty fast—over the course of about 10 minutes—so I didn't really have time to think about it. I guess when something like that happens, your instincts take over. You just react . . . you don't have time to think. We practice emergency procedures all the time, so it was pretty much ingrained in my head what to do. I suppose my actions in this situation showed me how well I was trained to pilot the plane.

After this mission, I wasn't allowed to fly for a week, which is Air Force procedure; they need to observe you before you get back in a plane to make sure you're okay. After the week was up, I performed my first flight. I had to go up in a two-seat F-16 (which we don't use often; 99 percent of the time we fly single-seat planes), so someone could observe me and make sure I didn't freeze up or panic while I was flying. I was fine and went back to my normal flying schedule. Since that incident, I haven't experienced any fear of being in the air, but my sense of awareness is heightened; I feel and notice more things in the plane than I did before. Every little rumble gets my attention.

Rising to Every Challenge

Pilot training was definitely hard work, but all you're really learning in flight school is how to fly basic maneuvers and use the instruments to get from point A to point B. Now, the kind of flying I do involves weapons, and the *easiest* thing I do is the actual piloting of the F-16. The hardest part is employing all of the weapons and the radar, and doing everything else that has to be done while flying. It's really challenging because there's so much more to know and be responsible for, and a lot more pressure to perform. You're out there and your life is at stake, not to mention the lives of everyone you're flying with. You're actually training to go into combat, not into a sterile environment where you don't have to consider these types of dangerous situations.

My only actual combat experience so far has been in Iraq. I've been deployed twice for Operation Southern Watch and Operation Northern Watch. Basically, we fly in and defend the no-fly zone (regions established by United Nations Security Council Resolution 668 and monitored by the Air Force for almost 10 years, prohibiting Iraq from military air operations against Shia and Kurd minorities) to ensure that Iraq doesn't violate the policies that were set up in 1991. Typically, a deployment like that lasts around three months.

During these deployments, I lived on an Air Force base and stayed in a dorm-like room. It's tough to be in a foreign country (I've been deployed to Saudi Arabia and Turkey), and you don't have some of the luxuries you have in the United States. But although it was hard to be away from home, I stayed very busy, so that helped pass the time. Plus my family and friends were supportive and sent me letters and care packages . . . emails helped, too.

Whenever someone's deployed, I'm sure they feel a little nervous at the thought of going into actual combat. I got through these feelings by reminding myself that we're prepared; we train for this stuff every day. The only difference is that instead of a simulation, we have real weapons. I think we're all pretty confident that we can go out there and perform any mission assigned to us because that's our job and we've been trained well.

It's a great feeling to know that I'm defending my country and its values. Like many people, I'm proud to be an American. But it feels different to know that I'm actually out there fighting for the American flag. A lot of what we do occurs all over the world and when you see the American flag flying, you feel so proud.

To this day, people come up to my parents and say, "Your daughter can't fly in combat. We don't allow women to fly fighters in combat." But guess what? We do. Women were first permitted to fly in combat in 1994, and now nothing restricts what women can do in the Air Force. It's true that, historically, this has been a man's job, but more and more women become fighter pilots all the time. The rules have changed. Now we can do anything in the Air Force that men can do, and it feels great!

I wanted a hot job and that's what I got. I know that I'm a pioneer and that some people still don't agree that women should be fighter pilots. I hope they'll eventually see the light, because being a fighter pilot doesn't have anything to do with gender, just ability and motivation. I never use the fact that I'm a female to get special treatment in the Air Force; I try to blend in with everyone else. I think that's the only way to integrate the armed forces. Fighter pilots have such a strong bond because we depend on each other for our lives. In my squadron, my peers accept me as a sister the way they accept each other as brothers, and they treat me the way they treat the male fighter pilots. It will take time, but sooner or later, being a female fighter pilot will mean nothing more than being a fighter pilot.

A Behind-the-Scenes Look at the Job

Favorite Part: I love how adventurous this job is. Day after day you get to go really fast! Flying the F-16 is also a lot of fun; it's a very maneuverable plane, so you can do anything with it. Every time you go out for a mission, you give it everything you have, and afterward, you go over every detail with your squadron of what you did in order to learn from the experience.

Least Favorite Part: Due to pilot cutbacks from military downsizing in the last decade, there's a shortage of pilots, and the ones we have seem to be overworked. Our hours are very long, so by the end of the week you're really tired. It's just a limitation of the Air Force right now, but hopefully that will change.

Hours: We typically work five days a week, around ten to twelve hours each day. My starting time in the morning depends on the flying schedule for the base. Some weeks we fly early, so I'll have to be in at 5:30 A.M.; other weeks we'll fly at night, and I won't have to come in until 10:30 or 11 A.M.

Dress Code: Every day I wear a green flight suit made of Nomax, which is a fire-retardant material, with a T-shirt underneath and combat boots. The suit is like a big, green bag that zips down the front, and it's definitely made for a man; when I go to the restroom I have to take the whole thing off!

Work Environment: The base itself is like a little city, including housing facilities. Our squadron has its own building where we work, and our jets are parked in front. When we aren't flying, our other duties are carried out in different sections of the building. Most of my ECP work takes place in the Vault, which is a secure section where all of the classified information is stored. I don't actually live on the base; that's reserved for married people.

Education/Skills: To fly in the Air Force, first you have to be an officer, and then you must be selected for pilot training. To become an officer you need a college degree in any major and to put in a certain amount of time. Another option is the Air Force Academy, which is a four-year institution. If you go there, you earn your degree while training to be an officer. I was a second lieutenant (which is the lowest ranking officer) when I finished college at the Air Force Academy. Now I'm a captain.

The biggest skill needed for my job is hand-eye coordination. Believe it or not, most of the fighter pilots I know grew up playing video games! Playing sports, an instrument, or anything that requires quick reactions is a great benefit.

Personal Qualities: To succeed as a fighter pilot, you have to be dedicated, confident, aggressive, and willing to push yourself. You need to do so many different things . . . it's a really dynamic job and you can never just "get used to it." It also helps to be pretty thick-skinned. For example, during debriefing after a flight, we basically offer each other constructive criticism for three or four hours. No one holds anything back, and every move you made gets picked apart. You have to be able to sit there and take that kind of intense critiquing without taking it personally. You learn to handle the criticism with the training. It's not like we are trying to hurt anyone's feelings, we just want everyone to get better and do well.

To be successful in the military, you must be disciplined, have a sense of honor and duty, a desire to serve others, and the ability to take orders and respect authority.

Perks and Rewards: The biggest reward is how cool it is! I often run into people who say, "Ever since I was little I've dreamed of being a pilot." I think I take it for granted because I fly all the time, but I know there are many people who would give anything to do just once what I do every day.

HOT TIPS

   🔥   Concentrate on doing well in school. To get accepted into a military academy, good grades are a must. The Air Force Academy in particular is one of the most selective colleges in the country and requires that you take four years of English, four years of math (including Algebra, Geometry, Trigonometry, and Calculus), basic science courses (like biology, chemistry, physics, and computers), and social science courses (like history, economics, government, and behavioral sciences). Even if you're not looking into getting into a military academy, you'll still need good grades to join the armed forces.

   🔥   Leadership qualities are important to your success in the military. Now is a good time to take on challenges that will give you leadership experience. Consider running for student government, becoming a youth group leader at your church, organizing a fundraiser, or taking on any other position that requires you to lead and set an example for others.

   🔥   If you are seriously interested in the Air Force Academy, you can take a tour of the campus (located in Colorado Springs, Colorado), which is available for high school students. The daylong tour gives you the opportunity to see the campus and dorms, take classes, eat lunch in the dining hall, and ask questions.

   🔥   Stay in shape. You'll need to be physically fit to make it in the military, so now's a good time to start a regular fitness program. Find something you like—such as jogging, walking, biking, or organized sports like basketball or soccer—and staying active will be easier. The Air Force Academy places a strong emphasis on sports and physical fitness since involvement helps instill leadership, confidence, teamwork, endurance, agility, and a competitive spirit.

🔥 Stay away from drugs and other illegal activities. This is a no-brainer no matter what career you choose, but the military, especially military academies, are looking for candidates who demonstrate strong moral character. Any brushes with the law or drug and underage alcohol use could keep you out.

WORDS OF WISDOM

Some people get their civilian pilot's license or take private flying lessons when they're in high school or college—but that's not the only route to becoming a fighter pilot. I went into this field completely cold, with no flying experience whatsoever. You *do*, however, need to get a college degree and become an officer, or you can go to the Air Force Academy like I did, and work to get accepted into pilot training.

Find Out More!

Bogeys and Bandits: The Making of a Fighter Pilot by Robert L. Gandt (New York: Viking, 1997). Eight trainees (including two women) are followed from start to finish as they undergo the grueling process of becoming Naval fighter pilots. This book gives an up close view of the difficulties and struggles they encounter along the way.

Flying
P.O. Box 53647 • Boulder, CO 80322 • (850) 682-7654
www.flyingmag.com
This magazine for aspiring pilots contains interesting and exciting stories, articles about flying, detailed information about new products and planes, a calendar of events, and a questions and answer section.

United States Air Force
www.airforce.com
Find information at this site about 150 careers in the Air Force. Also included are educational opportunities, officer programs, details about basic training, and local recruiters.

The Ninety-Nines
Box 965, 7100 Terminal Drive • Oklahoma City, OK 73159 • 1-800-994-1929
www.ninety-nines.org
This organization was founded in 1929 by 99 women pilots for female support and advancement in aviation. The site offers information on great pioneers of aviation and women pilots making history today. Also find scholarship, grant, and award opportunities for young women in the aviation industry.

HOT *Job...*

Wedding Planner

and Business Owner

As the owner and operator of A Perfect Wedding, Inc., I help brides and grooms create a vision for their wedding and do everything I can to make their dream happen. I help make all the arrangements—from the invitations to the menu, to the cake and flowers. I suggest sites for the ceremony and reception, plan the wedding's design and decor, add creative touches, make a schedule of things to do before the big day, track all of the details, and oversee the actual wedding day from start to finish.

Home Base: Fairfax, Virginia

Number of Years in the Field: 9

Personal Philosophy: "Love what you do and success will follow."

When I was a child, my favorite and most prized possession was a bride doll—a precursor to my future, perhaps? Maybe, but I never thought about becoming a wedding planner until after my own wedding. Like most brides, I had a lot of ideas about how I envisioned my big day, but I didn't know how to carry them out. So I hired a wedding consultant (consultant, coordinator, and planner are terms used interchangeably in this business) to help me. Unfortunately, though, not everything went as planned. When my wedding day came, many of the details we discussed and planned didn't get implemented. For instance, my wedding cake ended up having four tiers instead of three, didn't look like the one I picked out, and leaned like the Tower of Pisa! I'd specifically requested that no green garlands be draped on tables, and that was the first thing I saw when I walked in. To top it off, I had ordered a magnificent champagne fountain, but the wedding coordinator over-filled it and it didn't start working again until midway through the reception. Despite my slight disappointment (this was the happiest day of my life, after all!), I still thought being a wedding coordinator seemed like a great job. I've always been extremely organized and detail oriented, and I felt that I would get a lot of enjoyment from making things easier for other brides.

I started coordinating weddings at a local historic church. They often had four weddings per day and needed someone to make sure one event didn't run into the next. At the same time, I began taking professional development courses through various wedding consultant associations. This combination of hands-on experience and coursework helped me become more familiar with the logistics of planning a wedding, including all of the industries, businesses, and vendors involved. Only after I had acquired this in-depth knowledge of the field did I feel comfortable setting up my own business and calling myself a wedding planner.

Because I've always been a fast learner, it only took me about six months to get my business started. Training courses that usually take six months to a year to complete only took me six weeks. I also researched and met vendors in my area, including everyone from photographers to caterers. I have a lot of drive, energy, and focus and I worked toward my goal full time, right from the start. What's important to note, though, is that a business is an ongoing learning experience—whether it's discovering new wedding service providers or keeping up with current trends. Opening the business was easy; perfecting it has taken years!

In recent years, several movies have depicted wedding coordinators and the planning process—which are fun for me to watch. But despite what you might see in the movies, consultants aren't flippant with the client's money and they certainly don't fall in love with the groom—if we did we wouldn't have any business! But some films have accurately portrayed the nuts and bolts of this career—meeting with clients, discussing an infinite number of details, and bringing creative ideas into play.

Many couples dream about their wedding day for a long time and know that it's one of those special moments that will always be remembered. They want a wedding that reflects their tastes and styles. They want something that, in years to come, when their children, family, and friends look at the photos or video, they'll see the couple's personality showing through. It's my job to get to know each couple and help create that vision. Brides and grooms tell me all the time that I make their dreams come true (I tend to hear a lot of thanks and warm words; it's a definite perk of being a part of one of the most joyous events in a person's life!), but I feel more like a dream catcher than a fairy godmother. I consider my role to be someone who catches sight of another person's dream, and then makes it happen.

Event Planners Must Be Ready for Anything

Most of the weddings I plan are held in traditional locations, such as churches, historic mansions, gardens, museums, country clubs, and hotel ballrooms. But even traditional weddings can become wild events, like the time we had a fire, flood, and a bee swarm all at the same function!

The wedding was held at the place where George Washington grew up, now called River Farm. About 150 people were in attendance and we had planned for various aspects of the reception to be held in different areas of the home. The fire started when a guest inadvertently knocked over a candle and walked out of the room, not realizing it had set the linens ablaze. When I walked in and saw huge flames shooting up to the ceiling, all I could think was, "I can't believe it! George Washington's family home is going to burn down on my watch!"

I closed myself in the ballroom, which probably wasn't the smartest thing to do, but I didn't want the guests to walk in and see the room on fire. I grabbed some tablecloths and started beating out the flames. At that moment, the caterer walked through with a big vat of hot water for tea and yelled, "Get out of the way!" as he threw the water over the fire. The two of us kept beating at the flames and just when we finally put it out, somebody came running in with a fire extinguisher. Before we could stop him, he blew foam over the entire mess. To make matters worse, dessert was scheduled to be served in that room in 10 minutes!

I was racing around scouting the house for a different room to serve dessert. Although harried, I felt safe because all the guests were outside in two tented areas, off the terrace and on the veranda. But while I was searching for a new room for the dessert, an unexpected storm kicked up and down came torrential rain. It was dry under the tents, but it rained so hard that the ground around the tents flooded and water came seeping in. No one seemed too fazed by this, though; the guests were still on the dance floor, dancing in puddles.

But that's not all. At the beginning of the reception, the wedding cake was sitting under this beautiful little portico, and several bees were flitting around it. A guest came along and stuck her nose right in there to get a closer look at the cake. She had on heavy perfume, which caught the attention of the bees, and they went after her, chasing her around the area. I should have known right then that it would be a rough night.

At the end of the evening, feeling like I'd been through an event planner's worst nightmare, the site manager came up to me and said he'd call me Monday about the insurance for the fire. The mother of the bride overheard and said, "Fire? Was there a fire?" No one had even known! I breathed a sigh of relief knowing that the bride and groom were unaffected by all the chaos and thought to myself, "I'm so happy that despite the fire, despite the flood, and despite the bees, I still did my job and the wedding turned out beautiful!"

Weddings of All Shapes and Sizes

The average cost of a wedding in the Washington, D.C., area is about $25,000 to $35,000 (the average nationwide is around $20,000). The largest budget I've worked with was $225,000 with a guest list of around 350 people. Most of my events are what I would call "high end," in the high five-figure dollar range. I've been asked to plan weddings of 700 or 800 people, but I generally decline the offer because that amount of people is just too crazy to work with.

One of the most memorable weddings I've done was also the smallest; just 30 people, and it was fabulous. The bride and groom initially called and said, "We've been engaged for a while, but we haven't really thought about a wedding date . . . we've done nothing." They asked me to plan their wedding and said they needed it all done in two weeks, but they wanted it to look like it was planned for a year. The couple worked for the same company, and both of them were being transferred to Australia several weeks later. They wanted to make sure their wedding didn't look like it was just "thrown together" and wanted to know if I could pull it off. I said, "Let me think about it." I did (for about 10 seconds) then said yes . . . how could I say no to such a great challenge?

Since they were moving to Australia, I kept thinking, "What can I do that will make this wedding really special for them?" One of the ideas I came up with was using Australia's national song, which is "Waltzing Matilda," and having them dance to that. We also used eucalyptus—the country's national flower—in their floral arrangements. Everything was planned down to the last detail; no stone was left unturned, from having pewter place cards, to specially designed menu cards, to floral arrangements that matched the wallpaper in the room. I didn't sleep for about two weeks, but it was one of my favorite weddings. A few weeks later, the wedding was featured in the local newspaper because it was a perfect example of how wedding planning has changed over the years. Because of job demands, couples often want to do things quickly.

While my specialty has become more expensive weddings, they aren't the only type of event I do. Other times I work with people who have very little to spend and rely on me to plan a beautiful wedding on a shoestring budget. These weddings are just as much fun to plan and often require more creativity. I recall one couple who had very limited funds for their wedding because they were both in graduate school. It was smart of them to contact a wedding planner to help; a wedding consultant probably saved them more money than if they had planned it all themselves. I was able to assess their needs, and together we figured out what they could do themselves and what made more sense for me to plan. I found a caterer who gave them a great price and even threw in the wedding cake for free! They kept their guest list small, only inviting their relatives and closest friends. Every one of the 50 people there was delighted with the intimacy and beauty of the occasion.

Putting It All Together

When I help a couple plan their wedding I usually get to know them pretty well because it can take up to a year to plan all the details. During our time together I make an effort to find out their favorite foods, music, movies, colors, and anything else that's important to them. I also try to gain insight into their personalities so we can incorporate that into the overall plan, which helps make their wedding truly unique. There are certain things that almost every wedding has, such as flowers, cake, music, and food, so I try to use what I learn about the couple to create different elements that will make their particular event stand apart from every other one. For example, I may have a family crest or monogram put on the linens. Or I'll include a special food or drink, such as a margarita bar if the couple met at a Mexican restaurant. Or I'll try to incorporate a significant piece of music, like "Take Me Out to the Ballgame," to represent a favorite memory between the bride and her father.

The majority of my time, though, is spent arranging all the different services needed for each wedding and planning ahead for future ones. On any given day I could be dealing with six or more weddings, each in various stages of preparation. I have to match couples with vendors (wedding service providers) who I think will be able to meet their specific needs, work within their budget, and suit their personalities. I may also be working on a schedule for a ceremony and reception. For weddings happening that week, I need to contact all the vendors involved so I can keep track of any last minute details. I also could have a final walk-through meeting scheduled at the reception location. In the midst of all that, a bride may call with questions about etiquette or protocol. For example, she may want to verify how the ushers should seat guests at the ceremony or what an appropriate gift for her bridesmaids might be. Then I'll be off to meet clients at a florist shop or photographer's studio to iron out details for a wedding to be held the following year.

But days aren't my only busy times—I often get calls from prospective clients who want to schedule evening appointments with me. To be a wedding planner you have to work all day and be available in the evenings, too. I usually book after-hours appointments three or four nights a week. When a new client arrives, they "interview" me; we'll sit down and discuss what they need and what they want. Good chemistry is so important between a couple and their wedding planner. After all, it's one of the most important days in their lives and a lot of trust is involved. Personalities need to be in sync to make it productive. We also spend a lot of time together, so it's pretty important that we like each other!

While some of my evening appointments are relatively short, others can last up to three hours. Those are usually "finals," where I sit with the bride and groom about a month before the wedding and we go over every single detail of the event. We review the schedule for the wedding day, get the lineup together (the order in which everyone will come in and leave the ceremony), and figure out who's paired with whom (such as bridesmaids, groomsmen, and flower girls). Finally, I review any questions the couple may have regarding etiquette and protocol. While the days can be long, it's worth it to create amazing events and memories for each couple.

The "Big Day" Makes for a Long Day

On the day of a wedding, I'm there from beginning to end, making sure things flow smoothly and anything that could possibly go wrong is taken care of. I usually show up about two hours ahead of time. It's my responsibility to oversee all of the logistics. Flowers and programs are arriving, candles have to be lit, chairs need to be set up . . . any number of things could be happening. Everything has to move quickly, because there's generally a short turnaround time for events. Most wedding locations book both a day and an evening event, so sometimes we have only an hour or so to bring in everything we need to set up and make it all look perfect.

The night of the rehearsal, I hand out a schedule to the entire wedding party (as well as to the immediate family) that details everything that will be happening on the big day, including where everyone will be. When I develop a schedule, it's very detailed, starting early in the morning and continuing through the entire day. For instance, I'll plan the bride's day, noting her hair and makeup appointment, what time she needs to arrive at the church (or wherever the nuptials are taking place), when the preceremony photographs will be taken, and when she needs to be ready to walk down the aisle. The rest of the itinerary takes her through the course of the reception, ending with the couple's departure.

I can't tell you how many times such a detailed itinerary has come in handy. It's my job to be incredibly thorough and execute everything well, and it pays off in many situations. Once a groom thanked me profusely for the schedule. He had had an important question to ask the bride but didn't know where she was. Using the schedule, he was able to telephone her at the salon where she was having her hair done and get the question answered. It's these kinds of "mini-emergencies" that make a little extra planning and detail really pay off.

Creating a Fairy Tale

I like every wedding to be different, and work on every last detail to make it very special and unique for each couple. I usually start with a wedding that has no date, no site, and no particulars—just two people in love who want to get married. Sometimes a client will have a huge amount of money to spend and they'll put their trust in me to design and produce a memorable event. They hire me because they value my opinion and expertise, and because they want me to handle everything. In return, I create an event where they have the time of their lives.

Other times I'll be working with a much smaller budget. When I suggest a concept, plan every part of it, bring it to fruition, and see my clients thrilled beyond all expectation, it's an instant source of gratification. I love being able to make a wedding come out looking twice as expensive as it really was, and knowing my clients are very impressed by what I've accomplished. I love it when the guests walk into the reception and their jaws drop when they see what I've created for the bride and groom. It's the best feeling when the look on their faces says, "I've never seen anything like this!"

Aside from attending to every last detail, another aspect of my job is trying to put the couple at ease by working with them and their family dynamics. For instance, I may have to mediate between the bride and her mother because they have very different ideas of how they want things done. I try to address any potential problem areas before the event so I can then focus on keeping things running smoothly. And sometimes it gets pretty hectic! For example, before the ceremony I could have a line of people all waiting to ask me a question. I may be sewing a button on a groomsman's tuxedo jacket, speaking to a photographer about camera positioning, and listening for the music to cue, all at once. It's not easy to juggle so many things at once, and it takes practice to pull everything together without becoming unglued. But that's my job—not only to stay calm regardless of what's going on, but to keep the bride and groom calm, too.

Even though a wedding is a happy time, it's also a stressful and emotional day for the bride, the groom, and their families. So many of their hopes and dreams are pinned on that one day. Usually, when the bride and groom take one look at me at the wedding they become very calm; they realize I've been with them the whole time, planning, helping. They trust me and know I'm there to take care of everything. Planners do this all the time; no matter how big or small, no matter what the size of the budget, every wedding is special.

This Is Their Day

I tend to get really close to many of my clients; they share their feelings with me throughout the planning process, and I come to know their families as well. I usually remain detached, calm, cool, and professional during an event, but there are exceptions. If a couple has had a lot of outside stress to deal with during the course of planning and their emotions start to really flow during the wedding, it's pretty hard not to empathize with them and shed a few tears of my own.

Carol helps a bride on the way to the altar.

My greatest hope for every couple I work with is that they relax, enjoy the moment, and focus on their love and commitment to each other. Weddings go by very fast, and I feel that it's my responsibility to ensure that they remember their own true happiness of that day for the rest of their lives. And I believe I do just that!

A Behind-the-Scenes Look at the Job

Favorite Part: I love working with people and being part of the most special moment of their lives. I also enjoy that each job is unique, allowing me new challenges at every turn. Each week I'm in a different location working with a different client. I could be in a tent with high winds and rain one week and in a hotel ballroom overlooking the city the next. One thing's for sure, it's never boring!

Least Favorite Part: Occasionally I run into someone who doesn't understand what a coordinator can and can't do and isn't open to working with me. This can definitely be frustrating, but it can also be an opportunity to win them over and prove how great working with a wedding consultant can be!

Hours: Ten- to twelve-hour days are common in this industry, particularly on wedding days; consultants are the first to arrive and the last to leave. During the week, office hours are generally 9 A.M. to 6 P.M., but three or four nights a week I schedule an evening appointment, usually from 7 P.M. to 10 P.M. Friday nights I'm tied up with rehearsals and, of course, weekends and holidays are popular times for weddings. This is basically a six-days-a-week job. I take Sundays off, but also have the flexibility during the week to schedule hours off here and there.

Dress Code: When I'm at a wedding, I usually wear something dressy (depending on the wedding, of course). Since the wedding coordinator is not a guest, a formal gown isn't necessary; a nice pantsuit or, my favorite, the "little black dress," allows me to work and still fit in with the environment. When I'm in the office I dress casually, but business suits are a must for meetings and appointments.

Work Environment: Daily work takes place in the office. Mine is at my home where I have a separate office used just for planning weddings. It has a mahogany desk and bookcases loaded with wedding and resource books, and the walls are covered with huge photos of weddings I've planned or coordinated. I have all the basics a wedding coordinator needs to set up shop: computer, fax machine, copier, printer, and telephone. As long as you have these, you can pretty much work anywhere.

Meetings outside the office are held at any number of places—floral shops, a photographer's studio, catering facilities, a restaurant over lunch, or the wedding site itself. Weddings and receptions are planned in all different locales, such as churches, gardens, hotel ballrooms, historic mansions, country clubs, and museums.

Education/Skills: A variety of coursework can prove valuable to a wedding consultant. Business and marketing classes are great if you plan to work for yourself. Psychology is helpful, especially when working with stressed couples or their difficult parents! And courses in art design are good because they can help you design a room or create a concept. Associations in the industry offer classes and workshops to learn about the field of bridal consulting and some colleges even offer a degree program in events management. I majored in journalism and my writing skills have been very helpful in developing brochures and literature, ad copy, and letters for my clients. Once you're ready to get started, join a professional association.

Personal Qualities: You definitely have to be a people person, and diplomacy is key. The groom and bride may have completely different ideas about what they envision for the wedding, and neither may agree with what you recommend. Somehow you must find a way to bring them together and make everyone happy. And if you work for yourself, you've got to be detail-oriented, disciplined, and motivated to make your business a success. You also need to have expert organizational and time-management skills.

Perks and Rewards: This is a very social type of job! I always receive invitations to teas, luncheons, dinners, and receptions from vendors I work with or managers of hotels or other venues. I also get to travel to great places. I've been to London and Rome to study the European wedding market and to the Caribbean Islands to check out places for destination weddings. After the wedding, many clients send you home with a monetary tip, a special gift, fabulous flower arrangements, and delicious wedding cake.

HOT TIPS

- As a high school student, take whatever business and marketing courses you can. Writing classes are also helpful as communicating well with your clients both verbally and in written promotional materials is crucial.

- Help organize a school dance or an event for a club, religious group, or sports team you're involved with to see if you like planning and handling lots of details.

- Intern, apprentice, or volunteer for an experienced wedding consultant or events company. The experience will be invaluable.

🔥 Get a part-time job at a florist shop, catering business, or photography studio. It's a great way to earn some spending money while you learn about the vendors involved in planning a big event like a wedding.

WORDS OF WISDOM

If you're positive, enthusiastic, and really love what you're doing, it shows. The only way to do this type of work is be really thorough, so before you decide to call yourself a wedding consultant, planner, or coordinator, know your business. It's not just about fluffing the train as the bride walks down the aisle. You have to know all the wedding service providers in your area—how they work, what they offer, what they charge, and how their personality works on wedding day. You've got to be well versed in every facet of the industry, and keep up with new products, businesses, trends, and up-and-coming vendors. Be prepared to work long hours and most weekends. If you stick with it and are persistent, your hard work will pay off. This is a fun and exciting career, and truly a hot job by any standard!

Find Out More!

Easy Wedding Planning: The Most Comprehensive and Easy-to-Use Wedding Planner by Elizabeth H. and Alex H. Lluch (San Diego, CA: Wedding Solutions Publishing, 2000). This easy-to-use planner helps a bride-to-be and others interested in learning about the wedding planning industry. It spells out all of the necessary preparations and includes a time table for keeping track of all the details.

Gala! The Special Event Planner for Professionals and Volunteers by Patti Coons with Lois M. Baron (Sterling, VA: Capital Books, 1999). This book is a great tool for anyone interested in learning to plan big events. Find advice for putting together any event. Checklists offer step-by-step guidance through the planning process.

The Knot
www.theknot.com
The Knot offers a complete guide to everything wedding related, from 99 ways to save money to setting the perfect table. Learn the ins and outs of putting together the ideal event. Also available are fashion tips and resources, city-specific trends in weddings, and lots of other specific information.

Association of Bridal Consultants
200 Chestnutland Road • New Milford, CT 06776-2521 • (860) 355-0464
www.bridalassn.com
The Association of Bridal Consultants has been one of the professional organizations for the wedding industry since 1981 and has about 2,500 members in 28 countries. It's a membership service organization, designed to increase awareness of the wedding business and improve the professionalism of members.

HOT *Job...*

Zoo Director

of the Smithsonian Institution's National Zoological Park

I run the National Zoo, which is a 163-acre public park in Washington, D.C., with more than 3,500 animals as well as native and exotic plants.

Home Base: Washington, D.C.

Number of Years in the Field: 12

Personal Philosophy: "Don't let anybody tell you that you can't achieve your dream."

I grew up on an old dairy farm in Connecticut with a menagerie of domestic animals. We had everything from cats and dogs to horses, goats, and parakeets. Being around them helped me learn about animals' needs and how to meet them as well as establish a strong caretaking connection. In fact, I was so connected that when I first envisioned a career, I knew it had to be with animals. I'm not sure the word "conservation" was in my head, but I knew I wanted to work with nature.

I decided that becoming a vet was the path for me, and training in veterinary medicine would give me a valuable skill. It was important to me to enter a field that was related to nature and wildlife, because in the long run, I really wanted to work with wild animals. After college I went to veterinary college for four years and then participated in a zoo medicine training program to become a zoo veterinarian. In 1994, when I passed the board-certifying exam to become a specialized zoo vet, I was the thirty-fifth—and youngest—person to receive this distinction.

I started working at the National Zoo in 1995 as an associate veterinary medical officer. I worked to become a supervisory veterinary medical officer, then the head of the Department of Animal Health, and then the Zoo Director in June 2000. I'm very passionate about my role at the

National Zoo and see it as twofold: I have a responsibility to all of the creatures housed here as well as to all of the people who work here. While the animals deserve the best care possible so they can thrive and live wonderful lives, the employees deserve my complete support so they're free to express their talents and reach their goals to better the zoo and help promote conservation. I think of my job as the leader of a team—and I strongly believe in teamwork. It takes a lot of hard work to run the National Zoo and I couldn't do it without the talents and skills of the dedicated people who work here.

As the director of the zoo, I have a very busy schedule. In addition to overseeing the care of the animals (which necessitates having an extensive knowledge of their anatomy, behavior, diet, and reproductive nature), I'm also responsible for the business side of things. This means preparing budgets for running the entire operation (including the Conservation and Research Center, a 3,200-acre facility in Front Royal, Virginia) as well as promoting the efforts of the zoo by giving speeches, doing interviews, and attending special events and fundraisers. I'm also responsible for planning for the future of the park, so it continues to meet the needs of the animals and our visitors in the best way possible.

What Goes on at the Zoo

So much more goes on at a zoo than exhibiting animals. One of my goals is to make people aware of all the wonderful things that happen behind the scenes. The zoo provides education on many levels, and we try to make learning as interactive and personal as we can. At the exhibits, visitors can read signage to learn about each animal and its habitat. Animal demonstrations also are going on constantly. For example, our elephants are exercised and have their feet checked each day. During any of these demonstration-type activities, zoo personnel narrate what's happening so the public can watch and ask questions to enhance their learning experience. Our visitors can see other activities, too, such as pandas being given fresh bamboo or a sea lion having its teeth brushed.

But visitors don't have to count on zoo staff to gain information. Just watching the animals is also educational. When animals are in a place where they feel free to perform their natural behaviors, people can watch them in action and learn what they're all about. If visitors want a more in-depth experience, we also conduct formal types of education. For instance, we host day camps and summer camps for children. We also organize weeklong workshops for teachers to teach them how to instruct their students about wild animals.

No matter what type of experience visitors are looking for, zoos really do play an important role, both for the visitor and the animal. Our mission is to study, celebrate, and help protect the diversity of animals and their habitats. Our vision for the future is to broaden our public outreach programs, modernize our oldest exhibit areas, and renew our role as a leading center for zoo animal care, reproductive biology, and conservation research. The earth and its inhabitants depend on biodiversity (the earth's variety of plant and animal life and their ecosystems) for survival because every plant and every animal plays a vital role in maintaining the balance of the earth's ecosystem. When that balance is disrupted, it can have a negative ripple effect, posing a threat to everything from the water we drink to the air we breathe. That's why conservation has become an important issue for most zoos; we must take an active role in eliminating the human-caused threat of plant and animal extinction to protect the earth's biological balance.

Today's zoos are involved with global conservation, research, and education efforts. Most prominent zoos no longer simply exhibit animals. Zoos of the twenty-first century have evolved into valuable resources for the preservation and protection of the earth's plants and animals. Some animals, like the giant panda or the Sumatran tiger, are on the edge of extinction because their numbers are so low. By studying and understanding an animal or a plant, we have the opportunity to do everything within our means to secure its future.

At the National Zoo, we have a long tradition of on-site and in-the-field scientific study of endangered species. The zoo population can provide a safety net or a fallback to ensure the survival of a species. In the zoo world, we manage the breeding of the different species that we care for through the Species Survival Plan (SSP). The SSP was put together by zoos in 1981 and is administered by the American Zoo and Aquarium Association.

The SSP ensures that the offspring born in zoos are as genetically strong as they can be. Essentially what we're doing is genetic matchmaking, which means we carefully plan the breeding of a species in order to achieve a healthy, genetically diverse population. If not enough animals within a species have a diverse genetic background, they lose things like resistance to disease or adaptability to new environments, and a species can go extinct. Cloning is the absolute opposite of ensuring the future of an endangered species. It creates animals that are genetically the same, and that's exactly what we *don't* want. Animals need to adapt and evolve in order to survive, and the only way to do that is to produce offspring with a diverse combination of genes. The more diverse the male's and female's genetic makeup, the healthier their offspring will be.

To create a more diverse combination of genes within a species, we may send an animal from this zoo to another zoo for the sole purpose of breeding. Animal exchanges like these promote a healthy captive population. For example, for a self-sustaining, captive population of sloth bears or Komodo dragons, a certain amount of each species (the number is different for each species) is needed in captivity. Moving animals from zoo to zoo to breed prevents one male from fathering an entire population of a species, which puts that species at risk for survival. Without breeding exchanges, promoting genetic diversity would be difficult for zoos.

The Giant Pandas: An Endangered Species

When visitors come to the zoo, one of our goals is to educate them about animals and their habitats. We try to raise awareness that the earth and its creatures are in danger; if we don't start taking better care of both, we could lose a lot of the earth's natural resources—including our animals. By making the zoo a fun learning experience, we can teach people about the plight of animals in jeopardy and the importance of each species to our world.

One animal that the National Zoo highlights to demonstrate conservation is the giant panda. It's one of the most critically endangered animals in the world. Approximately 1,000 pandas are left in the wild, most living in the high mountain ranges of central China. These black and white wooly bears have distinct markings around their eyes, ears, legs, and shoulders and have thick coats that protect them from the cold, rainy weather of their mountainous habitat. About 140 giant pandas live in captivity (zoos and breeding centers). The majority of them are in captivity in China.

The biggest threat to the survival of giant pandas is habitat encroachment and destruction. A panda's diet is 99 percent bamboo, and as more bamboo forests in China are cut down for wood and farming, the pandas lose their primary source of food and nourishment. When land is cleared to construct new roads and build towns, the pandas' habitats become fragmented. This means the animals become separated from each other and the number of potential mates dwindles. When an animal species has no choice but to mate within a small population, the genetic diversity decreases rapidly, leading to illness, sterility, and eventually extinction.

Other reasons for the giant panda's decline include traps set by farmers (meant for other animals) and illegal hunting. Although the Chinese government has established strict laws (punishment can be life in prison) to protect these animals from poachers, some hunters still kill the animals and sell their skins on the black market, usually for huge sums of money.

Pandas also have a low reproductive rate; a female panda can only mate once a year and give birth to as many as two cubs, although it's unusual for more than one to survive. Because the female panda has such a limited opportunity to mate, and a pregnancy doesn't always occur, it will take a long time to rebuild this declining population.

To help secure the future of this amazing species, the National Zoo has been a world leader in conservation efforts to save the giant panda from becoming extinct (along with the U.S. Fish and Wildlife Service, the San Diego Zoo, Zoo Atlanta, World Wildlife Fund, the Conservation Breeding Specialist Group, the American Zoo and Aquarium Association, and the China Wildlife Conservation Association). In April 1972, the National Zoo received its first pair of giant pandas, Ling-Ling and Hsing-Hsing. They were a gift of goodwill from China's leader, Mao Tse-tung, to commemorate President Richard Nixon's visit to China earlier that year.

The giant pandas were a symbol of friendship between the two nations and were adored by millions of visitors during their long lives at the zoo. Unfortunately, the pair never successfully bred, so no cubs carried on their legacy. Ling-Ling died of heart failure at age 23 in December 1992, and Hsing-Hsing died in November 1999, from a kidney disorder related to old age.

The deaths of Ling-Ling and Hsing-Hsing were difficult for the zoo and our guests; the pandas truly had become both a love and fixture of the facility. In 2000, through a series of negotiations and the granting of special permits from the United States Wildlife Services, the National Zoo made a deal with China to bring two more giant pandas to the Smithsonian National Zoological Park. The bears are on a 10-year loan to the National Zoo under an agreement with the China Wildlife Conservation Association; using private and corporate donations, the National Zoo will send China $1 million each year to continue research, breeding, and conservation efforts for this endangered species.

We were all excited about the new additions to our facility and on November 27, 2000 (coincidentally the one-year anniversary of Hsing-Hsing's death), I flew to China to bring the two pandas to Washington, D.C. I traveled with panda keeper Brenda Morgan and curator Lisa Stevens to the China Research and Conservation Center for the Giant Panda in the village of Wolong, Sichuan Province. There we met Mei Xiang and Tian Tian, who were simply amazing. Mei Xiang (pronounced may sh-ONG) and Tian Tian (pronounced t-YEN t-YEN) were both born at the breeding center and had been selected for the National Zoo based on their potential to breed. In other words, the center made sure the two bears were genetically diverse so they wouldn't need to be exchanged with other zoos or centers. The male, Tian Tian, was born on August 27, 1997; his name means "more and more." The female, Mei Xiang, is a year younger and her name means "beautiful fragrance."

Lucy lunching with Tian Tian.

During our weeklong stay, we toured the panda breeding facilities and met with our Chinese colleagues to discuss the pandas' transition to the United States and how we would continue to work in partnership to protect these endangered animals. When it was time to leave China, I was very excited to accompany these enchanting bears to their new home. I knew they would be happy in all the space that awaited, and they would be enjoyed by a lot of people for many years to come.

At 5 A.M. on December 6, Tian Tian and Mei Xiang were placed in special shipping crates and loaded onto trucks for the three-hour drive to the airport. There was a convoy of nine vehicles from Wolong, with press cars riding next to us, flashing their cameras to capture photos of the pandas' journey. With so much media all around us, we affectionately decided to call them the "Pandarazzi!" (Freelance photographers who agressively pursue celebrities for candid photos are called paparazzi.)

Once we arrived at the airport, the pandas were loaded onto a jet that had a big picture of Tian Tian on the side and had been given the name "Panda One" for the special event. The pandas were placed at the front of the plane in their crates near the cockpit, and the cabin temperature was kept at 53 degrees to keep them comfortable. One hundred and ten pounds of fresh-cut bamboo, as well as treats of carrots, apples, and biscuits, were loaded onto the plane for the bears to eat during their long ride to Washington, D.C.

Once the bears were settled and we were ready to take off, I breathed a sigh of relief. It was wonderful to be in China and meet so many people devoted to preserving the giant panda, but I was anxious to get the animals to their new home, some 10,000 miles away. The flight went smoothly; the animals were happy and content, not exhibiting any type of stress (pandas will honk if they are in distress). They seemed very relaxed and continued with their normal behavior of eating and sleeping while on the plane—a very good sign!

The total flight time was 18.5 hours with a stop in Anchorage, Alaska, to refuel the jet and switch pilots for the last leg of the trip. When we arrived in D.C., the police escorted us to the National Zoo where we were greeted by the media and a crowd of onlookers. The bears were unloaded from the trucks and carefully led from their crates to their newly refurbished $1.8 million Panda House, complete with air-conditioned grottoes (artificial caves), trees for climbing, shade, and a hand-painted mural of their native home, the mountains of Sichuan Province. Right away, the pandas seemed happy and content, exploring their new surroundings, playing with each other, and eating lots of bamboo!

Tian Tian and Mei Xiang were quarantined for 30 days so they could receive their vaccinations and acclimate to the climate, the time zone, and eating American bamboo. On the cold winter morning of January 10, 2001, the pandas were introduced to the public—including dozens of TV crews. More than 3,000 people visited them on their first day in the limelight and the story was featured on the news that evening across the nation! It was great to see that these two bears, these icons of conservation, could command this much publicity. It was an encouraging sign that people were interested in the plight of the giant panda and hopefully other endangered species as well.

While having Tian Tian and Mei Xiang at the National Zoo will bring enjoyment to staff and guests as well as awareness to the cause of conservation, it'll also give us the opportunity to study their behaviors and reproductive biology. All of the research we do is meant to assist us in learning more about the pandas, so we can help the species survive. A big part of our research is simple observation. Observing the pandas gives us the opportunity to see what they like and what they don't like—and it also gives us a chance to get to know their personalities.

Another way we study the pandas is by giving them "enrichments" and seeing how they respond. Every day we give the animals at the zoo different objects (like frozen fruit bars or burlap sacks) to stimulate them and pique their curiosity. Not only does this activity give their keepers a way to study and observe their behavior, it also seems to be fun for the animals.

The enrichments are usually different each day because variation challenges the animals and provides them with new and interesting activities. For example, one enrichment we give the pandas is a rolled-up sheet that has a little bit of food hidden inside it. Tian Tian is a very busy bear and he'll tear the sheet apart to get the food as quickly as he can. Mei Xiang, however, is more purposeful in her actions. She'll take her time unrolling the sheet, finding each piece of chow as she goes along. She's much more deliberate and doesn't miss a morsel. Tian Tian, on the other hand, misses pieces of food because he's so busy ripping up the sheet that some of the pieces get left behind!

Bringing the pandas to the National Zoo has been a huge success. By studying these animals and learning about their behavior we're continually making progress toward saving this species from extinction. Visitors want to see and learn as much as they can about these incredible creatures, too. Mei Xiang and Tian Tian are really ambassadors for our conservation effort in China. They represent the tip of the iceberg of a much bigger effort to show Americans how amazing their species is, to actively study them, and to contribute to saving them in the wild.

Working toward saving the giant panda is just one of the many roles I have as Director of the National Zoo—one that probably best highlights my determination and motivation for conservation efforts. But whether I'm trying to raise awareness for the zoo and its many efforts, working on a plan to build new habitats for our animals that will encourage well-being and natural behavior, or anesthetizing a giraffe with the rest of the vet staff for a hoof trim, my overall goal remains the same—to show how amazing the world is and to help protect it and *all* its life.

A Behind-the-Scenes Look at the Job

Favorite Part: It's never the same thing twice. On any given day, I could be examining a rhinoceros, giving an interview, meeting with colleagues to discuss future plans for the zoo, or figuring out ways to raise funds for various zoo projects.

Least Favorite Part: An important part of my job is to convince people that the zoo deserves the resources it receives so we can continue our work. But it can be frustrating to continually have to justify what the zoo represents and the importance of its research and conservation efforts. I sometimes wish more people understood how valuable animals are to our world.

Hours: I never work less than 60 hours per week and plenty of weeks I work 80–100 hours, including a little bit of time working on the weekends when I'm in town.

Dress Code: Most days, when I'm working in the park, I wear a pair of pants with a surgical scrub top, like the ones doctors wear in an operating room. A seamstress specially designs them for me. Each one has animal prints on them, including one with pandas and one with lions, zebras, and elephants. If I have an administrative or business meeting, I wear casual business attire.

Work Environment: The National Zoo is a 100-year-old park along D.C.'s Rock Creek Park. It's actually located in part of a national forest, so it's very beautiful. Whenever I enter the zoo, I feel as though I've entered a preserved or protected area. There are lots of very old trees, and of course, hundreds of plant and animal exhibits. It's just an incredible place to work and visit.

Education/Skills: Getting accepted into veterinary school is competitive, so it's important to concentrate on studies in high school, especially math and science courses such as algebra, geometry, calculus, biology, chemistry, and physics. There are 27 accredited four-year vet colleges in the United States (most of them are located at state universities) and while you don't have to have a bachelor's degree for admittance, most require three to four years of college coursework before you can apply for admission (requirements vary depending on the school). The majority of students who do get accepted into vet school have their bachelor's degree. I received my bachelor's degree in biology from Brown University and my D.V.M. (Doctor of Veterinary Medicine) from the University of California, Davis.

Personal Qualities: A strong desire to care for and protect animals is essential for becoming a veterinarian. Their health and welfare depends on the decisions you make on their behalf, so you must be comfortable assuming a tremendous amount of responsibility. Good observation skills are also necessary, since you'll need to diagnose and treat animals in emergency situations and will be required to make appropriate decisions about their condition quickly.

Although vets work with animals, they must be able to communicate well with people, too. That includes having a good relationship with work colleagues as well as the owner/caretaker of the animal being treated. Vets must be able to clearly explain the treatments and procedures they are administering and educate the owner/caretaker on how to best care for the animal. Finally, vets must show compassion for the people and animals they work with, especially when the animal isn't doing well.

Perks and Rewards: I'm very energized by the animal world and I get to interact with different animals everyday, as well as with the people who study and care for them. I'm also energized by seeing people visit the zoo and making a connection with the animals. I can stand among a group of visitors looking at an animal exhibit and not be the least bit bored. It's fun to see how they react and hear what they have to say.

HOT TIPS

🔥 Get experience working with animals in different settings—such as an animal shelter, a veterinarian clinic, a kennel, a stable, or a zoo—you'll broaden your background and may discover an area of animal care you're most interested in pursuing.

🔥 Read about animals, everything from your favorite creatures to animals you've never heard of before. Spend time reading about scientists who have made important contributions to the animal world. If you're passionate about caring for animals, the more knowledge you have, the more you'll be able to make a difference in their lives.

🔥 Develop good study habits. Working hard to achieve top grades in high school will help you through the nearly eight years of college courses it takes to become a licensed veterinarian.

🔥 Visit zoos, aquariums, wildlife parks, farms, ranches, and any other facility that allows you to observe and appreciate animals, so you expose yourself to different species.

🔥 Researching a career as a veterinarian now will give you the opportunity to see if this career is right for you. If you decide becoming a vet isn't for you, it doesn't mean you have to rule out working on behalf of animals. There are plenty of other options to explore, including becoming a wildlife photographer, a park ranger, a writer, a researcher, an animator, a teacher, an animal trainer, a docent (zoo volunteer), a zookeeper, a veterinary technician, or a fundraiser for the protection and preservation of animals.

🔥 Put your own conservation efforts to work. Reduce, reuse, and recycle!

WORDS OF WISDOM

There's no one right path that will lead you to the job or career that is right for you. You have to create opportunities and be willing to work at getting what you want in life. Becoming a veterinarian is competitive, so you need to have the motivation to study and work hard toward achieving your goal. But if it's what you really aspire to do, go for it!

Find Out More!

Opportunities in Zoo Careers by Blythe Camenson (Chicago: VGM Career Horizons, 1998). Learn all about different careers working with animals, including wildlife, zoo animals, and marine animals. Interviews with professionals working with animals are an added bonus.

ZOO Book: The Evolution of Wildlife Conservation Centers by Linda Koebner (New York: A Forge Book published by Tom Doherty Associates, Inc., 1997). In cooperation with the American Zoo and Aquarium Association, Koebner details the inner workings of modern zoos and how they are working to save some of the world's most endangered species. Learn about the history of zoos and how their role has changed to become prominent education, conservation, and research centers.

Smithsonian National Zoological Park
3001 Connecticut Avenue NW • Washington, DC 20008 • (202) 673-4800
nationalzoo.si.edu
The 163-acre Smithsonian National Zoological Park was established by an Act of Congress in 1889 "for advancement of science and the instruction and recreation of the people." Log on and get information about the zoo and see more than 200 pictures of animals. Webcams allow you to watch animal demonstrations and hear lectures.

Maureen Holohan

HOT *Job...*

Publisher, Entrepreneur, and Author

I came up with the idea for a book series about girls who love sports called The Broadway Ballplayers. For three years I wrote and self-published the series and toured the country promoting my books. In 2000, I landed a book deal with Simon & Schuster, a major publisher, which will help get the books into the hands of more readers.

Home Base: Wynantskill, New York

Number of Years in the Field: 4

Personal Philosophy: "Life is too short to do everything well so choose something you enjoy, work hard at it, and you will reach great heights."

Ever since I was a kid, my two passions have been basketball and writing. In high school I excelled on the court, but during my senior year I tore the anterior cruciate ligament (a major ligament that gives your knee stability) in my knee and underwent reconstructive surgery. I had already earned a full athletic scholarship to Northwestern University and a lot of people said my basketball career was over. But I didn't listen to them. After sitting out my freshman year (because of my injury), I played ball the following four years at Northwestern. My sweetest memory as a collegiate athlete was competing in the 1993 NCAA (National Collegiate Athletic Association) Women's Tournament.

Even though I stood out on the basketball court, I was really quiet in high school. Writing was my way to have a voice, to be heard. As a junior, I was the sports editor for the school paper, and my senior year I became the primary editor. My love of journalism grew, so when I went to Northwestern University, I chose it as my major. At Northwestern's Medill School of Journalism I was surrounded by a lot of incredible writers. They could turn out the most amazing copy, and I'd sit next to them thinking, "I'm the worst writer in the world."

Despite my lack of confidence I still really wanted to be a writer, so I kept pushing myself to improve. If you had asked my basketball teammates about me, they probably would have told you that I was never the best athlete on the floor, but they'd also say I worked harder and was more determined than anybody. I applied the same principle to writing. I kept working at it and one day my professor pulled me aside and said, "Others might be able to write a good paragraph or chapter, but you're the one who's going to finish the book."

Those words meant a lot to me and I took them to heart. I had a big assignment due for a journalism class that involved writing a magazine article. While I was trying to figure out what I could write about, I attended a high school basketball tournament where three police officers performed at the opening ceremonies. They rapped to the kids about staying in school, off drugs, and out of trouble. I thought they were really good, so I went up to them and asked if I could do a story on them. They said, "Sure," so I followed them around for about a month and wrote the article. It won the 1994 Randolph Hearst Journalism Award, which amazed me. It also surprised a lot of people at Medill. I think a lot of the students saw me more as an "athlete" instead of an aspiring writer. Sometimes determination can make all the difference in the world.

Playing Ball Overseas

After graduating in 1995, my first passion was still basketball, so I decided to give professional ball a try. This was prior to the birth of the WNBA (Women's National Basketball Association) and the now defunct ABL (American Basketball League), so the only opportunity for women to play basketball professionally was to play in another country. In September of that year, I went overseas to play for two months—but it felt like two years. I started in Greece, went to Hungary, and ended up in Israel. The whole experience felt like a bad dream. I had no money, one of my teammates was only 15 years old (and she was one of the better players), and overall, the level of competition was not at all what I was used to. Bottom line: I wasn't challenged in the ways that I had been in college, much less to the high level that I was expecting.

When I returned home, my goal was to try out for the ABL, which was being formed while I was in Israel. I trained hard, was in the best shape of my life, and seemed to be playing really well. But in the process, I tore the arches in my feet and, to make matters worse, I didn't even make the cut.

Always Have a Plan B

Obviously, playing professional basketball wasn't working out, so I needed a plan B. My journalism degree was something to fall back on in case I didn't become a professional athlete. The time had come to use it. Instead of writing magazine or newspaper articles, I came up with the idea of creating a book series called The Broadway Ballplayers. The series would be about a group of strong, confident girls who play all kinds of sports, including soccer, volleyball, softball, and of course, basketball. The stories would be loosely based on the neighborhood where I grew up and would feature a diverse cast of characters that live on a fictional street with a not-so-fictional name, Broadway Avenue. With a strong desire to make it work, I started writing.

Molly tells the first story. She's a lot like me; she's strong-minded and always seems to find herself in some sort of predicament. She is fiercely competitive in every sport, practices constantly, and won't back down from a confrontation with anyone. Other characters include Penny, Rosie, Wil, and Angel. Like Molly, they have their flaws and weaknesses, but they're all interesting, likable girls. Penny is a natural athlete. Wil is an excellent student who plays hard even though she doesn't excel at sports. Angel comes from a strong religious family. Rosie is a quiet girl whose father is always pushing her to be "the best."

While I was working on the first book in the series, *Friday Nights, by Molly*, I gave basketball lessons in order to buy groceries and pay the rent. Once the manuscript was finished, I sent it to several publishers and was turned down by all of them. After a while, I started to take it personally. It was like they were saying, "Your life, what you're writing, and who you are, doesn't matter to us." Their message seemed loud and clear—*girls' sports stories aren't important.* It didn't seem fair to me that a boy could go to the bookstore and find a lot of books and magazines about guys playing sports, but there was nothing similar for and about girls.

It was definitely a tough time. First, I had been rejected by the American Basketball League even though I had done everything I could to make it. Now, I was getting rejected left and right by publishers. I had desperately wanted both—to be a basketball player and a writer. These were my two passions and I was not about to give up.

After a certain point, I thought about starting my own company. I figured the only way to get my book published was to do it myself. I began reading books about self-publishing and how to start your own business. My goal was to prove to the publishing world that stories about confident, athletic girls are entitled to a prominent place on the shelf. Girls deserve the opportunity to read about female athletes who are just as tough and talented as boys . . . because we are!

As I tried to get my business going, a lawyer friend of mine played devil's advocate (someone who expresses opposing viewpoints to present a balanced picture) for a while, telling me I didn't know how hard it would be. He kept saying things like, "You'll need lots of money," and I would reply, "Well, I'll get a loan." It wasn't easy, but I found a way to make it work. The parents of a child who took basketball lessons from me knew what I was up to and agreed to co-sign a loan. The money enabled me to print my first 3,000 copies of book one. I wrote the story, and my mom, my sister, my neighbor Harry (who prides himself on finding typos in the *New York Times*), and kids I knew all served as my editors. I found a young woman at an illustrator's convention to do all of the illustrations for my first book, and *Friday Nights, by Molly* was released in September 1997.

In June 1997, I had surgery on my right foot to repair my arch. I was on crutches trying to run my new company out of a rented room in an apartment, and my books arrived. I had no space for them, so the people who co-signed the loan had to store them in their living room while I hobbled around selling them, which I did in less than eight weeks!

Because I'd planned to have a series of books, I knew I needed to keep writing. (It's important for a series to have new installments regularly or readers are likely to forget about the characters and lose interest.) Even though I was busier than ever trying to sell my first book, I worked on books two and three, *Everybody's Favorite, by Penny* and *Left Out, by Rosie*, and released them in February of 1998. A year later, I released books four and five, then six and seven. I wanted to pace myself to be sure the books weren't coming out too fast. My goal was to release one book every six months. By March of '99, The Broadway Ballplayers series was ranked the number-one selling sports series on Internet bookseller Amazon.com.

Selling the Books

To get the books in stores, I needed to grab the attention of my target audience—8- to 12-year-old girls who love basketball or other sports. I called every college in the Evanston, Illinois, area that was holding summer sports camps and talked to the coaches. I offered to speak to their campers for free about my basketball experience and the importance of having a "plan B," if they'd let me hand out flyers for my books. It worked and I was on my way.

When I give a talk, students often will be more interested in the fact that I was a professional basketball player and what kind of car I drive than my career as a writer. But what I try to get them to focus on is, no matter what their dream, it's important to have something to fall back on if it doesn't work out. I tell them how my biggest dream was to play basketball professionally, but when it turned out to be more of a nightmare, I had to answer the question, "What do I do now?" My example usually brings home the point about the importance of having a plan B.

Then I go to the chalkboard and show them what it took to set up a company. I explain how little the author and publisher make from selling books (usually over 50 percent of the money goes to the bookstores and distributors). You also have to pay for the cost of producing the book on top of all business expenses such as rent, travel, paper, postage, and supplies. It's easy to see there's not much left over.

I must have traveled to at least 50 sports camps the summer before The Broadway Ballplayers came out, but it paid off. I received 500 preorders for the first book, each of which I had to ship individually. But getting into a major bookstore like Barnes & Noble or Borders was another story. Through my research I discovered I needed to set myself up with a wholesaler (a company that distributes merchandise to retail stores), so I called a wholesale book distributor, filled out a bunch of forms, and waited. That process took about a month. Then, in order to actually get a bookstore to order one of my books from the wholesalers, enough customers had to ask for it or special order it when it wasn't on the shelf. That was the hard part. I had to figure out a way to let readers know about The Broadway Ballplayers series so they would want to buy the books. I decided the best way was to plan a promotional tour and go from town to town to tell people about my books.

My First Book Tour

The first book tour I set up (with funds from investors in my company) included Michigan City, Indiana; Toledo and Cleveland, Ohio; and Buffalo, Rochester, Syracuse, and Albany, New York. I called my family and friends and asked if they knew any teachers or principals who could help me get a foot in the door to speak to their students. My plan was to arrange an event at a local bookstore, like a book signing, then find a school nearby and set up a talk. I'd ask the bookstore to have at least 10 copies of The Broadway Ballplayers available for purchase at my signing. During the day, I would speak to hundreds of kids at school and ask them to come to the bookstore that evening where they could buy my books and I would sign them.

In the first two and a half years, I visited more than 125 cities and 450 schools and sold more than 65,000 books. It was pretty exhausting; by the time I reached my 100th city, Orlando, Florida, I actually fell asleep at a book signing! It was definitely a "no-frills" book tour and I stayed at more cheap hotels than I can count.

While I was on the road, I kept calling the children's book buyer at Barnes & Noble, begging to get my books in their stores. Finally, she had to order the books to meet the demand I was creating. I also established a track record as a presenter and people started calling me back. Word got around that I was a good speaker. It helped that I was young (once a school principal actually asked if I had brought the author!) and kids responded to me.

The Book Contract!

Soon the challenge became not only getting the books into stores, but also keeping them on the shelves. That may sound easy, but it's not. It got to the point where I realized that although I was hesitant to give up part of what I had created, if I wanted to take it to the next level and sell more books, I had to compromise. Up until then, I had made all the decisions about my books and had complete control over their marketing and sales. But in order to sell more books, I needed to find a publisher who could get the books into more stores. Having someone else involved meant I would lose some of my control and I was a little apprehensive about that prospect. I was fortunate to hook up with one of the best agents in New York City for young adult literature. I was very nervous, but I knew the best decision was to get the help of a professional publishing house.

I signed a contract with Pocket Books, which is a division of the big New York publisher Simon & Schuster. One of the first things I worried about was if they'd create an image for the new book cover that didn't fit with my vision of what The Broadway Ballplayers should look like (a diverse group of girls from different backgrounds) and miss the whole point of my books. But once I started working with them, I was relieved to find we were on the same track. They scheduled the re-release of book one, with a brand new cover, for December 2000, followed by regular releases of the rest of the books in the series. This arrangement relieved me of the pressure to sell my books myself, and more importantly, it's given me more time to write new books for the series.

The Writing Process

A lot of people have asked me how I went from being a journalism major to a juvenile fiction author. My answer is that I don't think of my books as fiction. The characters are very real to me and I describe them as if I were a journalist reporting on actual people. To accomplish that authenticity, I did my homework. I spent six months doing research and read a lot of other juvenile books, especially series such as Nancy Drew, The Hardy Boys, The Baby-Sitters Club, Sweet Valley High . . . anything I could get my hands on. I studied the language, dialogue, and plot in these stories to see which had realistic characters. It bothers me when I read a young adult book and the language talks down to the readers or uses words they'd never say.

The age group I write for (8- to 12-year-olds) is a lot smarter than many writers give them credit for. I felt that a lot of the books I read talked down to kids, that the dialogue wasn't authentic, and I didn't want to make the same mistakes. For example, this is the age when a lot of girls begin to struggle with self-esteem issues, and I wanted to address that at the same time I was telling a story. I find that the secret is to "show" the characters' self-esteem through their *actions* and even in the confidence with which they carry themselves. Creating strong characters who lead by example works better than simply saying, "Rosie has a lot of self-esteem and confidence." It's taken me a while to get a feel for how a successful story works. First I develop the plotline by coming up with a basic premise as well as a subplot. Then I decide how the secondary characters, the antagonists, will help bring the plotline off the page. Even though all my characters are athletes, I try not to dwell on the "play-by-play," which can get a little boring. The books aren't only about sports and the fun part is coming up with a solid plot that I can weave sports into.

Once I get the basic structure, I usually can write a chapter a day. This first draft isn't my best writing, but to me the biggest enemy a writer faces is a blank screen. Until you get something on it, it's an ongoing battle. I jot things down and then go back and rework it until I get it right. Sometimes my best ideas come to me in the shower; I've even thought about putting a dry-erase board in there! I've also had good luck in the swimming pool and while I'm driving. I guess doing routine things allows your mind to clear so you come up with original concepts.

A lot of people help me out, but my sister is my best editor. It's funny, because we talk about the characters as if they're real people. I'll tell her, "Penny wouldn't say that!" and my sister will respond, "Yeah, the last time I talked to her she was really upset about it."

Right now, I'm putting all my focus on becoming the best writer I can be. I want to work as hard as I did when I was on the basketball court. I recently finished a story that my editor told me I needed to rewrite. I could have given up or complained, but I didn't. I stayed up until 3 A.M. to get it right on the second try. The editor emailed me the next day and said, "You got it!" By listening to the editor's comments, I learned how to improve my writing. I realized that her goal was to help me become a better writer the same way my coaches taught me to be a better player. Whether I'm the head of my own company or have a small role as part of a team, I always want to have a positive attitude. And it's that positive outlook and willingness to struggle that I want to convey to kids through The Broadway Ballplayers.

A Behind-the-Scenes Look at the Job

Favorite Part: I love the incredible freedom I have as a fiction writer. I don't believe in writing a fairy tale in every book, but my goal is to give kids a sense of hope. I think they need that . . . everybody needs that. I also think it's fun going into a meeting with a group of adults who are a lot older than me and everybody thinks I'm younger than I am and I don't know what's going on . . . and then showing them otherwise.

Least Favorite Part: The feeling of never being satisfied. I tend to get so caught up in wanting to get better that I seldom stop to smell the roses and appreciate what I've done, and that's not good . . . it's not healthy. I'm a very happy person and I don't complain, but I always want to be better—as an athlete, a person, a sister, a daughter, a writer, and definitely as a businessperson.

Hours: My best writing time is between 10 at night and 2 in the morning. I usually go to bed around 1 or 2 and get up at 9 or 10. During the day I give basketball lessons and work out, so I'm in perpetual motion throughout the day.

Dress Code: When I was starting, I dressed like a businessperson to give talks at schools. But that was kind of silly because the kids couldn't relate to me when I was dressed in a suit, especially since I look pretty young. Unless I have a meeting, there's no need for me to get too dressed up. Now I wear a Broadway Ballplayers T-shirt, sweatpants, and sneakers, whether I'm doing lessons or giving a talk. When I write, I wear the same thing.

Work Environment: I write pretty much everywhere—in bookstores, in my office, my bedroom, wherever. I listen to classical music. It's hard for me to write with other kinds of music or the television on; I find that my mind starts listening to what's playing or repeating the words instead of focusing on the computer screen. The funny thing is, I have no trouble writing effectively with a basketball game on. I think the background noises are so second nature to me that I can block out the actual game and keep my focus on what I'm doing.

Education/Skills: To succeed in this field you need an incredible work ethic and very thick skin. Just as in sports, there will always be someone telling you you're not good enough. I know that when my feet hit the floor in the morning, I'd better be ready to run (so to speak). I have a degree in journalism, but writing is really about practice and experience; write as much as possible and experience all you can to stay fresh.

Personal Qualities: As an athlete, a writer, and an entrepreneur, I face risk and rejection every day. Being all three means I can get a triple dose. If you're not willing to take the rejection, plan on getting knocked on your rear end. But you do have a choice—you can choose to focus on the rejection or on the people who believe in what you're doing. You need the ability to look to the right people for support, the willingness to put yourself on the line, and the desire to work like crazy.

Perks and Rewards: I know that no matter what ends up happening with my books, my effort has been for a great cause. Proof of that comes from the cheers I get at assemblies, or from seeing young girls get so many more opportunities than my friends and I had.

HOT TIPS

- ⚑ Read anything you can. Knowledge is gained from reading books, magazines, and newspapers, and finding styles you like helps shape your writing style.

- ⚑ Write for your school newspaper or school literary magazine. The experience will help you develop your skills and talent as a writer and give you that first taste of seeing your words in print.

- ⚑ Write in a journal. You can write about yourself, your best friend, or your favorite place. Or rewrite a story on the news and add your own flair.

- ⚑ Be open to meeting all kinds of people—everyone has something they can teach you, and vice versa. Pay attention to what people do and how they say things. I've collected a lot of material by observing people. And I always remember funny stories, great names, and cool places I may be able to use in one of my stories.

WORDS OF WISDOM

Everybody always says that with hard work anything is possible, but it helps to be good at something. To get better, have a coach, mentor, teacher, or someone to follow. Read, practice, and imitate. From that, develop your own style. Find something you have an incredible passion for and if you're good at it, the combination of these two things will give you the best chance at success. If it doesn't work out, that's where that "plan B" comes in handy.

Also, experience as much as possible. Life is too short to do just one thing—think of all the other experiences you'd miss out on! I recently tried out for the WNBA and didn't make it. While I was disappointed, I wasn't devastated. I knew I had tried my hardest. But when I looked around at the faces of the other players hoping to make the team, I saw that they wore the same expression I once did, that if they didn't make it, they would feel like they had nothing. They were hungry to play ball, far hungrier than I was. They were probably wondering what they would do tomorrow if they didn't make it. I, on the other hand, had 50 things to do by Monday for The Broadway Ballplayers ... my plan B!

Find Out More!

Careers for Bookworms and Other Literary Types by Marjorie Eberts and Margaret Gisler (Lincolnwood, IL: VGM Career Horizons, 1995). There are many careers for people who love to work with words. This book explores jobs in book publishing, newspapers, magazines, think tanks, libraries, bookstores, and the television and film industries.

Write Where You Are: How to Use Writing to Make Sense of Your Life: A Guide for Teens by Caryn Mirriam-Goldberg (Minneapolis: Free Spirit Publishing, 1999). Anyone can be a writer with this guide to learning how to express yourself on paper. From the beginner to the experienced writer, this book will offer helpful hints, inspiring suggestions, and will help you understand yourself and your potential through writing.

The Broadway Ballplayers
www.bplayers.com
The official site of The Broadway Ballplayers offers fans a complete list of books in the series along with a synopsis of each one. Also available is a list of all the players (characters) in the series. Check out book tour dates and Maureen's school visits.

Young Writer's Nook
www.youngwritersnook.com
A resource for young writers ages 8 to 18 that provides information about writing and publishing. Find informative articles and helpful links that will answer any questions about all kinds of writing. Also find advice on how to write a short story (or poem, or article, etc.), where to submit it, and how to get published.

Betty Lennox

HOT *Job*...

Professional
Basketball Player

*Guard for the WNBA
(Women's National
Basketball Association)
Minnesota Lynx*

I love basketball, and I feel really blessed to be
living my dream: playing professionally for the WNBA
Minnesota Lynx. When I'm not playing, I'm training to become a better athlete
by lifting weights or working out on the treadmill or bike, or in the pool.

Home Base: Houston, Texas

Number of Years in the Field: 2

Personal Philosophy: "Never give up. Faith plus education plus determination
equals success."

I started playing basketball with my brothers when I was 5 years old. I
have a big family (five brothers and three sisters!) and I'm the youngest
girl. My brothers let me play ball with them, but they didn't go easy on
me just because I was a girl. They played hard and I was always getting
hurt. When I'd run crying to my mother, she would tell me that if I came
back in the house, she would make me stay inside. "If you want to keep
playing, you have to learn to play rough, too," she'd say. I wanted to keep
playing, so I always went right back out. I guess playing against the boys
gave me my determination, and it also made me fearless; they taught me
not to be intimidated or afraid of anything.

My sisters saw how tough it was to play with the guys, but they
encouraged me to hang in there. They used to say, "Betty, we see potential
in you. Don't give up on your dream to play ball professionally." I started
playing on a basketball team when I was in the fifth grade and have been
playing organized ball ever since. I've pretty much lived for the game. I
played all through high school. My first year of college I played for Butler
County Community College in El Dorado, Kansas. The next two seasons

106

I played for Trinity Valley Community College in Athens, Texas, and we won the Junior College National Championship (1996–97). Playing ball at a junior college helped prepare me to play for a four-year university. I was offered a basketball scholarship to Louisiana Tech, and in 1998 we went to the NCAA (National Collegiate Athletic Association) Championships, finishing as runners-up to Tennessee. During my senior year, I earned Sun Belt Conference Player of the Year honors.

But what I wanted more than anything, was to play basketball professionally. Back then, playing pro ball *really* was a dream because the WNBA didn't even exist. I just knew playing professional basketball was something I wanted, and I wanted it so bad.

Joining the WNBA

On April 24, 1996, the board of governors for the NBA (National Basketball Association) announced the formation of a women's professional basketball league, the WNBA, with the first game set for June 1997. Val Ackerman, who had been Vice-President of Business Affairs for the NBA, was named President of the WNBA. Sheryl Swoopes (of the Houston Comets) was the first player to sign a WNBA contract.

The first season there were eight teams. The Eastern Conference consisted of the Charlotte Sting, the Cleveland Rockers, the Houston Comets, and New York Liberty. The Western Conference included the Los Angeles Sparks, the Phoenix Mercury, the Sacramento Monarchs, and the Utah Starzz. When the league was formed, everything was so new that teams had to be named, uniforms designed, logos created, and even basketball colors chosen (the official Spalding WNBA basketball is orange and oatmeal)!

The historic first game was played on June 21, 1997. The Los Angeles Sparks went up against New York Liberty at the Great Western Forum in Inglewood, California. Liberty won, 67–57. During the first season, there was a lot of excitement and support from fans. NBA players like Charles Barkley, Shaquille O'Neal, and Karl Malone and celebrities like Penny Marshall, Rosie O'Donnell, Tyra Banks, Spike Lee, and Susan Sarandon were among the thousands of fans that came out to watch.

The WNBA's opening season was very successful for a first-year professional sports league. In fact, it was one of the most successful first-year leagues in the history of professional sports. Part of its success had to do with the season's schedule, which began in the summer when the sports calendar isn't crowded with a lot of other professional sporting events. The WNBA was able to have its games broadcast on NBC, ESPN, and

Lifetime. More than 50 million viewers watched the televised games during the first season. The fans really came out to support the players; game attendance was larger than anyone had expected. With each game the excitement grew, and since the WNBA's initial season, the league has grown to sixteen teams, including the team I play for, the Minnesota Lynx, which was added in 1999.

Every year, 64 players from colleges and universities around the country and the world are chosen for the WNBA draft. Of those 64, only 12 (the top players who are practically guaranteed of getting signed to the WNBA) are invited to attend the draft. The rest watch on TV or the Internet to see if they'll be added to the official player roster.

Right out of college, I was in the top 12 for the 2000 draft, so I was invited to the event, which took place at the NBA Entertainment studios in Secaucus, New Jersey. The WNBA sent me a free plane ticket and also paid for my hotel and meals. I spent a day being interviewed by the press before the draft got underway. Broadcasters and TV cameras were everywhere, so it was very nerve-wracking sitting in that room and waiting. My palms were sweating I was so nervous! But I was one of the lucky ones; I was the sixth draft pick, so I only had to wait about 20 minutes before my name was announced.

I headed up to the podium after Brian Agler, the general manager and head coach of the Minnesota Lynx, called my name. Val Ackerman, the president of the WNBA, handed me a jersey with my name on it. I held it up, smiled, and had my picture taken by the press. I was really nervous standing in front of everyone, but was also extremely happy because I had made it into the WNBA!

Playing Pro

It was exciting being drafted to play professional basketball, but because it happened so soon after I finished my last game at Louisiana Tech University (LTU), I didn't have time to adjust to pro ball, mentally or physically. From a mental standpoint, I didn't have the chance to psyche myself up or even find out what was expected of me as a professional athlete. And physically, my body was tired from playing a full season at LTU.

My body had to adjust immediately. As soon as I finished my last game in college, I headed straight to the four-week WNBA training camp. The camp gives players a chance to get ready for the season, and it gives the coaches an opportunity to see what everybody needs to work on. I think I had less than a month between my last game at Tech and the start of camp.

We had two four-hour practices every day, which meant we were playing basketball eight hours a day. We had to play hard the whole time. For the first time, I was playing hard-core ball year-round. I had to will my body into handling the intensity of going for that long without any kind of break, as well as pushing myself 100 percent every day. I quickly discovered that playing professional basketball is a lot more challenging than playing college ball, and physically, it was a pretty tough adjustment. The pro league is extremely intense and it's harder to maintain your focus and strength.

Besides being tired, I got knocked around pretty badly during training camp. I broke my little toe, and endured black eyes, busted lips, and twisted ankles. I had experienced injuries like this playing ball in college, but they weren't as bad, because the play wasn't as rough as pro ball. Hits and shoves from other players that simply knocked me around at LTU now literally knock me on my rear end.

The level of pro ball is intense. Unlike in college, you're expected to play a very physical game. It surprised me that the coaches let the rough play—like forceful shoving—go on at practice, and that the referees didn't call more fouls during the games. In order to be successful, you *have* to play that way; it's a requirement of the job. Even though my brothers used to play rough, this style was never figured into my dream of being a professional athlete. I'm a strong person and I play tough when I'm going for a shot or defending my area, but I never thought basketball could feel so punishing.

I knew having an attitude or running my mouth off only would make things worse. It was okay to be emotional about the game—as long as my emotions didn't negatively affect my attitude. I had to really focus, will myself to hold it together, and keep my mouth under control. I would say to myself, "If this is what you want to do, you've got to learn to take it." As much as I loved basketball, it got to the point where I started to question myself: "Is this your dream? Is this what you really want to do?" The answer was, "Yes," but looking back, I think it was a test to see how badly I wanted to play the game at this level.

For the 2000 season, the Minnesota Lynx only had five veterans (returning players), which made my first season even more challenging. As a rookie, I had to step up to the plate right away and prove that I deserved to be on the court. It was like going from being a big fish in a little pond to a little fish in a big pond without time to get used to the new water. Rookies were involved in every play, every drill, and every game; we didn't spend much time on the bench. We couldn't take our time watching and learning and gradually absorbing how things were done. You either handled it, or you were out of the game . . . period.

When it came to *how* we played, the rookies weren't cut any slack or given a break. No one said, "Oh, a rookie made a mistake but it's okay . . . she's just a rookie." All the newcomers, myself included, were treated just like the veterans who'd been playing pro ball for years. We were expected to play like the pros from day one! We had to know what to do, know how to run the plays, and consistently work hard to get the ball in the basket.

Betty at the hoop against the Sting.

Head coach Brian Agler knew I was passionate about the game when he signed me to the Lynx. He knew what my skills were—that I was aggressive offensively, quick, and a good rebounder and defender, and he expected me to live up to my capabilities. He treated me like a veteran. He didn't say, "Betty, do this and I know you'll learn from it." Instead, he would say things like, "This is how you're going to set up the next play and if you mess up, you're coming out of the game." It was a lot of pressure, but everything was happening so fast that I didn't have a chance to react to it. I just got in the game like I was supposed to.

When I'm having a really good day on the court, I feel like I'm in a "zone," like I'm doing everything right. But it doesn't feel effortless. It feels as though I'm working really hard, but that all the daily hard work and practice is paying off during the game. It's like you're doing so much, and the crowd is cheering for you because you're the one who's getting it done . . . not just the person scoring, but the player making a good defensive stop, a good hustle, or a turnover or steal. It's so amazing to play when you can't even hear yourself talk because the fans are so enthusiastic and loud. You're trying so hard, and everything comes together. You feel like it's worth all the hard work and sweat. If I was the type of person to brag—which I'm not!—it's the sort of feeling that would make me want to say, "You can't stop me!"

After my rookie season ended, I looked back and realized what an experience and accomplishment it was to get through the first season as a professional player. I made it and I was successful. I was named to the 2000 All-WNBA Second Team, and voted a Western Conference reserve in the 2000 WNBA All-Star Game. Despite all of the tough practices and injuries (and getting knocked on my bottom!), I really enjoyed being able to live my dream. My game still had some weaknesses and I still wasn't used to the roughness, so my first off-season goal was to train extra hard in the weight room and become a lot stronger. It's my job to work as hard as I can so that I can hold my own on the court and be as strong as the more senior players.

Training for the Job

I have two hobbies in life: basketball and lifting weights. Training in the weight room keeps me in shape to play and is a way for me to work on areas of my body that I think are weak. I know if I build up my muscle strength, I'll improve my game by having more power on the court. The routine I do is a combination of the workout that the trainer from the Lynx taught me, as well as moves I've always done on my own.

Most days I spend at least three hours in the weight room. People are always asking me what I could possibly do in the weight room for three hours, but I have a lot to accomplish in that time. I lift weights six days a week and take Sundays off, except for going in the pool for an easy work-out. Mondays I train the muscles in my upper body, Tuesdays I do lower body exercises, Wednesdays I work the upper body muscles I didn't work on Monday, and I'll keep alternating like that. This kind of workout is part of my job as a professional athlete. It's a lot more intense than the training I needed as an amateur player, and you really don't need to push your body this hard when you're in high school—in fact, it could be harmful.

In addition to strength training with weights, I also work out on the treadmill and the stationary bike. I'll run for 15 minutes, then ride the bike for another 15. That's the most I'll do, though, because I usually do my cardio workout right before basketball practice and I want to make sure I still have some leg strength left to get through practice. If my legs are too tired, I won't last on the court. Aside from helping me with my game, working out helps me feel good on the inside and look good on the outside—I love working out and the way I feel when I'm in shape.

Practicing is a huge part of being a professional athlete, and our head coach loves holding practice. Each session is really long, starting at 9 A.M.

and going until around 2 P.M. It's important to warm up and be prepared for whatever he may have planned.

Before we start, each player takes care of whatever needs to be done for her to get the most out of the practice. For example, if someone has an injury or needs to get her ankle taped, she'll go to the training room to see the athletic trainers for treatment, which may include soaking her foot in a whirlpool, a massage, or whatever. Next, we do individual warm-ups on the court, then we get into a circle, sit on the floor, and stretch as a team.

Once we're done stretching, our warm-up continues with easy drills to loosen up our bodies for the more intense parts of practice. First we do a dribbling drill. We'll jog slowly and bounce the ball as we move back and forth across the floor, working on ball handling and control. After that we'll do some type of running drill—like sprinting up and down the court to warm up our legs. Once the warm-up is over, then we *really* start working.

Practice is very organized—one person isn't down at one end of the gym doing one thing while someone else is on the other end doing something different. Our team has three coaches: our head coach Brian Agler, and two assistant coaches, Heide VanDerveer and Kelly Kramer. They break up the team into groups so that each group can work on different skills, like rebounding, speed work, guarding, shooting, or defense. Drills begin with players paired up to work one-on-one. Once we've run through a drill with each pair of players, we do it again but playing four-on-four. Then we'll go three-on-three, and two-on-two, and continue to breakdown the drill. This is what we do for the entire practice. It's exhausting, and we all work up a sweat. The coach never shouts, "Okay, water break!" so when you're not in the mix of whatever's going on, it's up to you to drink a lot of water so you don't get dehydrated from sweating so much. Practices are definitely grueling, but they're all in a day's work as a pro basketball player.

Even Pro Athletes Need Support

A lot of people ask me if I've had a defining moment as a pro athlete when I realized, "Wow, I'm really living my dream." But I'm very hard on myself and I have high expectations; I have a ladder to climb and more steps to take before I make it to the top. So I tell them that my defining moment is still to come.

At the end of my first season, I was excited to win the 2000 "Rookie of the Year" award, which is voted on by a panel of sportswriters and broadcasters who regularly cover the WNBA. The trophy is gorgeous; it's small but it has a huge crystal on it and was designed by the Beverly Hills jeweler Tiffany & Co. It was truly an honor. Winning the award had a lot to do with the support and confidence of my family, coaches, and teammates who taught me to strive for the best and to always work hard.

A lot of people want to credit me for my success as a ballplayer, but I feel like I'm not the one who needs to be credited. As a spiritual person, I really have to thank God for the opportunities I've had. I think God has helped me to do all this. I even have a pregame ritual of praying before we run onto the court for a game.

The other major influence in my life is my family. Coming home from a game, I usually get about eight different phone calls from them, which really makes me feel important. My family supports me to the fullest and is behind me as much as anybody could be, and that means a lot. Since I've done so well in the WNBA, they've really let it go to their heads! My sister said to me, "Since you're not the type of person to be big-headed, I'll be bigheaded for you!"

I guess timing is everything. Playing for the WNBA is such a new opportunity, had I been born earlier, it wouldn't have existed. I never would have thought I'd end up where I am, but I'm ecstatic to be playing for the Minnesota Lynx.

A Behind-the-Scenes Look at the Job

Favorite Part: Knowing that I'm living my dream is the best feeling. It's not about money, it's about doing something I love. It's part of who I am; when you say "Betty," you say "Basketball." The hours are long and the training is tough, but it's all about the love of the game . . . and that's what I have.

Least Favorite Part: The only thing I don't like is how physical the game is. When I came out of college, no one warned me that the WNBA could be like the NFL! I'm a strong person, and very physical, but I never thought I'd get knocked around as much as I do. But that's the way it is, so I'll have to become physically stronger and give a little back!

Hours: My hours are different depending on what's going on. During the season, practice takes up almost the entire day. On game day, we get to the arena and shoot hoops from around 9 A.M. to noon. Then we watch basketball films for about an hour and have about three hours left to do whatever we want (most of us just want to rest). Two hours before the game we go back to the gym and watch more films. The game usually starts at 7 P.M. and lasts for about three hours. It's a pretty long day.

My responsibilities as a player for the WNBA don't end when I step off the court. I'm involved with the WNBA's two primary community outreach programs: "Be Active," which teaches boys and girls, ages 11 to 14, how important it is to play and be fit, and the "WNBA Breast Health Initiative," which is a partnership with the National Alliance of Breast Cancer Organizations and promotes the issue of breast cancer and the importance of early detection.

Dress Code: I have two uniforms; one for home games, which is white, and one for away games, which is green. Our jersey is V-cut at the neck and sleeveless, and the shorts go to the knees. The jersey is made out of a nylon material that really absorbs sweat. For practice, we wear a reversible jersey that's black and white with "Lynx" written across the front and our number on the back (mine is 22). Since we're sponsored by Nike, we can choose to wear either the "Lisa Leslie" or the "Dawn Staley" basketball shoes.

Before and after games, as well as when we're traveling, we have to dress in "business" attire, such as nice slacks or dresses. We're not allowed to wear jeans, sweats, tennis shoes, or anything casual like that.

Work Environment: Our team has its own practice facility, which is downstairs from the main floor where we play games. It's a great gym. When we're traveling to games, we fly and stay in hotels, two women to a room. A charter bus usually meets us at the airport and takes us to our hotel and the sports arena for practices and games. There isn't much time to sightsee or go to the movies when we're on the road because our schedules are pretty tight, but occasionally we do get to go shopping!

Education/Skills: Being a professional athlete is more than just scoring points on the court. You've got to score points in school, too. Some athletes have a reputation of not reading or writing well because they put too much effort into their game and not enough into their studies. I'm an average student and I had to spend hours and hours on my schoolwork, but it was worth all the hard work because I earned my college degree in psychology!

Before a player can enter the draft and be part of the WNBA, she has to use up her four years of college eligibility (play for four years at the college level), although she doesn't have to complete her degree. Most pro athletes have been training for their sport for many years by the time they make it to the professional level. Aside from being athletic and having a passion for the sport you play, to be successful at the pro level, you need to be competitive, dedicated, a team player, and not afraid to push yourself a little further each day.

Personal Qualities: If you want to be successful as a professional basketball player, you have to have a positive attitude and an open mind. Because the season only lasts between three and four months, a lot gets poured on you in a short period of time. You don't have time to have a bad attitude. If you've got time for that, then you're holding yourself back. A negative attitude will distance you from the coach and the other players, which makes you difficult to coach and play with. You have to be a team-oriented "people person" to be successful at this level of play.

Perks and Rewards: Traveling to different places can be a lot of fun. I've had the opportunity to visit many different states, and even go out of the country to play ball. A lot of ballplayers go to other countries in the off-season to get more experience and playing time. I went to Israel for a few months after the 2000 season ended, but I returned early because of the political upheaval there at the time.

HOT TIPS

▲ Join a basketball team at school, the AAU (Amateur Athletic Union), the YMCA, or some other organized team so you can get the experience and practice you need to become a great player.

▲ Keep up your grades. If your grades aren't good enough to get into college, your chances at a career in basketball are pretty slim. Something to keep in mind: Basketball scholarships are given to people who have basketball talent—but who also display academic know-how.

▲ Find out about the basketball eligibility requirements and scholarships at different colleges and universities. Talk to your coach, look on the Internet, or write to the athletic department of the college you're interested in attending. Your high school counselor can give you the address of any college or university you are considering.

▲ Attend camps and training clinics to improve your skills as a player. Your coach or physical education teacher can help you find some in your area.

▲ Athletes need to take care of their bodies from the inside out. Now is a good time to start eating nutritiously to fuel your body for the added demands you're placing on it. Get in shape with a fitness program you enjoy. Besides practicing for the sport you're involved in, participate in other types of fitness activities just for fun, like riding your bike, inline skating, or dancing.

▲ Enjoy the game!

WORDS OF WISDOM

No matter what you want to do, don't limit yourself to things that come easy to you. Find something you want to do, set a goal, and work toward it. If you want to play basketball, always work hard and be the type of person who wants to impress the coach as well as yourself. If you're happy with yourself and with the coach, and he or she is happy with you, you're going to be successful. Work outside of practice to improve your game. When it comes down to it, that's where you really prove yourself. When you put in extra hours to better yourself as an athlete, whether it's shooting baskets or lifting weights, it shows that you're willing to go the extra mile for the team.

Find Out More!

WNBA: A Celebration: Commemorating the Birth of a League by Kelly Whiteside (New York: Harper Horizon, 1998). Colorful photo scrapbook of the WNBA's first season from the moment it was announced to the championship game. Included are stories about the players, officials, and coaches, including their excitement over the WNBA's birth.

Sports Illustrated Women
P.O. Box 61981 • Tampa, FL 33661-1981 • 1-800-950-5150
sportsillustrated.cnn.com/siforwomen
Discover the accomplishments and challenges of professional players while getting tips for improving individual performance in this magazine dedicated to girls and women in sports.

Amateur Athletic Union: Girls' Basketball
www.aaugirlsbasketball.org
Dedicated to promoting amateur sports teams and physical fitness programs, the AAU is a good place to start for anyone interested in playing sports. For more experienced basketball players, the organization offers a division that puts young women one step closer to playing at a professional level.

Sports for Women
www.sportsforwomen.com
This site offers information about women's sports at all levels: college, professional, extreme, and Olympic. There are features on female athletes, advice from professionals, news stories, scores, and standings.

The WNBA
www.WNBA.com
The official Web site for the Women's National Basketball Association. Stats and information on players, coaches, and teams are available, as well as season schedules.

HOT *Job...*

Disney Imagineer

Imagineering is the design, master planning, construction, and project management group for The Walt Disney Company. We design and build theme parks and resorts around the world. My job is to oversee all phases of a project, from the brainstorming of ideas to opening day.

Home Base: Pasadena, California

Number of Years in the Field: 14

Personal Philosophy: "Have fun, do what you enjoy doing, and you won't ever get bored."

I started working at Disney in 1976 wearing a muumuu and selling souvenirs in Adventureland for $2.40 an hour. I was an 18-year-old college student going to California State University at Fullerton and I needed a part-time job, something with flexible hours. So I worked weekends, nights, summers, and holidays at Disneyland in Anaheim, California, wearing a costume (employees, also known as "cast members," wear "costumes," not uniforms) and selling souvenirs. I enjoyed my job at the theme park and soon became a permanent part-time employee, which meant I wasn't just seasonal help.

Three years later, when I was a senior, I needed an internship to earn upper-division credits for my major, which was English. It didn't really matter what I did as long as the job was at least eight hours a week and allowed me to apply my liberal arts/English background. Since I was already part of the Disney team, I checked into internships with Disneyland. As it turned out, they were looking for someone to write employee operational manuals. Not very exciting stuff, but it was just what I needed to earn my college credits.

About six months later, a full-time job writing operational manuals for the Tokyo Disneyland project opened up. The job was based in the Anaheim office, so I applied for the position and was hired—which meant

I had to quit going to school during the day and take night classes after work (as well as continue my internship). Even though I had to add an additional semester to my education, I knew that when I finished school I would be employed as a writer. It was unbelievable to me: I had a degree in English, which everyone told me would be worthless if I didn't become a teacher, and before graduating from college I already had a full-time job.

In 1987, I learned about an opening for a writer and producer in Imagineering's communications department. I interviewed for the job and was hired, and that's how I became an Imagineer. It was that simple. Some of the different projects I became involved with early on had to do with writing and producing videos for art galleries and pavilions at Epcot (a Disney park at the Walt Disney World Resort in Florida). One of the videos I produced featured three respected female Japanese artists and was used inside the Japan pavilion gallery.

Taking on whatever assignments came along, I eventually ended up becoming a design administrator, which is a junior producer. I worked with the creative team directing the work and ensuring everything was done on time and on budget. For one of my assignments, I worked on a water park called Typhoon Lagoon at Walt Disney World in Florida. Midway through that project I was promoted to show producer. Now I'm an executive producer, which is a vice-president level position.

The hardest question for me to answer is, "How do you get a job in Imagineering?" Some people have a design background and some don't—obviously I don't, but as a writer I still have creative experience. It's not a big secret that there's no *one* way to get your foot in the door here. Once you do, you move from project to project, learning from the people you work with along the way. Being the producer for various projects made me realize that this is truly what I like doing. I love producing something I can help design, build, open, and watch people enjoy.

A Different Kind of Storyteller

Imagineering is really about telling stories, and everyone has a different responsibility in bringing that story to life. For example, one part of the telling may be for someone to design a ride system that goes from 0 to 60 miles per hour in three seconds. Someone else does the writing, another person paints it, and so on. We all come at it from different angles, but each of us has the same point of view in terms of what the story is, how to make the theme consistent, and how our particular part supports the shared vision of the design team.

It's like building a house: one person designs it and another puts the foundation down. Someone else figures out the framing and still another adds the final coat of paint. And there's that one person who makes sure everybody is doing his or her job so the house turns out the way it was intended. That's what I do.

We're pretty meeting-oriented at Disney, whether it's to brainstorm something new or get updates on projects in the works. This is especially important for someone in my job. I don't sit and draw, so I don't need solitude. I actually need to talk to people to find out what's going on. During the course of any given day I may have several scheduled meetings, or I may just pop in on a few people. This is how I'm able to keep track of all the projects I'm responsible for. I've usually got six to eight projects that I'm involved with at once, all in different stages of development. If one of them really takes off and becomes big, I'll devote most of my time to it.

Getting ready for a pitch to management with the project team.

I do a lot of emailing and communicating on the computer, too. My office is in Glendale, which is about 45 minutes north of Disneyland and its new expansions, California Adventure and Downtown Disney, located in Anaheim. Communicating via computer allows me to talk back and forth with the project manager in Anaheim without leaving my office.

Getting something "onstage"—which isn't just an attraction but anything a guest can see, smell, touch, or experience, including the plantings and walkways—begins when we're given a problem to solve or a new attraction to create. The size and scope of the attraction isn't always known. For example, we might be told, "We need a new theme park in Orlando. Come up with a theme." That's a pretty big assignment, but not as big as being told, "We need something to go right here, on this particular piece of land." Or the challenge could be, "We want a new ride for Blizzard Beach," which narrows down our options. Once we've been given more guidelines, such as the budget, the project gets narrowed down even further.

What the Imagineers are asked to do can be very broad. Other times we're given an assignment that's very specific, yet still not entirely defined, in that we may or may not have a story line or complete description of what the project should be. Regardless of how much or how little we're given to work with, it's up to our team to fill in the blanks. To do that, we'll weave together architecture, graphics, landscaping, smells, music, color, film . . . anything you can see, hear, touch, and smell to tell a story.

When I started working in Imagineering in 1987 and received my first assignment, it changed my entire outlook about my career. I was assigned to the team that was working on Typhoon Lagoon, Florida's second water park (River Country was the first).

Since I was promoted to show producer midway through the project, I went to work in the field. This meant moving to Florida and overseeing the actual installation of the water park. It turned out to be the most incredible learning experience I could ever imagine! In a year's time, I probably learned more about construction and the design process than I would have learned in school.

Creating Typhoon Lagoon

Every ride or attraction that we build has a story line or a "legend" behind its creation. The legend of Typhoon Lagoon is that many years ago, there was a little resort village in an unnamed tropical area that was hit by a typhoon, upturning everything. The earthquake and volcanic eruption that followed left the village in shambles. Following this cataclysmic event, the inhabitants rebuilt their town, turning it into a 56-acre water park where guests can surf and splash in a wave pool, snorkel with live sharks, or zoom down the "Humunga Cowabunga" slide with its 51-foot drop.

The attraction is a big, tropical, volcanic oasis. As visitors approach the water park, they're greeted by a volcano that erupts every 15 minutes and spouts a 50-foot flume of water like a geyser. A series of signs read:

> A furious storm once roared 'cross the sea,
> Catching ships in its path, helpless to flee,
> Instead of a certain and watery doom,
> The winds swept them here to Typhoon Lagoon!

Because we have a sense of humor at Disney and like to cover every detail, all sorts of props are scattered around Typhoon Lagoon. Guests can see marooned boats that look like they have been shot through roofs, debris strewn all over the place, and buildings that are completely leaning to their sides. One building, supposedly an old hotel, is now a dining resort. It used to be called "Placid Palms," but we crossed that name out and in its place, wrote, "Leaning Palms." Typhoon Lagoon looks as if the wind blew through it and left behind this little jewel of a water park. We had a whole mythological theme going when we were creating ideas for this exotic water attraction.

Once the concept for Typhoon Lagoon was established, our team had to figure out how to design the park so that all of the details supported the story line. Take the "Leaning Palms," for example. During construction we realized all of the dormer windows at the top of the building were perfectly straight. That wouldn't work since it was supposed to look like a typhoon had blown through the building, making everything crooked. So what did we do? We tilted the windows. We had a lot of fun with the story, graphics, props, and even the planting of all types of foliage, including palm trees.

Being part of the team that created Typhoon Lagoon was a pivotal experience for me. Up until then I'd been doing what I was trained to do and could do well: writing and producing. But with that project, I discovered that I loved seeing things go from the two-dimensional drawing phase to the three-dimensional building phase, and beyond to something you can actually ride, touch, and really experience.

It was the first time I was on a major construction site, and it got in my blood. I decided that, of all the things the Walt Disney company had to offer, Imagineering was where I wanted to stay. I didn't need to go operate a park or work on the "corporate" side of things. *This* is what I wanted to do, and everything since has been amazing.

Supervising Splash Mountain

Splash Mountain in Orlando was the first new attraction for the Magic Kingdom park at Walt Disney World in 18 years, and I had the good fortune of working on it. Splash Mountain is a flume ride (a ride using a water channel), located in Frontierland, and it's based on the 1946 Walt Disney classic movie *Song of the South*. The 11-minute log ride follows the story of Brer Rabbit as he's chased through the backwoods and swamps by Brer Fox and Brer Bear. The ride ends with a 5-story drop at a 45-degree angle and everybody gets splashed!

A great part of being an Imagineer is that we get to have fun with the rides first, usually a year before the attraction opens to the public. Of course, since there are no lines and every detail has to be checked and double-checked, we just keep riding it. I'll never forget the first time I rode Splash Mountain. The scenes weren't even programmed and a lot still had to be done, but I could see that everything we had planned, all the details we agonized over, were going to come together. We went on that ride so many times—it got to the point where we'd ride with our eyes closed and guess where we were to make the ride less monotonous. I'd be on it to check a show scene, and once I'd passed that particular scene, I was basically just waiting to get off. After about 200 times you have to trick yourself into making it fresh in order to enjoy it!

When Splash Mountain was finished, I was really anxious to see the first people ride it. I took pictures of them, and I've still got the photos. As the guests got off the ride, I remember watching to see their reactions, if they were laughing and carrying on about their experience. Luckily they were, which meant our job was a success. It's a huge milestone to see our guests respond positively to all of our hard work. Working on and finishing a ride is the biggest thrill for me—probably the same thrill a guest feels while experiencing an attraction for the first time.

Building Blizzard Beach

The biggest, most comprehensive project I've ever been a part of was Blizzard Beach, the third water park located on Walt Disney World's 30,000 acres in Florida. This was the first time I was involved with a project from start to finish, from "soup to nuts" as the saying goes.

As always, step one was developing a theme, so we held a three-day meeting in Florida for the entire design team. We traveled to the two existing Disney water parks as well as a bunch designed by our competitors to get the feel for the whole water park idea. Then we locked ourselves in a room and started coming up with concepts and creating storyboards, which are sketches for the project. After we returned to California, the next several weeks were spent refining our ideas before presenting them to Disney's corporate decision-makers.

When you're developing something like the theme for a whole new park, it's a disservice to lock onto just one concept. If you only take one idea into your presentation, it will beg the question, "Okay . . . so what else have you come up with?" Some brainstorming sessions don't produce a lot of creative ideas, but with Blizzard Beach we were really clicking. When you start to click as a group, everyone is in sync and it becomes a lot of fun. We put our heads together and came up with four really solid ideas.

For brainstorming sessions like this one, we generally gather 10 or 12 very creative people called "Concept Designers." These are people who have a great affinity for coming up with fun, original ideas—things like, "I know, how about a water park that's really a ski resort?" I'm not good at coming up with ideas on my own, but once I'm given a concept I can usually make it better or help move it forward. This group, made up mostly of artists and writers, got together in a room and did what they do best—create! I was there, too, to help keep things moving in one direction. Of the four ideas we came up with, we all liked Blizzard Beach the best.

The story line of Blizzard Beach is that a businessman tried to open a ski resort at Walt Disney World Resort during a freak storm that dumped a ton of snow in the middle of this normally warm tropical paradise. Unfortunately, the plan was foiled when the temperatures began to rise, melting all the snow and ice. The ski resort never opened, but in its place, a Florida-style winter wonderland water park with 22 water slides was born.

We felt like Blizzard Beach was the craziest concept we could imagine, which was a good thing. Let's face it, no one else but Disney Imagineers would create a snow-capped 90-foot mountain in central Florida. "Mount Gushmore" would be complete with moguls, slalom courses, toboggan and water sled runs as well as "Summit Plummet," the world's tallest, fastest, free-fall waterslide where riders plunge almost straight down at speeds of 50 miles per hour! As excited as we were about Blizzard Beach, we thought we should still test ourselves by thinking of other concepts.

The senior managers who make the final decisions listened to our presentation very politely. When we were finished, they pointed to the one that had a Mexican theme and said, "This is the safe one. We should do this one." Then they looked at Blizzard Beach and said, "But we're going to do this one."

Making Blizzard Beach look like a snowy mountain in a tropical locale is just one of the many zany ideas that the Imagineers have created. It's such a fun concept, and so outrageous, just the thing the masterminds at Disney are so good at dreaming up.

Completing a New Attraction

It's difficult to explain how it feels to see something you've worked so hard on finally reach completion. Naturally it's rewarding, because it's exactly what you want to happen, it's what you've been working toward for so long. You're happy it's over and glad to be moving on to the next thing. But you come to identify yourself with each project, so you feel sad and kind of down when it's time to move on. Everyone here experiences these feelings.

It's emotional to let go of something you've invested so much of your time and creative energy into. You work and work and work, then your "baby" is turned over to someone else and they operate it. Visitors ride and experience it, and now the project doesn't need you anymore. One day you "own" it, and the next you have to ask someone if it's okay to come and see it. At the same time you can't help but think to yourself, "Hey, you knew opening day was coming—get over it!" There have even been times when I've counted the days until a project was over because I was ready to be done, but I still miss it.

No matter how difficult it is to finish a project, the ultimate reward is being able to visit one of our parks and watch guests enjoy an attraction that we worked so hard to complete. Seeing the smiles on their faces is a constant reminder that what we're doing still sets the standards for the industry, and I'm really proud to be a part of that.

A Behind-the-Scenes Look at the Job

Favorite Part: My job is just really, really fun! I don't think I could go to work every day and not enjoy myself; I couldn't stand it. I work with people who have great senses of humor, which is a blast.

Some days I get to visit either a competitor's amusement park or one of Disney's parks and go on some rides. Then I talk to my coworkers about my experience, what I liked and didn't like. Not many people can say that's how they spend their day . . . and get paid for it!

Least Favorite Part: Whenever I go to theme parks, I find myself studying the rides instead of simply enjoying the thrill. I end up studying all the little details; looking at the light bulbs that are burned out, what's not working properly, what needs maintenance. Sometimes I'm so busy looking at the mechanics of the ride I forget to sit back and say, "Wow! That was fun!"

Hours: Very few people in Disney Imagineering have "typical" work hours. I like to get to work when it's quiet—around 7 A.M.—and I generally leave between 5:30 and 6 P.M. This changes drastically when one of the projects I'm working on is in construction. Then I'll usually start around 6:30 A.M., because that's when contractors arrive at the site. During the construction phase of a project, I usually work Saturdays and Sundays as well as Monday through Friday.

Dress Code: We're very casual at Walt Disney Imagineering. There's no dress code so my wardrobe usually runs from nice pants to jeans, depending on my mood, the weather, and if I have any high-profile meetings that day. When you're out at a construction site, however, you have to adhere to certain safety rules, which include long pants (usually jeans), a hard hat, and steel-toed construction boots.

Work Environment: Imagineers are tucked away in a nondescript building in an industrial area of Glendale, California. No signage is in front of the building showing we're part of Disney, otherwise people might want to come in, thinking it was Disney*land*. Since we're a creative company, there are model shops, artist studios, and a sculpting studio within the building.

The company, in general, is really casual, so I wouldn't describe our offices as plush. But they're functional, and we're surrounded by some of the great art that our designers and artists produce here every day. Each artist has his or her own office, and almost everyone here has his or her door open. Sometimes a door will be closed and you can hear music playing, which generally means someone is focusing on a project, so we try not to disturb his or her creative flow.

My office is a mess! I have assorted storyboards leaning up against the walls, papers everywhere, and lots of cool stuff hanging up. I have a few caricatures of myself on the walls that the artists I work with have drawn for me. And there are lots of team pictures—me and a couple of hundred other people standing in front of our latest accomplishment. No one's wearing a hard hat though; we always wait until you can get out of your hard hat before taking the picture so we can see everyone's faces. Besides, no one likes hard-hat hair!

Education/Skills: The education required for a job in Imagineering really depends on your role. We have artists, writers, designers, engineers, architects, construction managers, accountants—you name it. There's no one way to get into this job because we have such a wide array of disciplines (more than 140!). I graduated with a bachelor's degree in English and came to Imagineering as a writer and video producer.

As for skills, you need to be able to think creatively; we call it "thinking out of the box." That's true for everyone who works here, not just the designers. For example, our engineers are highly educated, with degrees from schools like CalTech and MIT. But they have to think creatively just like everyone else. For example, they may be asked to design a ride where guests seem to drop faster than the speed of gravity—basically make the impossible possible. You're constantly challenged to stretch the limits in ways you didn't learn about in school.

Personal Qualities: A sense of humor is a must in this line of work. Our job is to design places where people have fun, and you have to have fun yourself in the process! We're also very passionate people who care deeply about the quality of the work we do. We don't leave our work at the office each night when we go home—we're constantly thinking about how to improve our product.

Being outgoing and a good communicator is helpful, too. We give a lot of presentations, what we call giving pitches, and if you come up with a great idea, you may be the one asked to speak in front of the corporate decision-makers to convince them to proceed with your idea. You need to handle situations like this, as well as communicate the passion you feel for the project. If public speaking isn't your strength, though, plenty of other people on the team can carry the ball. The important part is getting the idea presented well, not whether you did the actual presenting.

Perks and Rewards: You get the experience of watching people enjoy what you've designed and built. It is so rewarding to see. We also get to go on a lot of rides and call it research!

HOT TIPS

🔥 Get a part-time job at an amusement park or entertainment-related company. It doesn't matter if you're scooping ice cream, sweeping walkways, or operating rides. Experience the atmosphere, enjoy the rides, and think about what you would recommend to make it better.

🔥 Even if you're not an artist, take art and design classes to get a better appreciation of the medium you might be working in—and to learn to communicate better with the artists you'll be working with. Having a good idea is great, but being able to explain and show it brings it to the next level. Design classes can help you do this.

🔥 For fun, visit themed-entertainment environments, like shopping malls, family fun centers, or restaurants and see what kind of design story they tell. Ask yourself what does and doesn't work. Is the theme consistent? Do all the elements, such as the background music, lighting, and colors support the theme or story line? What would you change to make the look work better? Discovering whether you enjoy looking at an environment with this kind of eye for detail may give you an idea if becoming a designer is right for you.

🔥 Visit a lot of art museums and galleries. Inspiration can come from many places, but galleries and museums can be key. You can observe the use of line, shape, and color; see how artists create illusions that defy the laws of physics; and observe the reactions of others. And there's a bonus—you get to see good art!

⚜ Take design classes, workshops, or seminars. You can find these through art museums and community education programs or even through local vocational schools or colleges. Check with one in your area to see if they have a class you might be interested in taking. Also, many computer programs will teach you the fundamentals of design (there are some on designing amusement parks). Any experience you can gain in these areas will help give you an appreciation for the strength and power of art and good design.

WORDS OF WISDOM

Start believing in yourself right now! Find the thing that makes you feel confident and do it. I changed my major in college three or four times before I realized I was taking upper-division English classes just because I liked them. It turned out that was my field of interest and the one in which I was going to excel. I didn't have a clue what I would do with my degree, but I knew it would be a process I would enjoy and that's what counts. If you're doing something you enjoy, and you stick with it and keep working at it, you'll eventually become successful.

Find Out More!

The Fantastical Engineer: A Thrillseeker's Guide to Careers in Theme Park Engineering by Celeste Baine (Farmerville, LA: Bonamy Publishing, 2000). This book describes how engineers create the magic of theme and amusement parks, roller coasters, aquariums, and zoos. Experts provide information about their jobs and advice on gaining employment in the industry.

Walt Disney Imagineering: A Behind the Dreams Look at Making the Magic Real by the Imagineers (New York: Hyperion, 1996). The story of how the magic of Disney is made is told here by the Imagineers themselves. Full of artwork, photos, facts, and trivia, this book provides the chance to see the various phases of planning and development behind some of the Magic Kingdom's most exciting attractions. There are even plans for creations that were never built.

Disney.com
www.disney.com
An assortment of home pages provide crafts, recipes, party ideas, and other family activities. Also read up on Disney movies, TV shows, computer games, music, and theme parks. Information is available about the company, including career opportunities.

Imagineering Online Magazine
www.imagineeringezine.com
This online magazine provides extensive information on the mechanics of imagineering and the different facets that are essential to making concepts become reality. Included are a list of ideas meant to inspire students toward creating exciting and elaborate science fair projects.

HOT *Job...*

Special Agent

with the FBI (Federal Bureau of Investigation)

As an FBI Special Agent, it's my job to conduct investigations involving violations of federal laws. There's a lot of variety in what I do; over the years, I've worked in a number of areas including international terrorism (acts of terrorism or violence against the United States by a foreign country, like the bombing of a building or a bomb threat on an airplane), white-collar crime (crimes committed against banking institutions, such as an employee stealing money), and espionage (the stealing of government secrets, military technology, or defense information). The work is always interesting and challenging, and I love the fact that I'm now combining a longtime passion, flying, with my work— I'm also a pilot for the Bureau!

Home Base: Houston, Texas

Number of Years in the Field: 16

Personal Philosophy: "Never give up on your dreams."

*An alias has been used to protect the agent's identity

The seed was probably planted for my decision to become an FBI agent in August 1977, when I began my freshman year at Florida State University (FSU) in Tallahassee, Florida. I lived in a dormitory, but several of my classmates were members of the Chi Omega sorority, and I often spent my free time at the house with them. I figured if I liked the house better than dorm living, I would pledge to become a member.

On Saturday, January 14, 1978, a man broke into the Chi Omega sorority house and brutally beat and sexually assaulted several of the members as they lay asleep in their beds. Two girls died that night. One of them was my friend, Margaret Bowman. On that same night, my roommate came home late from a party at a fraternity house on campus. She was crying and shaking all over. After she calmed down, she told me that when she was parking her car in front of the dorm, a man walked through the bushes toward her and his shirt was covered with blood. She ran from him as fast as she could into the dorm.

The next morning, we awoke to hear of the horror that had taken place at the sorority house. When a description was given of the suspect, my roommate began to get hysterical; she knew it was the same man she had seen the night before. I went with her to the police station so she could give her statement. By Sunday evening, her father had driven up from Miami to take her home. She was one of several hundred female students that left FSU that week. As far as I knew, none of them returned to school that year. Although my parents begged me to come home, I decided to stay and finish the rest of my freshman year at FSU. I suppose I was a little scared, but I had a strong will to finish out the year.

In June 1978, I visited my former roommate for a few days in Miami. While I was there, two FBI agents flew down from Tallahassee to interview her regarding what she had seen that horrible night. We were both so nervous, but when they showed up they were so nice and normal, they put us right at ease. I was very impressed with the professional and sensitive manner in which they handled the situation. And the fact that they were dressed in business suits, as opposed to wearing uniforms, made them seem like regular guys instead of law enforcement agents. Even though I knew that under their suits they had guns, I didn't find them intimidating at all.

A man named Theodore Bundy was arrested a month after the FBI agents interviewed my friend. He was charged with the murders of the Chi Omega girls, and further investigation determined that he was in fact a serial killer who had murdered at least 36 women—maybe as many as 100—during the 1970s. He was convicted and sent to death row, where he stayed until he was put to death in the electric chair in January 1989.

Finding My Path

I'm a real people person—I enjoy giving of my time and helping people—so my original intent when I went to college was to become a doctor. I started taking all these high-level math and science classes, but quickly discovered they weren't my cup of tea; as a matter of fact, I dreaded them! My only relief at the time came from taking elective courses, especially psychology—I loved anything that studied the mind—and criminal justice. I realized I had an interest in learning what made a person become a serial killer, the kind of monster that Ted Bundy was. The psychological aspect of criminal justice was intriguing to me, and I was eager to learn more. Good grades also came easily to me in those classes and I found that I really looked forward to them. So the next semester I signed up for more criminal justice classes and less of everything else, and eventually changed my major to criminal justice with a minor in psychology.

Despite Florida State having a good criminal justice program, after spending the summer with my family, I decided it was too hard to think of going back. So in the fall of 1978, I began attending Palm Beach Junior College, which also had an outstanding criminal justice program. During the winter quarter, I took a criminology class and our big assignment was to pick a criminal-justice related topic to research and write a 25-page report. We were able to submit several different choices, but our professor had to approve our topic. I proposed a comparison of the role of an FBI agent to the role of a police officer. My professor really liked the idea and before I knew it, I was completely immersed in my research.

I was immediately attracted to the excitement and versatility that the Federal Bureau of Investigation seemed to offer. I'm the kind of person who doesn't like being confined to an office all day. With the FBI Special Agent position, there were so many options available that if I didn't want to sit behind a desk, I wouldn't have to. The more I learned, the more I felt drawn to this as a profession. Needless to say, by the time I finished my report, I was determined to become a Special Agent with the FBI.

Becoming an FBI Agent

As a Special Agent, you have the opportunity to work in any one of the areas the Bureau investigates, which include extortion (blackmail), terrorism (violence or threats of violence against the United States), drug trafficking matters, civil rights violations, kidnapping, organized crime, foreign counter-intelligence (the investigation of anyone visiting from a foreign country who is considered a "threat" to the United States), violent crimes (such as bank robbery), white-collar crimes (financial crimes), and other violations of federal statutes or laws.

There are different areas within the Bureau that agents can work and specialize in. For example, if you come into the Special Agent position with an accounting background, you may be placed on a white-collar squad. And if you find a new interest, such as becoming a firearms instructor or a polygraph examiner, other options can open up for you. The FBI has field offices and satellite offices in 56 major cities throughout the United States, and maintains liaison offices abroad in a number of foreign countries. The FBI is responsible for enforcing more than 300 categories of federal crimes.

The process of becoming an FBI Agent requires several steps. First, you fill out a short application (which you can get at any local FBI field office) and submit it to the Bureau. If you meet the criteria (you have to be a United States citizen, be at least 24 years of age, have a degree from a four-year college or university, and have no criminal record), you're sent a long application. The long application requires information about your family, friends and close associates, where you've lived, and jobs you've had. Once that is reviewed and you complete a formal interview, a detailed background investigation is performed, including a credit and arrest check, verification of your educational background, and interviews with personal and professional references, relatives, neighbors, and friends. After all that, you have to pass a medical exam and polygraph (lie detector test) before being eligible to enter the training academy.

The training academy is located on the Quantico Marine Base in Quantico, Virginia. It's basically like 16 weeks of boot camp; a third of your training is physical, a third is firearms training, and the remainder is class-room time (classes on white-collar crime and international terrorism, for example). You do a lot of running, push-ups, sit-ups, pull-ups, obstacle courses ... that kind of thing. I've never been much of a runner, so that part was kind of tough for me until I got up to speed. For those trainees who were police officers or came from a military background, the weapons train-ing proved difficult. They had to basically relearn everything, including how to stand and how to hold and use their weapons the "FBI way."

My first assignment after completing the training academy was at a satellite office of the Cincinnati Division (outside the main office) called the Columbus, Ohio Resident Agency. I was the only female agent in a 28-person office consisting of two squads. I stayed there about two years, working reactive crimes (bank robberies, fugitives, and drug trafficking matters) as well as white-collar crimes.

In 1987, I transferred to the New York office (our largest division, with 1,200 agents) and primarily worked foreign counter-intelligence (FCI), dealing with espionage (a foreign country stealing information deemed sen-sitive to U.S. national interest). I remained in New York until December 1991, when I was transferred with my husband (who was also an FBI agent at the time) and our infant son to the Houston Division. I worked FCI until after the birth of my daughter in 1993, then became part of the Joint Terrorism Task Force (JTTF). The JTTF consists of members of local and federal agencies who work together to investigate and respond to threats against critical U.S. infrastructures, such as secrets of the Department of Defense or U.S. chemical and biological warfare information.

In 1997, my supervisor at the JTTF was promoted to FBI Head-quarters, and at the same time, a good friend of mine became a supervisor for the Special Operations Group (SOG). The SOG is a unique squad that primarily conducts surveillance and works at an "off-site"—an under-cover location that looks like a regular business. The squad of 23 agents works with the Drug Enforcement Agency, the Houston police, and any other law enforcement agency during common or joint investigations. Since I was losing one supervisor and my close friend was taking over SOG, I felt it was a good opportunity to make a change. So I requested a transfer, and came to my current assignment with SOG.

A Day in the Life of a Special Agent

No two days are ever alike in this line of work. An agent may spend one morning meeting with a source (an informant or confidential witness) then typing reports all afternoon. The next day, the Special Agent may present a case before the Grand Jury or meet with the U.S. Attorney to prepare for trial on another matter. The SOG primarily works drug traf-ficking cases. Due to the nature of drug investigations, you might work drug surveillance all day and at the end, nothing happens. Drug dealers are highly suspicious of most of their clientele; they never know when one of them might actually be an undercover law enforcement or federal agent. If, during the course of their transactions, they become the least bit suspicious of the person they're dealing with or think they're being followed, they'll keep putting off the meeting or drug sale. That can be very frustrating.

On television and in the movies, FBI work is made to look pretty glamorous and the good guys always wrap up the case by the end of the show. In real life, though, it rarely works that way. There's a lot of behind-the-scenes work—the not-so-glamorous, time-consuming tasks that are often left out when law enforcement is portrayed on TV and in the movies. Duties such as gathering evidence, putting in countless hours of surveillance, writing reports, and meeting with informants play a big part in the role of a Special Agent. But despite the lack of glamour, there's an awful lot of satisfaction in this job. A Special Agent is a public servant. Whether making the streets safer or speaking at a college career fair, an FBI Agent plays an active role in the community in which he or she lives.

Taking to the Air

I've been fascinated with the idea of flying since I was a kid. When I trans-ferred to SOG (which also has the aviation wing assigned to it), the pilots

I worked with became my inspiration and my desire to fly was re-ignited. What had once been merely a fascination had suddenly become a career option! Over the next year and a half, I privately paid for a flight instructor, lessons, test, and in May 2000, I passed my check ride (a test of a pilot's skill and knowledge of an aircraft) and am now a part of a select group; as a part-time copilot for the Bureau, I'm one of eleven female pilots in the FBI.

Flying, while fun, is also a challenge. In the FBI we primarily fly single-engine airplanes, which have involved features such as retractable landing gear (which closes up into the airplane) and a variable pitch propeller (meaning the angle can be adjusted). So the actual flying can be quite complex. But by far the hardest thing about doing aerial surveillance is using the stabilized binoculars, which are high-powered binoculars that have a gyro (a mechanism within the binoculars that rotates at high speed and keeps them perfectly still) inside so when you look

Maria ready to take on another case.

through them, you don't see the movement of the plane; everything looks like it's perfectly still. For example, if I've got the eye from the plane, it's my duty to keep the subject in view. If the vehicle we're following makes a stop and the driver exits the vehicle, even from 4,500 feet in the air, I can describe the clothing the person is wearing and what he or she is doing.

Pursuing this new path in my career helped me to improve my time management skills. It also made me realize that when things are meant to be, and you have patience and perseverance, they will eventually happen. The next step for me is to get my Instrument Rating so that some day I can become a full-time pilot for the Bureau. I know it's going to happen, because I'm ready to make it happen.

Memorable Cases

I've worked many interesting and difficult cases, but one of the toughest ones I've been involved with was the crash of TWA Flight 800 in 1997. At the time, the FBI was trying to determine the cause of the crash. At one point we were concerned it was a terrorist act; then there was the possibility it was caused by a missile from a Navy ship.

Many months later, the ongoing investigation determined the plane was brought down by an explosion of fuel vapors in the aircraft's center fuel tanks. A spark had apparently ignited the gas tanks because they didn't contain any type of fail-safe system to detect a gas leak (the airline has since recalled all those planes and fixed the problem). The Bureau conducted interviews with immediate family members and friends of the victims to find out why they were on the flight, where they were going, and who they were going to see. The purpose of gathering this information was to determine if they had any enemies or international ties that would make them a target, or if a disgruntled former TWA employee may have been on board.

There were four victims on Flight 800 that were from Houston. One was a 37-year-old mother traveling with her two daughters. She was a prominent Texas crime victim's rights advocate who was a well-known figure in the community. The other was a 30-year-old woman who had been on her way to France to visit her twin sister when the flight went down. I was asked by the Special Agent in Charge to interview both families. As a parent, any case involving the death of a child is incredibly difficult for me to deal with, so those were really tough interviews to do. I later received a letter from the Director commending me on handling a challenging situation well.

Another memorable case involved terrorism. We knew of a terrorist subject who was collecting a lot of money in the United States and sending it overseas for terrorist-related activities. I developed a relationship with a source (someone who can help us with an investigation) who was close to this person, someone who had been used by the subject as a depositary (a person who is trusted to keep something for safekeeping) for the funds he had collected. Sometimes it can take months or even years to develop a relationship with a potential source—a bond has to be built before he or she will trust us enough to want to help. With the help of this source we managed to remove the money so it couldn't be accessed by the terrorist subject. It was very rewarding to keep money from possibly being used in terrorist activities or attacks against American citizens.

Juggling Family and Career

Sometimes it can be a real juggling act, combining a career in the FBI with a family and children. For a woman in a male-dominated profession like this, it can be especially difficult. If you decide to follow a career path into the FBI and have a family, it's important to find someone who is comfortable sharing the responsibilities at home—someone who isn't opposed to helping with cooking, cleaning, and taking care of the kids, and is a proponent of women in such a male-dominated job.

While I don't know for sure, it seems like a high percentage of women in the Bureau who are married are married to other agents. I think this really helps. A fellow agent knows what it's like day in and day out, what you're going through with a difficult case, and how draining it can be, for example, to be outside all day in 96-degree heat doing weapons testing. When you're working the late shift and dinner needs to be made and the kids need to be picked up, it takes a lot of pressure off to know your spouse is taking care of things.

Even though this can be a dangerous job, I don't fear for my life or my family on a daily basis. I take all the necessary precautions and know I am well trained to do what I do, so I don't think about it much. I feel very confident of how much protection I have around me, in terms of my own abilities, the abilities of my fellow agents, and a higher power watching over me. I don't think my kids worry, either. Our family has a strong faith in both religion and in ourselves, and my children know at the end of the evening, mommy is going to come home.

A Behind-the-Scenes Look at the Job

Favorite Part: To me, the diversity of my job is the best part. The everyday challenges I encounter and variety of the work really contribute to job satisfaction. Since Congress decides which federal statutes (laws) the FBI is responsible for enforcing (currently over 300), there's a wide array of classifications an agent can work during the course of his or her career. That basically means you can transfer to another area and work on something completely different on another type of squad (and even though it's up to you to find out what's going on in the new squad, the other agents tend to be very helpful in bringing you up to speed). It's almost like you can change jobs every few years if you want to. And if you don't, you have great opportunities to become very specialized in what you do.

Least Favorite Part: After a long day at work, I dread the occasional late-night phone call advising that something has come up and I have to work the weekend. The biggest concern for me when changes like this occur in my schedule is if it disrupts my family plans or causes me to disappoint my kids. As a Special Agent, you are on call 24 hours a day, 7 days a week.

Hours: I normally work Monday through Friday, and at least one weekend a month I'm called in to cover either Saturday or Sunday, or both. My shift is supposed to be alternating weeks of 7 A.M. to 3 P.M. and 3 P.M. to 11 P.M. However, since my assignment is with the Special Operations Group (SOG), which is a covert squad assisting in all investigative areas by providing ground and aerial surveillance, my hours are always subject to change—the crime world doesn't normally operate on a 9-to-5 schedule!

Dress Code: What an FBI Special Agent wears to work is directly related to what is on his or her schedule for that day. I'm assigned to an off-site unit, which is outside the main office of the FBI, so I can dress pretty casual every day. Otherwise, it's important that I dress so that I fit into the environment in which I'm working, and normally that's not the high-society side of town. When you're driving around a neighborhood full of crack houses (a house where crack cocaine is sold), you don't want to draw attention to yourself by wearing nice clothes and flashy jewelry.

Work Environment: I spend about 90 percent of my time working outside the office, either sitting in a car doing surveillance, in a plane tracking suspects, or conducting interviews related to cases we're investigating. The rest of the time I'm in the off-site office, which, on the outside, looks like a small office in a business district of the city. We park all our vehicles in an enclosed garage that is part of our actual office space. We keep them hidden because what we do is very covert (undercover). We literally drive up a ramp and into a garage that's large enough for about 20 vehicles and an electronic door closes behind each car that enters. Inside it looks like a small business, with 16 desks set up in bull-pen style (rows of paired desks lined up in one big room) and two computers where we check our email. The place is completely sanitized of anything FBI-related, though, because we don't want anyone who might come in, like an exterminator or telephone repair person, to know it's a government-related office.

Education/Skills: In order to qualify to become a Special Agent, you must be a United States citizen, at least 24 years of age, and have at least a bachelor's degree. There are four entry programs you can apply for, depending on your degree: law (requires a J.D. degree), accounting (you must have a B.S. degree in accounting or a related discipline), language (in addition to a degree in any subject, you must be proficient in a language that meets the needs of the FBI), or diversified (a bachelor's or advanced degree plus three or two years, respectively, of full-time work experience). I have a bachelor's degree in criminal justice from Florida Atlantic University.

Since 1994, I have been an active participant in the Bureau's hiring process. I'm a Phase II Assessor for the Bureau, which is the interview phase of this process, and means I am part of a three-person panel that conducts interviews of the applicants who make it this far. I've seen people with a wide variety of backgrounds become employed as FBI Special Agents. I've noticed that those who interviewed well usually had military, business management, computer, or law enforcement backgrounds. As far as skills, the FBI Academy provides you with all the special skills training necessary to do the job of a Special Agent.

Personal Qualities: This type of work requires you to sometimes work under very stressful situations, so the ability to stay calm in the face of adversity and make split-second decisions may be the one trait that could save your life. The other beneficial personality traits to have are patience, perseverance, and tenacity. You tend to do a lot of waiting, especially when you're on surveillance, and you have to be forceful and aggressive at times—yet persistent and sensitive to the needs of others—in order to interview people effectively and get the information you need. As a female agent, you also need to be comfortable in a profession that is basically 80 percent male without being intimidated into feeling like you have to prove yourself.

Perks and Rewards: The personal rewards in this profession come from simply doing your job well. The perks, however, are few, if any. I suppose one perk would be that if you like to travel, as I do, you can become involved in cases that take you to other states or even foreign countries. While working International Terrorism matters, I traveled to Europe twice on official business.

HOT TIPS

⚶ Maintain a healthy lifestyle; stay active and fit. Your health is always important no matter what you do, but to become a Special Agent you have to undergo rigorous physical training. You won't make it through 16 weeks of Academy training if you aren't in shape to begin with. And the job itself is physically demanding and rigorous.

⚶ Call or visit your local FBI office for brochures about the Special Agent position and other job opportunities. There are 56 field offices nationwide, and the inside cover of your local white pages will list the office nearest you. You might decide that there are other positions that interest you even more than becoming a Special Agent!

🔥 Read the *FBI Law Enforcement Bulletin,* which is available in many university libraries. It's easy to read and understand, and gives an in-depth view of the various areas of expertise that are available within the Special Agent position.

🔥 Stay away from drugs, gangs, alcohol, and illegal activities. The decisions you make now, as a teenager, can greatly affect whether or not you'll ever be accepted as a candidate for FBI Academy training. If you have any encounters with law enforcement, there is a good chance it will come out in the background investigation that every applicant goes through. Even though juvenile records are sealed and off-limits to the FBI during your background investigation (meaning they don't have access to information about minor crimes or first offenses), you'll still be given a lie detector test and asked about past drug use and other items.

WORDS OF WISDOM

Anyone can achieve goals; we all accomplish them every day. However, many people set their sights too low and settle for too little. As a young woman, you shouldn't limit yourself or your dreams—whatever "having it all" means to you should be your goal. Sometimes the things we desire don't come to us in the order we want them to, but that doesn't mean we should give up on them. If you want something badly enough, are willing to work toward it, and have faith in yourself, you can and *will* achieve your goals.

Find Out More!

John Douglas's Guide to Careers in the FBI: The Complete Guide to the Skills and Education Required to Be a Top FBI Candidate by John Douglas (New York: Simon and Schuster, 1998). This books describes the skills and education needed to become a top FBI candidate, offering helpful strategies to increase the chance of being accepted into one of the agency's many programs. Also read about the history of the Bureau, its organizational structure, and the stories of some of its agents.

Federal Bureau of Investigation
J. Edgar Hoover Building • 935 Pennsylvania Avenue NW •
Washington, DC 20535 • (202) 324-3000
www.fbi.gov
This Web site provides information about the FBI, including how the Bureau developed, facts and values, famous cases, news, career information, and more. The Kids and Youth Educational Page has games, tips for crime prevention (including Internet safety and a gang alert), interviews, and the latest information on school-based outreach programs sponsored by the Bureau.

Rebecca Taylor

HOT *Job...*

Fashion Designer

I absolutely love designing clothes, and starting my own business has given me the creative freedom I need to design my own unique collection of women's wear—everything from dresses and skirts to pants and coats. My clothes can be found in specialty boutiques like Scoop and top department stores like Barney's, Bloomingdales, Fred Segal, and Saks Fifth Avenue.

Home Base: New York City, New York

Number of Years in the Field: 10

Personal Philosophy: "Someone will eventually pursue the things you've been dreaming of, so it may as well be you."

I don't know if you'd call it flair, but I've always had a thing for clothes. As far back as I can remember, I absolutely loved dressing up. Even as a 4-year-old I would squeeze into my baby sister's clothes for the sheer fun of trying things on. When we were a little older and given the choice to pick out a new dress, my sister always preferred something pretty and blue, but I always opted for something more dramatic, such as a scarlet dress with a bold print. I guess I was destined for fashion from the beginning.

My parents really wanted me to become a pharmacist, but that's not what I saw myself doing. I dropped out of college and was kind of aimless for a while in New Zealand (where I grew up). I did all sorts of odd jobs (including working in a hospital and cleaning toilets in a hotel) while trying to figure out what I wanted to do with my life.

One of the odd jobs I had was working in a costume shop that made the costumes for Peter Jackson movies (a well-known New Zealand filmmaker). There I found a mentor who encouraged me and taught me pattern making. This was a huge breakthrough for me; I discovered that making patterns for clothing was something I really loved doing.

My experience working on movie costumes motivated me so much I decided to attend fashion school. I enrolled in the Wellington Polytechnic

School of Design (now called Massey University) and studied fashion design and construction, which is how garments are put together. The day I graduated, I packed my bags and got on a plane for New York City, one of the fashion industry's hot spots. At 22, I was young and had a meager $300 to my name. I couldn't even afford my own plane ticket; it was a graduation present from my parents.

Off I went, never thinking twice about what I was getting myself into. If I had stopped to think about it, I probably would have realized that moving so far away from home with no job and no place to live wasn't the smartest thing to do. But sometimes you have to go for it. I found my way to New York and through a friend, I got a job making tuna fish sandwiches (about 1,000 of them, actually) for a fashion show. The designer was Cynthia Rowley, an up-and-coming New York designer of romantic, feminine dresses and women's wear.

Making sandwiches turned out to be my "foot in the door." I suppose I was in the right place at the right time because I was hired by Cynthia Rowley to work full time at her apparel company. At the time her business was small and my position wasn't "job specific," so I was able to gain a lot of valuable hands-on experience doing everything from packing boxes and shipping orders to designing clothes. Working for her was such an incredible learning experience. It gave me an insider's view of the ins and outs of the fashion industry.

Girls Can Do Anything

Growing up in New Zealand, I remember an ad campaign with the slogan, "Girls Can Do Anything." It made me feel like anything was possible, a feeling I never lost. So with five years of experience in the fashion industry under my belt, I decided it was time to start a business of my own, designing and selling clothing for women. I didn't have a game plan or any type of formal business outline, I just knew I had to do it. I was encouraged by Elizabeth (Beth) Bugdaycay, who I met while we were both working for Cynthia Rowley. She was a great source of support for my talent and encouraged me to go out on my own as a designer. She even agreed to become my partner. I knew I couldn't sit around waiting for the right opportunity to come along, so I decided to go after my dream.

I bought some planks at a hardware store to make a table for my living room, so I could work out of my apartment. I purchased fabric, sketched some patterns, and made a few sample dresses. Once I finished sewing the dresses, I asked a fashion magazine editor I knew if she'd be willing to look at my small collection. She agreed to and liked what I had done. She was kind enough to put me in touch with a woman who ran a showroom (a place where buyers come to look at designs and place orders for their stores), and before I knew it, I was officially running my own business.

The Fashion Center of New York (also known as the Garment District) is a 4- by 6-block area that has thousands of showrooms. The Fashion Center is *the* place to be if you want to be a fashion designer. Retail buyers from all over the country go there to shop, place orders, and bring merchandise back to their stores to sell to their customers. A designer may have his or her own showroom or several different designers or manufacturers may share one, which is what I did when I first started my business.

Once I had space in the showroom, I set up shop and the very next day I had a $20,000 order from Saks! It sounds like it was really simple, but it definitely wasn't. Beth and I worked like crazy to get through the challenge of fulfilling that order. When it first came in, Beth and I looked at each other in shock, and it wasn't just over the excitement of the sale. The reality was we had $500 in the bank and had to figure out how to buy all the fabric and trimmings and pay people to make all the dresses. Financially, we didn't know how we'd manage, because at that time, money was so tight we couldn't even afford pizza for lunch!

Luckily, Beth is a genius when it comes to money. With her careful planning we scrimped and cut costs wherever we could. We begged people for special financing terms and hand-cut everything ourselves to get the orders out. It was quite an ordeal, but we did it.

Although our showroom was in the Fashion Center, that's not where we spent most of our time. When Beth and I started this business, we worked in a tiny office in the heart of New York City. It seemed like every 15 minutes a fire engine would pass by with its sirens blaring. It was so loud that if we were on the phone we'd have to hang up and call the person back once the truck had passed and it was less noisy. We didn't have a staff so we did everything ourselves, from hand-cutting patterns to packing and shipping garments for delivery. We didn't even have a voicemail system, which was a nightmare. The phones were always ringing and we'd have to stop what we were doing and answer them ourselves, making it difficult to get any work done. Our successes and challenges both seemed so huge.

Facing Challenges, Having Fun

If I had known in the beginning how challenging it was to start a clothing business, I doubt I ever would have given it a go. I never knew exactly how

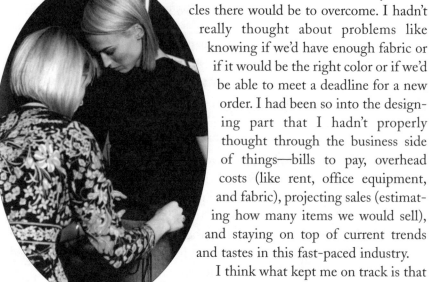

**Rebecca behind the scenes
with a model at a fashion show.**

much work it entailed or how many obstacles there would be to overcome. I hadn't really thought about problems like knowing if we'd have enough fabric or if it would be the right color or if we'd be able to meet a deadline for a new order. I had been so into the designing part that I hadn't properly thought through the business side of things—bills to pay, overhead costs (like rent, office equipment, and fabric), projecting sales (estimating how many items we would sell), and staying on top of current trends and tastes in this fast-paced industry.

I think what kept me on track is that I wasn't willing to give up and I never took the word "no" for an answer. When I started, everyone told me it couldn't be done, that I couldn't become a designer with my own label. I would show people my ideas and they would say, "No way can you do that," or "It'll be too expensive or too this or too that." But that just made me more resolved to do it. I'd say, "Oh, yeah," and then figure out a way to get it done because I believe there's always a way to get around obstacles. Sheer determination is what got me where I am today.

Big dreams or goals can feel overwhelming, so it helps when you're able to recognize when you achieve a small victory. It's important to acknowledge the steps you've taken: "Okay that's cool, I struggled with this but I got through it." Otherwise you begin to feel like you're not getting anywhere or that you're never going to reach your ultimate goal. Taking time to think about all the little triumphs along the way keeps you from taking them for granted, and you'll realize that you really *are* getting somewhere, that every day you're closer to your dream. You have to get up each morning, face the day's challenges, and solve whatever new problems come your way.

Every six months, Beth and I sit down and say, "Okay, where were we six months ago? Where are we now? Is the business growing and doing better?" It puts everything into perspective and helps us see that all the small steps we've taken are bringing us closer to where we want to go, which is to continue growing the business.

As our business has grown, we've been able to hire staff to help with all of the work, so there's not as much chaos as there used to be. We've also opened our *own* Rebecca Taylor showroom in the Fashion Center, where the buyers and the press come to look at the collection. When you enter the showroom, you pass through glass doors that have our company logo etched on them. On one side of the showroom is a wall that's covered with clear plastic padding and filled with lots of pink feathers. On the other side is an elevated platform where the models model the clothes. Pink neon lights underneath the platform give it the feel of a floating dance floor. The ceilings are very high and the clothing racks are suspended from them.

In addition to displaying our collection, we also use the showroom for conferences and meetings. We've created a meeting area that has two white leather couches and two very heavy white tables. The showroom itself is airy and light with huge windows and a balcony that overlooks the Hudson River. In the evenings when the sun sets over the water, the sky looks pinky-orange and it's really beautiful. Sometimes Beth and I will wander out to the balcony at the end of the day and have a glass of champagne and remind ourselves how fortunate we are to be making a living doing something we love.

Designing the Collection

Each season I design an entire new collection, everything from dresses, sweaters, and coats to pants and tops. My collection has been described as "feisty feminine." I always like to have a mixture of stronger-looking pieces and more delicate, feminine touches, so there's a sense of irony or contradiction.

I come up with ideas for things that I would want to wear. For example, I may design a flirty dress for dates with my husband, more casual pieces to wear to the office, and hip outfits for nights out with my girlfriends. I like creating clothing that makes women feel sexy and good about themselves when they put it on, things that are soft and feminine but with a bit of an edge.

I find inspiration for the clothes I design all around me, but mostly from things that are pretty and feminine. I like the romance of fairy tale books, old magazines from the 1930s and 1940s, Victorian flea markets, period costumes from the theater or the movies, and pictures of ballerinas. My idea source isn't limited by people; for instance, I love cats and other felines. Their fun, sexy, playful, and cute attitudes have been inspiration for several designs. For example, I once designed a faux-leopard print zip-up jacket with a hood (hoodie) and some animal print pieces dyed in bright pinks and oranges.

However, as much as I'd like to design whatever I want, there are some restrictions. I don't have the freedom to come up with *totally* crazy, wild stuff. The line I create has to sell and be profitable so that I can pay the people who make it. I also have to stay within the parameters of the current trends because that's what the public is looking at and that's what they want to buy. But I try not to be too trend- or decade-oriented, doing completely 1970s or 1980s looks, for example. I prefer to stay more current and focus on what feels right now as opposed to what felt right in the past.

The key to coming up with creative designs for each line is to be open to new ideas. Ideas can come from music videos, movies, or other pop culture trends. Style and fashion change quickly so I have to be up-to-date with what is going on in the world. When consumers want something different or there's a demand for a certain type of garment, designers have to react quickly and create what the consumers want to buy.

Getting the Help I Need

My biggest influence as a designer is my mom. When I was a little girl, she owned her own sewing machine and used to make all of my clothes. I never had a store-bought pair of jeans until I was 12! Now my mom flies all the way from New Zealand to help with the final preparations for my runway shows. She's very talented and helpful, especially when it comes to the detail work that makes the line look beautiful. She'll sew or embroider or do whatever it takes to put the finishing touches on the garments I've designed. I couldn't do it without her.

The weeks leading up to a fashion show are incredibly intense and very exhausting. We work a lot of late nights as well as weekends to get ready for the big event. The collection needs to look exactly the way I've envisioned it, so it takes a lot of effort to get it just right. The way I look at it, a design is a work of art in progress, so if a dress isn't working or doesn't look fresh enough, I'll start all over. Agonizing over a creation and wanting it to be perfect before it's presented to the press and buyers is part of the job.

By the time the fashion show gets underway, Beth and I are usually feeling pretty tired and fragile. My mom is very loving and gives us a lot of moral support. She also indulges us with snacks and makes sure we're eating right to keep up our energy level so we can handle the extra workload prior to the show.

Being busy all the time goes with the job of being a fashion designer. I like to keep involved in every aspect of developing the Rebecca Taylor collection, whether it's picking fabrics, overseeing production, meeting with buyers, deciding on colors, or planning for the next fashion show. But my favorite thing, what I love more than anything, is designing the line. The more I get to do it, the more fun I have. I have a great time creating clothing for women that makes them feel pretty and girly when they put them on.

It's also thrilling to see a celebrity wear something from the Rebecca Taylor line. Jewel, Cameron Diaz, Julia Stiles, Robin Tunney, Ashley Judd, and Courtney Love have worn clothes from my collection. Equally exciting to me, though, is when a regular girl walks by wearing a top or a skirt that I've designed. To me, that's the ultimate compliment. It means she actually liked the piece enough to buy it!

A Behind-the-Scenes Look at the Job

Favorite Part: There are so many positives to my career. It's great to have the creative freedom to design and have my own business, too. Being the boss also has its advantages. There are days when Beth and I will be working hard, putting in long hours at the office, and I'll say, "Saks is having a sale on shoes." The next minute we're heading out the door in search of shoe bargains!

Least Favorite Part: It's an awful feeling when I design something new, put it in a showroom and the buyers don't quite get it. Inside, I feel deflated. When you're a young designer, sometimes the buyers don't want to take a chance on your line if you're doing something before anyone else is doing it. But once a more seasoned designer does the same thing, they'll say, "Oh, okay, that's cool, we just never knew it was cool until so-and-so did it."

Hours: My hours are typically 9 A.M. to 8 P.M., Monday through Friday. When we started the company, Beth and I used to work every single weekend, but now I make a point of saying things can wait until Monday. There are always things that need to be done and it would be so easy to drift into the office on Saturday or Sunday to work for a few hours. But I have to set boundaries, otherwise I'd be there all the time. It's not good to "go, go, go" all the time. Everyone needs a break now and then.

When we have a runway show coming up, however, the hours I put in are a different story. I'll work six days a week, then the two weeks right before the show I'll work every day—and night.

Dress Code: I'm a jeans, sneakers, and T-shirt kind of gal. Ironically, my partner Beth is the one who likes to dress up. I think about clothes all day long so the last thing I want to think about when I get up in the morning is what to wear to work. I also run around a lot during the day, working with dresses on the mannequins, going to fittings, or kneeling on the ground pinning dresses, so it isn't feasible for me to be all dressed up. I do keep a pair of gold high heels under my desk, though. When I have meetings, I'll put them on with my jeans and they give me a feeling of confidence.

Work Environment: My work studio is in a big, open loft with huge windows on one side of the building, which makes it fairly bright. Nobody really has offices. Instead, lots of tables with loads of fabric and trimmings are all over the place. In addition to working in the office, I also travel fairly frequently for business. I go to Tokyo a lot as well as Los Angeles, Paris, and London. I'll look for beautiful fabrics and shop the stores so I can see what's selling in other markets. It's important to look and see what other parts of the world are showing, regarding their fabrics and designs. If you just look at the New York market, you'll limit yourself creatively. You've got to be open to new ideas and influences.

Education/Skills: Fashion school teaches you how to make patterns and put garments together, which is vital to this industry. You can't design something if you don't know how to put it together, and you can't instruct the people making the clothes if you don't know what you're talking about.

Many design firms are now using CAD (computer-aided design), so it's to your benefit to learn how to use a computer. Using the CAD program allows a designer to create a garment on a computer and change the color from blue to orange, or the sleeves from short to long with the click of a button.

Personal Qualities: You've got to love clothes! Having an appreciation for the way a garment looks—from the way it drapes a body, to the color, the fabric, and the lines—is key for a designer. And a good imagination is critical for coming up with fresh ideas, which is vital in this field.

A designer also needs to express herself clearly. She needs to take the vision in her head and communicate it to the people who are making the garments so that pieces come out the way she envisioned them. Fashion design is a competitive industry, so talent, creativity, an eye for color and detail, a sense of style, and the confidence to create garments that are creative and fresh will help you get ahead in this business.

Perks and Rewards: Every season I get a new wardrobe, anything I can create, in any color that inspires me. The only thing I have to buy are shoes. Equally cool is all the market research I need to do for the job, which is a fancy way of saying I get to do a lot of shopping!

HOT TIPS

◊ Learn to sew. Find a relative, neighbor, or friend who can teach you or find out if your school offers a home economics class that includes sewing. Another good way to learn is to contact a fabric store in your neighborhood to find out if they offer introductory classes.

◊ Window shop at different clothing stores and read fashion magazines like *Vogue, Teen Vogue, Glamour, Mademoiselle, In Style, Lucky, Elle,* and *Bazaar.* You'll get a good sense of what the current fashion look is as well as how styles change depending on the season and how popular culture (such as movies, recording artists, and sports) can influence the kind of clothes we wear. Determine what elements you like and don't like, and work toward developing your own sense of style.

◊ Get a part-time job at a clothing store. You'll learn what the public is buying and it may help you decide if the fashion world is for you. Fashion design seems like such a glamorous field, but a lot of hard work is involved and you should get a taste of it before you commit to design school. Working directly with customers also gives you the opportunity to find out what they like and don't like as consumers.

◊ Visit museums hosting fashion or costume exhibits and look at fashion history books to get a feel for how fashion has evolved throughout the years. Note what's changed as well as how some style elements are repeated through the years.

◊ When you watch movies or TV, pay attention to the costumes. See what the costume designers have fashioned for the actors and figure out what works and what doesn't. Just for fun, come up with ideas about what you would do different.

◊ Buy a sketchpad and practice drawing garments or other items you like. This is good sketching practice (something you'll spend a lot of time doing if you become a fashion designer) and will help you begin to notice the details in garments.

WORDS OF WISDOM

As you begin to take an interest in fashion, read magazines and shop the stores so you can see what's out there. It's important that you take in what you see, digest it a bit, and then develop your own sense of style. Don't get too trend-oriented; it's a dangerous path to follow because it can seem too contrived. Instead, stay true to your own sense of design. Whatever career you choose, have fun and enjoy what you're doing—it will show through in your work.

Find Out More!

Careers in the Fashion Industry by John Giacobello (New York: Rosen Publishing Group, 1999). Learn about the history of the fashion industry and find detailed descriptions of the different aspects of fashion, including design, retail, modeling, makeup, journalism, and photography. Included are interviews with professionals and advice and suggestions on how to get started.

Fashion: The Twentieth Century by François Baudot (New York: Universe Publishing, 1999). This book explores the evolution of fashion during the last century. Popular designers from the last 100 years are profiled and historical events that affected the styles of the times are discussed.

Fashion Careers: The Complete Job Search Workbook by Wendy Samuel, et al. (New York: Pocket Productions, 1999). This guide offers advice pertaining to all fields of the fashion industry. Find sample résumés and interviews to help in search for employment. Also included are worksheets that identify fashion talents and help determine the area best suited to individual goals and skills.

HOT *Job...*

Space Plasma Physicist

for the National Aeronautics & Space Administration's (NASA) Jet Propulsion Laboratory (JPL)

My job is to come up with theories and ideas for studying all sorts of space phenomena such as icy bodies in space (namely comets), and the atmosphere of earth and other planets. I'm also the Project Scientist for the U.S. Rosetta Program and a member of the Galileo flight team.

Home Base: Los Angeles, California

Number of Years in the Field: 15

Personal Philosophy: "I'm inspired by something John F. Kennedy said on September 12, 1962, at his address to Rice University students in Houston, Texas: 'We choose to go to the moon in this decade and do other things, not because they are easy, but because they are hard.'"

I was a smart kid and my parents knew it. They also wanted all of their kids to go to college, so we took college prep courses in high school and were expected to get good grades. When it came time to decide what to study in college, I was absolutely *not* interested in anything that had to do with math. I *hated* math. I wanted to be a journalist or a history major, but my parents said, "No." They wanted me to be an engineer.

We lived in the Silicon Valley, an area in California known for all the high tech companies located there, and my parents thought engineering would be a field where I could make a reasonably good salary. "You're never going to make money as a historian," they said. And they couldn't see me as a journalist. So they agreed to pay for college if and only if I agreed to become an engineer. Bribery works when you're 18 and don't know any better!

In the end, I didn't like engineering. But while I was in college, I had an opportunity to work at Ames Research Center, which specializes in new technologies research for NASA. I was hired through my school to work in the engineering department, but I eventually transferred to the science department because I thought it was so fascinating. During my junior year, I switched my major to earth sciences because science was fun and I was successful at it. I've never regretted becoming a planetary scientist—I love the research and the science. The only thing I do regret is the long hours. Unfortunately, if you're not willing to put in the hours, somebody else will.

I work in Pasadena, California, at the Jet Propulsion Laboratory (JPL), which is the lead U.S. center for robotic exploration of the solar system. My expertise is in gas kinetic theory, which means I study the thermal conductivity (the ability of a substance to conduct or transmit heat) inside icy bodies such as comets or icy satellites. It also means that I study how molecules migrate through the icy bodies, allowing for the release of gas. It's not unusual for scientists to work on more than one project at the same time. At JPL, I have dual roles; one is the project manager for the U.S. Rosetta Mission, the other is a member of the flight team on the Galileo Mission to Jupiter.

The Rosetta Mission

The Rosetta Mission is a joint NASA-ESA (European Space Agency) project created to study the comet named 46P/Wirtanen. Comets are relatively small (a few miles in diameter) bodies of ice, rock, and carbon-based molecules. When comets orbit close to the sun, the intense heat from the sun produces a cloud of gas and dust. As the gas and dust move away from the comet, they form the comet's long tail, which can be thousands of miles long and sometimes seen from the earth. Since comets are made up of the same chemical compounds that formed the solar system itself, studying these "dirty snowballs" is important because they provide scientists with key information about the early origin of our planetary system.

The Rosetta mission is named after the Rosetta Stone, which is the ancient tablet that provided the key to unlocking the secrets of the Egyptian hieroglyphics. The ESA is spearheading the project and NASA is contributing instruments and scientists to read the data. Typically, a mission like this will have a project manager and a project scientist who are dually responsible for its management. In this case, the Rosetta mission has two of each: a project manager and a project scientist who represent the ESA and a project manager and a project scientist who represent NASA.

The Rosetta orbiter will be the first spacecraft to orbit a comet and will be launched on January 12, 2003, for its eight-year journey to Wirtanen. It's scheduled to reach the comet on November 29, 2011. Since the orbiter will pass far from the sun (where it's very cold) as well as within the earth's atmosphere (bringing it relatively close to the sun) it has been designed to withstand extreme temperatures, both hot and cold. The Rosetta lander (a probe or surface science package) will self-eject from the spacecraft and land on the comet's surface. It will send back data regarding the composition and structure of the comet's components. The rest of the spacecraft will orbit the comet for two years, studying the nucleus (or center) of the comet and collecting data that will help scientists decipher critical evidence about how the giant planets (Saturn, Jupiter, Neptune, and Uranus) formed some 4.6 billion years ago.

When the Rosetta project began, NASA contacted JPL and instructed them to assign both a project manager and scientist to it so that American scientists would have a voice and representatives in this joint endeavor. I was selected by JPL to be the project scientist. One reason I was chosen was because I'm young—since the project has a very long life, they didn't want someone who might retire before it was completed! Part of my role as the project scientist involved serious discussions with NASA headquarters to convince them that this was a valuable project to spend money on. Once the spacecraft is assembled and in flight gathering data, the project scientist's role shifts: if any of the instruments are competing for resources, the project scientist decides what will happen.

For example, the instruments may compete for attitude, which is the spacecraft's angle of orientation relative to Earth. All the instruments are pointed in a particular direction, so if someone wants to look someplace other than where the instruments are pointed, the spacecraft must be turned to a new direction. Instruments also compete for power; since the supply is limited, when all of the instruments are in use, each instrument may not be able to reach maximum capacity. For this project, JPL's project scientist represents only the American portion, so the European project scientist will have the final decision (since they're spearheading it). But that person will help organize the American response to the problem.

Once the first data point comes down, meaning that the orbiter and lander have provided information, everybody gets to "feed at the trough"; we'll eagerly analyze data, write papers, and compete to explain what it all means. I'll participate in that, too, which will be the fun part and a welcome change from working with the instruments. This data analysis frenzy will continue throughout the mission and last for a few years afterward.

In September 2001, my role with the Rosetta Mission changed—I was named project manager for the American portion of the project, but we're out of money for the U.S. portion. Now my job is to assemble a team to put together information we can present to NASA headquarters to convince them to give us more money. I consider this new assignment a wonderful challenge because I get to capitalize on my interpersonal and negotiating skills (hopefully all those years in high school on the debate team and student government will pay off!).

The Galileo Mission

My second role at JPL is as a member of the Galileo flight team, which I've been part of for about seven years—I was hired when I first graduated as a neophyte (beginner) with a Ph.D. Galileo is a NASA unmanned spacecraft whose mission is to study Jupiter and its moons in detail. Jupiter is the largest and most massive planet in the solar system—it's about 300 times more massive than Earth—and like all of the planets, fills us with questions. The spacecraft was named after the first modern astronomer, Galileo Galilei, who made observations of space using a crude telescope in 1610. He was the first to spot Jupiter's four largest moons orbiting around the planet: Io, Europa, Ganymede, and Callisto, now known as the Galilean satellites (moons).

The mission was launched on October 18, 1989, from Cape Canaveral in Florida with the Galileo spacecraft flying through the earth's orbit aboard the Space Shuttle *Atlantis.* It was propelled onto its interplanetary flight path by its own motor system, passing by other planets on the way to Jupiter to gain additional energy from the gravity of each planet. Galileo finally arrived at Jupiter in December 1995, six years after its launch.

Multiple cameras and 11 scientific instruments are on board the Galileo spacecraft. Their purpose is to measure and study the atmosphere, satellites (moons), and magnetosphere of Jupiter and send the data back to the scientists on Earth who try to figure out what it all means. Each one of the instruments was designed and built for a specific purpose, such as the magnetometer, which senses magnetic fields in the spacecraft's immediate environment and the near-infrared mapping spectrometer, which measures the thermal, compositional, and structural nature of the Galilean satellites. My job on this mission is to monitor a console as it registers data from the spacecraft to make sure the instruments are working properly. If something goes wrong, I relay the information to the instrument engineers who can repair problems through computer technology. An older spacecraft (which Galileo is, since it was built in the '80s) can develop a corrupted area of memory in its computer system. If that happens, scientists must reprogram around it. They write a new program and uplink it (transfer it) to the spacecraft using giant telescopes aimed at the deep space network. Unmanned spacecrafts are a lot like VCRs—they can be programmed using a remote control!

I'm also the person responsible for planning the instrument observations schedule down to the microsecond. Many scientists and scientist teams want to use the information-gathering capabilities from Galileo, and it's my job to organize these requests. Scientists have to take turns sharing what little time is available on the instruments. Using the Galileo instruments is not like using a telescope where only one person can use it at a time. Multiple requests can be met at once or consecutively. To work out the logistics, we gather in a big room and negotiate as a group. If instrument use can't be agreed upon, I make the final decisions.

Scientists have theories, developed through years of study and research, to explain most phenomena in our world. One theory was that the moons of Jupiter (which we know are made of water and ice) are dead and dormant, with no activity. The calculations show that they should be frozen solid; it's very straightforward. When the Galileo project was in the development stages, many of the principle instrument investigators were so convinced of how quiet it would be that they didn't want to do many observations near those moons.

But once we started collecting data, we were really surprised. We discovered that one of the moons, Ganymede, had an atmosphere and a magnetosphere. In order for a moon to have both these situations occurring, there has to be activity inside of it . . . it can't be frozen solid! These findings were profoundly different from what we had expected. To this day, no one has a reasonable explanation for why that's possible. Even scientists—who rely on proven, reproducible findings—can't deny the evidence. That's one of the amazing things about *being* a scientist—we're always striving to explain phenomena like this.

Another exciting find occurred when the spacecraft flew by Europa, one of Jupiter's other moons. Despite several science-fiction tales that there might be life on Europa, the consensus was that it, too, was frozen solid. Surprise! When we began taking detailed measurements, we discovered that not only is the surface *not* a billion years old like we thought (it's a lot younger), it might even be active right now. That's how *not* frozen solid it might be. Now, there's a lot of speculation about whether there may actually be an ocean there, and possibly life. We still don't know for sure; nothing is proven yet. But for me, this discovery essentially transformed science fiction about life on Europa into potential science fact, a perfect example of what is so phenomenal about the work I do.

Unpredictable Days

The first thing I do when I arrive at work is check my email and figure out what is urgent enough to warrant an immediate response. I may have an idea of what I'd like to accomplish on a given day, but typically the messages I get will supersede whatever plans I have, which can be annoying.

The most urgent issues to address are related to the Galileo project. Because the flight is in progress, anything that I need to check or create (such as an instrument sequence) needs to be done right away. Or I may need to look at data to figure out how to play it back or attend a flight-team meeting to discuss the status of the Galileo project. In between handling the Galileo issues, I address any emails pertaining to Rosetta. I also spend time reading any pertinent information on the upcoming Rosetta mission.

In the afternoon, I try to find time to do my own science. I might gather information and use it to formulate new proposals or write scientific papers. I may create theoretical models or codes on the computer, trying to figure out what I want to do next with the information I've formulated. I really need to concentrate when I do this kind of work, so I'll retreat to a separate office to avoid interruptions. When I come out of hiding, my coworkers will joke by saying something like, "Oh, you finally showed up!"

But it's rare that I get to do what I've planned. Not only do I need to deal with all the regular unexpected details and events, but, at any given moment, a crisis may occur. This means we drop everything and work to resolve the problem, for example, the Thanksgiving Day anomaly (problem) with the Galileo project. The spacecraft was damaged and most of our staff was required to report to the office. Before Thanksgiving I had told my boss, "Look, my family has said that after 20 years of being a guest at Thanksgiving dinner, it's my turn to be the host . . . to buy and fry. No way will they be understanding if I have to work that day." Sure enough, just as the turkey was ready to come out of the oven, my beeper went off and my family went berserk. Putting it mildly, they weren't thrilled that I might have to go into work.

Fortunately, I didn't have to go to the office right away, but around 11 P.M. I had to wake up my crew to let them know we had a problem. We ended up saving the spacecraft, a feat that was a culmination of contingency planning, emergency planning, and working around emergencies that we hadn't prepared for—that's what it's always like around here. We were commended by NASA Administrator Daniel Gouldin and called heroes in the newspaper because of the level of effort that we put forth that day.

Searching for Answers

Scientific subjects being studied today are so complicated that science is no longer a single person sitting alone in a lab coming up with theories and trying to prove them. Instead, scientists collaborate in teams. Most people are experts in one particular area, so teams consist of scientists with different specialties. Together, they can make an idea come to light. Because I want to study the atmosphere of Ganymede (one of Jupiter's moons) and I'm not an expert in chemistry, I collaborate with a chemist who can tell me if the reactions I'm predicting are actually possible. Someone else might be working on a proposal about particle bombardment (interplanetary materials like meteors or "shooting stars" that hit Earth or other planets) and he or she might ask me to participate by providing a theory for how the particles get off the ground, which is my expertise.

In some ways, being a scientist is like being an entrepreneur. *You* come up with an idea for a project and you have to convince investors to give you the money to work on it. *You* know the idea is wonderful, but the investors may be skeptical, so you need to persuade them that the project is worthwhile. Scientists like myself spend a lot of time writing proposals with detailed budgets in an effort to convince NASA to fund us so we can continue with our scientific research.

This part of being a scientist brings a certain amount of anxiety. If a project you're involved with winds down and you don't have another one lined up, you're out of a job. We ensure job security by coming up with a scientific question, writing a proposal for how we'd like to try to determine the answer, and doing everything we can to get NASA to pay for it. Sounds pretty straightforward, but it's actually a very long and complicated process. There's a lot of competition, and you never know if funding will be available or if your idea will be selected. I've decided that's why so many people around here have gray hair!

Contact, the 1997 film based on the book by Carl Sagan, shows what it's like to be a scientist struggling to raise money for a project you believe in. It is a pretty accurate portrayal of what it's like to be a female scientist in a male-dominated field. Most scientists, like artists, have a sense of inspiration about what they do; it drives them to do the hard work—including raising money and overcoming personal obstacles like gender bias.

Finding the Open Door

When I was a teenager and my parents steered me away from choosing history or journalism as my college major, I never felt like they had slammed the door on my dreams (in fact they still paid for my degree even though I switched majors). And while I was open to giving engineering a try, I had no idea what to expect. About halfway through college, I began to realize that I was struggling. It wasn't because my courses were hard, it was because I was bored. I wasn't the least bit interested in engineering.

I realized this when I took a class in earth sciences and found that I wasn't bored by it *at all!* It was easy for me to do well because I truly enjoyed what I was learning. Then, when I started working at Ames Research Center and discovered planetary sciences, I was hooked. I had found something that registered so strongly for me that I forgot all about the fact that I loved writing and poured myself into this new passion.

I believe that we ultimately do the things we love, regardless of the path we may have been put on. It's certainly worked out that way for me. I love science, I love astronomy, and I love my job. But for the last eight years, in addition to my work at JPL, I've developed and written for the Web site, Windows to the Universe. It's a site about science, planets, and stars. It's been a huge success, and being able to write for that has helped fulfill that long-ago passion for me. Twenty years after changing my focus, I've rediscovered my love for writing and am doing what I had initially wanted to.

In addition to the Web site, I've also written a series of books for young children that tell a fun story while teaching them about earth sciences and the universe. They have yet to be published, but I know that when they are, it will be because I have the unique qualifications to write them—something I wouldn't have had if I had pursued my original path. In my family we always used to say that when one door closes another one opens. I guess you could say a back door opened for me, one I never even imagined, allowing my original dream to become a reality . . . thanks to my career as a scientist.

A Behind-the-Scenes Look at the Job

Favorite Part: It's been an exceptional experience working on the Galileo project, bringing down really mind-bending data, the kind of information that changes the way we think about things. In quieter moments, it's given me an immense sense of pride to be a part of that.

Least Favorite Part: Without question, the long hours are the worst part of my job. Because of societal expectations, I think it's more difficult for a woman than a man to spend a lot of time on the job. In our society, it's still often perceived that the woman takes care of the home and children. You may be seen as someone who's not devoted to your family and you have to be really sure that you are willing to dedicate a substantial amount of time to this field. On the other hand, maybe you're the kind of person who will force a change in the culture allowing you to have a family and a demanding career. Just be aware that to make a contribution as a scientist, you will be faced with some hard choices. I have seen women who have managed to have both a career and family, but it is not easy to devote yourself to a partner, children, and your job and give each the attention they deserve.

Hours: I work about 60 hours a week, but there have been times when I've steadily put in 70 to 90 hours. The demands are so great that you need all the time you can find to get the job done.

Dress Code: I can get away with looking just about any way you can imagine! It's perfectly fine to show up without my hair done, in jeans and a T-shirt every day. In fact, wearing dirty jeans with holes in them gives you more credibility than a suit and tie in this field. If you look too put together, people will think you're putting more time and effort into your appearance than your work. As a project scientist, I do have meetings with NASA and the media, so I wear a suit for those occasions. I've also started making sure my nails are manicured and my hair looks relatively coifed, which makes me feel more professional . . . and boy, do my coworkers give me a hard time about that!

Work Environment: Unlike what a lot of people might think, I don't work in a high-tech lab with fancy machinery all around me. To the contrary, I work in an office environment full of cubicles. My cubicle is located in one collective area with those of the rest of the team working on the Galileo project. Mine has a door, and when I really need to concentrate—like when I'm reading, doing calculations, or working on new proposals—I shut it. We have a protocol regarding closed doors: if you knock and the person doesn't respond, you don't burst in. But that still doesn't prevent interruptions from the telephone or email, and it doesn't stop people from knocking on my door. So I have another office that's quieter, one where I hide when I need to do some heavy thinking. Luckily, only my manager knows about this second office, so I'm bothered only in more urgent situations.

Education/Skills: I have a bachelor's degree in geophysics, a master's degree in geophysics and space physics, and my Ph.D. in space plasma physics. Pursuing a scientific career such as mine requires advanced degrees. If earth sciences or planetary study is of interest to you, be sure to keep up with math and science, including chemistry and physics.

Personal Qualities: The ability to see things in a different way, to "think outside the box" is what it takes to become a good scientist. People who are intellectually oriented will be successful in this field. The scientists and engineers at JPL are some of the brightest in the country, and in order to be that good, they tend to be very focused and not particularly social. On the other hand, in order to understand the environment we work in and be able to negotiate with headquarters or the Europeans, it helps to have excellent interpersonal skills. If you have to be in front of the media, like I do, good communication skills are key. Since science can be incredibly technical and complex, it's important to be able to educate the media and the public about the projects we're working on, so that they comprehend what we're talking about.

Perks and Rewards: The U.S. Rosetta Program is a European mission, so I travel overseas a lot. I fly over there twice a year, and sometimes I'll stay a little longer and make it into a vacation. I've been to London, Amsterdam, and Paris, and next time we're going to Italy. The last time I was in Paris, I was scheduled to fly home on a Friday, but it was $1,000 cheaper for the government if I stayed until Monday. I thought, "Well, to help out the U.S. government, I'm willing to do it!"

HOT TIPS

🔥 Math and science classes are a necessity if your goal is to become a space scientist. They're the foundation for everything you'll do, whether you aspire to become an astronaut or make an important scientific discovery.

🔥 Concentrate on keeping your grades high. Scientists are smart people, usually at the top of their class. You won't go far in this field if your grades are low to mediocre.

🔥 Join a debate team, or some other activity that forces you to speak, debate, argue, or lecture in front of people. Whether you're working on a team project or presenting your ideas to your colleagues/peers, good communication skills are essential to most scientists.

⚶ If you have the opportunity, take computer classes at school, community education centers, or the library. Today, most scientific work is done with computers, so you'll need to have proficient computer skills.

⚶ Read everything you can about astronomy, rockets, astronauts, and anything else that interests you about space. The more knowledge you have, the better informed you'll be about which area of expertise you'd like to pursue.

WORDS OF WISDOM

I believe that people need to be multi-dimensional—there needs to be more to you than just science. Once you get into graduate school, the demands of a science career are so great, they'll crowd out your other interests. Stay well-rounded and keep up with your hobbies. You'll enjoy your career much more if it doesn't consume your life and keep you from doing the other things that you love. If you like to play an instrument, play it. If you like to climb mountains, climb.

Find Out More!

DK Handbooks: Stars and Planets by Ian Ridpath (New York: DK Publishing, 1998). This thorough field guide for beginning astronomers offers a general introduction to astronomy, information on stargazing equipment, a glossary of terminology, and the history of each cosmic feature's discovery.

Windows to the Universe
www.windows.ucar.edu
This Web site is all about science, planets, and the stars. Claudia helped create it and is coauthor of the information on this site. Log on and catch a glimpse of her smiling face!

Women of NASA
quest.arc.nasa.gov/women
This Women of NASA Web site aims to encourage and provide support for young women interested in math, science, and technology careers. The interactive site offers live chats, Web casts, and profiles of women working in these fields at NASA.

NASA
300 East Street SW • Washington, DC 20024
www.nasa.gov
Located in the nation's capital, NASA headquarters oversees the operations of the agency's many facilities across the nation. Visit the Web site for information on the newest space discoveries, photos from current missions, career and visiting information, and links to the agency's many facilities (including the Jet Propulsion Laboratory).

Janice C. Molinari

HOT *Job...*

Independent Television Producer

and co-owner of Brisun Productions

Being a filmmaker, whether I'm working as a director, cinematographer, or producer allows me to take my passion for storytelling and turn it into a meaningful experience for an audience. When I'm hired to produce a television program, I'm responsible for the creative vision of the show as well as developing a budget and arranging the financing, bringing the talent (cast and crew) together, and coordinating the entire production, from start to finish.

Home Base: Towaco, New Jersey

Number of Years in the Field: 10

Personal Philosophy: "Get out there and find something that inspires you enough to want to exceed your limits."

I've learned that you need to be open to whatever comes your way. You may have your heart set on one particular goal and hit a bump in the road, but that bump may take you in a new direction, somewhere you never thought of going. That's what happened to me.

I originally thought I wanted to be a big feature film producer like Steven Spielberg or work on major TV programs, but what I found was that I love doing documentary-style programs because they're so real. It's not the direction I had necessarily wanted to go in or one that I had even considered, but I was guided in this direction and it's become my passion. What I love most about working on documentary-style programs is being able to tell someone's story in a way that makes viewers think—or makes them realize something about themselves that they'd never thought of before.

In the beginning of my career, I didn't think I had enough experience to become a movie or TV producer, so I thought I'd start in advertising and learn to produce 30-second commercials. I majored in communications (with a concentration in film studies) at Fordham University in New York City and during my senior year I got a job at an ad agency—I absolutely hated it. But, even though I didn't want to be part of the advertising world, I still didn't have enough confidence to go for my dream—producing TV shows or feature films.

After leaving the ad agency, I landed a job at *MTV Sports* in the production management department, working on things like budgets and booking travel arrangements for the show. I was very active throughout high school, playing basketball and softball and running cross-country, so I was excited to be working on a sports show. Although the job didn't allow me to work on the actual production end of *MTV Sports,* my department was in the same area of the building, so I got to work side-by-side with the people who were producing the show.

One of the first shows we did was about winter hurricane surfing (surfing on big waves created by offshore storms) at the New Jersey shore. Normally, production management doesn't go on shoots (where we film the show), but this one was about two hours from my house, so I asked the producer if I could tag along and lend a hand. I went on the shoot and took the 16-millimeter camera my dad had given to me for college graduation. On my own initiative, I shot three rolls of black and white film. I didn't have a clue what I was doing, but I was eager. I asked the producer if he would mind taking a look at my footage. He ended up using almost all of my footage in the surfing piece and said he wanted me at the next shoot.

So that's how I got my start. In addition to fulfilling my duties as a production manager, I would go on location for *MTV Sports* with a film camera and shoot. Even though I had taken film classes in college, I didn't have much experience, so things always seemed to go wrong. The film would be overexposed, grainy, or scratched because I didn't clean it properly. Or the lens would be half on and I'd get a funky picture. It was always something, but it actually became a "look." I was always trying to get shots that were unique; it wasn't unusual to see me rolling around on the ground shooting the camera up at the athletes.

Because the producers of the show wanted to create something that was different from other shows—something with an edge—the mistakes worked. I think it was this unconventional, no-rules approach to shooting (along with just experimenting and making some mistakes that actually looked good) that helped with the look of the show.

During this time, I also had the opportunity to work with a lot of experienced cinematographers (the professionals who do the actual shooting of the film), so I was able to learn all about the camera and how to shoot film correctly. I had learned the basics of operating a film camera and lighting techniques in college, but it wasn't until I got my job at *MTV Sports* that I became more skilled and started to develop an eye for composing interesting and different shots. That, combined with my unconventional style (and interesting mistakes!), are what made the producer see something in my work.

The Making of a Filmmaker

My second year at *MTV Sports*, I was hired as a cinematographer. I spent a year shooting film there, then decided to work on my own for a while because I wanted to branch out and try shooting for other kinds of programs. I became a freelancer and worked for myself, being hired by different companies. This was great because I could still be hired to produce segments and do shoots for MTV, but because I wasn't officially working for them anymore, I had the opportunity to work for a variety of other clients and challenge myself in new directions.

In 1993, I found myself doing something I never could have imagined. Every year from July 6 to July 14, the Fiesta de San Fermin, otherwise known as Running with the Bulls, is celebrated in Pamplona, Spain. Every day during the festival, bulls are let loose from a corral at one end of town and are herded through barricaded streets to a stadium (the Plaza de Torros) at the other end of town for the bull fights. I was covering the event for *MTV Sports*.

I was running with the bulls and filming at the same time so our viewers could get an idea of how crazy it gets. I started the run and was moving along thinking, "Okay, this isn't a big deal." I kept looking over my shoulder wondering, "Is this it?" Then there was a surge from the crowd behind me. There were wall-to-wall people and it became insane. The bulls were back there and everyone started to run. Elbows were flying and people were getting punched and slammed up against the side of the barriers lining the route trying to get out of the way of the bulls. I started to panic and thought, "What did I get myself into now?"

I kept filming, trying to get something that would be usable. I figured if my camera work was shaky and my footage was all over the place, it would show what the run really felt like. The course is a little over a mile long and at the end of it, all the bulls funnel into a tunnel that leads into the stadium. One of my coworkers had told me that when I got to the tunnel I should stay to the left side because when the bulls come around the corner, they swing to the right. So, as I was running along, my mind was racing with one major concern, "Get to the left, get to the left." Wouldn't you know that as I approached the tunnel, I was on the right. Several bulls had already passed by me, so I figured it would be safe to make a move. I looked over my shoulder and began to cut over to the left-hand side of the tunnel only to stop in my tracks. A huge pile-up of 15 to 20 people was laying on the ground and I didn't want to step on them. I wound up getting pushed down by the people running behind me, then more people fell on top of me.

I couldn't breathe and all I kept thinking was, "This was a stupid thing to do and now I'm going to die and my dad's not going to be too happy about it."

I had heard that a rocket is sent up to signal when the last bull enters the arena. Because I hadn't heard any noise from a rocket, I figured there had to be at least one more bull nearby. I began to feel relieved as people started to get off me but then I realized I'd be more vulnerable if I was closer to the top of the pile. Trouble was looming.

As I was pushing to get up, I heard a bull on the cobblestones behind me. The next thing I knew, his hoof connected with the back of my right knee and he pushed it back down onto the ground. Then he stepped on my shoulder but his hoof lifted off me and he stepped between my head and my camera, which I was still holding with my right hand. The camera was off at that point because I'd gotten knocked around so much and lost power. I didn't see the bull, but I could smell bull all around me. I was dazed but heard the rocket go off so I knew it was safe to get up. The last bull had to be in the arena.

I made it into the arena and limped over to the MTV production crew. I was in shock and started to pass out. The medics came over, sliced up my jeans and saw that my leg was swollen. The bull had damaged the ligaments in my knee as well as burst a blood vessel, causing my knee to fill up with blood. Twice I had to go to the hospital to have it drained with a needle.

While I was recuperating at the hotel the following day, the assistant camera person knocked on my door and said, "Janice, check it out." She had a stack of newspapers in her hand and I had made the front page. There was a color photo of me running with my camera, two bulls directly behind me and six bulls at my side. I was so surprised because when I was running, I had no idea how close they were to me; I was just trying to get the best footage I could. So in addition to a great story, I also came home with some lasting souvenirs—a copy of a newspaper with me on the cover and some serious bruising on my knee!

Work Is Always an Adventure!

For the next three years, I worked as a freelance cinematographer, which gave me the time to learn more about producing as well. In 1996, *MTV Sports* asked me to come back to the show as a producer, which was a *big* promotion. Basically it meant I would be running the entire show, from deciding what stories we'd be covering to directing and editing. The first feature I produced was on B.A.S.E. jumping, which stands for Building, Antenna, Span, Earth. People jump off of things like bridges, cliffs, or buildings with a quick-release parachute. This sport is vastly more dangerous than skydiving because you're much closer to the ground and if your parachute doesn't open immediately, you're dead. B.A.S.E. jumping is legal in some countries, but in the United States it's only legal one day a year, in one place, off the New River Gorge Bridge in Fayetteville, West Virginia.

The idea for the show was to have Will Oxx, a seasoned B.A.S.E. jumper, teach a skydiver (Joe Jennings) how to B.A.S.E. jump and follow them through Joe's learning process. We filmed Joe practicing off a bungee tower attached to a bungee cord, from a hot air balloon, and then a bridge. For the big finale, we took Will and Joe to Angel Falls in Venezuela, which is the world's largest waterfall (it's about three times the size of the Empire State Building) so we could capture their 14-second free-fall on film.

The production crew and I flew to the city of Canaima and from there we took a 45-minute helicopter ride to our makeshift location headquarters (base camp), which was in the middle of the Amazon Rain Forest. It was another 25-minute helicopter ride to the bottom of the falls. The helicopter could only hold half our group of 18, so every morning we'd split into two groups to fly to the film location.

Our base camp provided the barest form of living. We stayed in open-air huts with outdoor cold-water showers and bugs crawling all over the place, including baby tarantulas. We'd been taking malaria pills, which make you have really vivid dreams—mine were about snakes. A giant anaconda skin hung as a decoration inside the hut where we ate breakfast, so that didn't help matters.

We were scheduled to be at Angel Falls for five days; three to prepare for the shoot and the last two to film a bunch of jumps. Our intention was to get a total of five jumps on film, which was ambitious considering the element of danger involved. But five would give us the camera coverage we needed to show the jump from a variety of angles and then edit them all into a single jump.

From the start, production ran behind schedule. The weather turned bad as soon as we arrived. It rained, and it rained *hard*. We basically sat around waiting for the rain to stop. By the end of day four, we still hadn't filmed any jumps because the weather wasn't cooperating. At one point, I noticed Joe sitting on a rock all by himself. He was looking up at the falls talking to himself, saying, "Okay, I can do this. I'm getting ready. It's going to happen." My audio guy happened to record it because Joe's mike was on. "Roll the camera," I said. "This is going to be part of the story." So we filmed him sitting alone, contemplating the jump. We'd need something to fill the half-hour show, especially if we never got the jump.

Each day, we'd have to pack up all of our equipment by 4 P.M. and be ready to fly back to our base camp because the helicopter pilot couldn't fly after dark. At 3 P.M. on day five, the clouds suddenly disappeared. In a matter of 10 minutes, it was entirely clear. "All right, let's go, we're doing this now," I said and eight of us piled into the helicopter to get to the top of the falls.

At this point everyone kicked into high gear, excited that the jump was finally going to happen. Everything started happening fast. I was using a walkie-talkie radio to

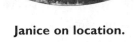

Janice on location.

communicate with everyone, "Where's the medic? Is the camera down below at base camp ready to roll? Is everyone harnessed?"

We had one camera on Will that would roll as he was free-falling. One of our Venezuelan guides (who barely spoke English and was definitely not a cinematographer) manned another camera at the top of the falls. I showed him the camera and said, "Just push this button." My coordinating producer, Meaghan, bravely climbed 15 to 20 feet down from the falls (with a guide and a harness) and stood with one foot hanging off the ledge of an outcropping and held the third camera in her hand. I was strapped into the doorframe of a moving helicopter with the fourth camera, shaky legs and all. We also had a cinematographer positioned at the bottom of the falls with another camera equipped with a 600-millimeter lens, which is a super zoom lens. We needed as many shots from different cameras as possible because we were only going to shoot one jump, not five like we had hoped. When you edit, it's important to show something from many different angles to make the piece more dynamic.

Will and Joe finally got to jump, and it felt like my heart leapt right up to my throat. I kept thinking, "If they die, it's my fault, they're my responsibility." But at the same time, as I was flying in the helicopter filming the fall, it hit me that this was the most incredible shot I could ever imagine. They leapt from the outcropping of the rock at the top of the falls and fell away, growing smaller and smaller. They fell for 14 seconds, which seemed like an eternity. By the time they opened their chutes, we had passed by in the helicopter, so I couldn't see them anymore. The moment was so exciting because I had wanted to shoot B.A.S.E. jumping for years. It was also a little frightening because B.A.S.E. jumping is such a dangerous sport, and Will and Joe could have lost their lives. But what an amazing sight it was to watch them fall away from the falls! Everyone started celebrating immediately. Joe and Will were successful, everyone got their camera shots, and we were done.

Editing Footage

What keeps my job interesting is that it constantly changes. One week I might be running with the bulls and the next I might be in the office on the phone setting up the next adventure or sitting in a quiet edit room putting together a story with the footage we've shot.

Editing the footage you've shot is what shapes the story; it's what makes it come alive. When you shoot film, your aim is to get something original, something that is aesthetically a little bit different (such as interesting camera angles), so that when you begin the editing process, you have great material to work with. The better the material, the better the story will turn out.

The first thing I do when I start editing is review all of the footage we've shot and log it so I know what I've got. Next, I weed through it to find the parts that will highlight the story best. I sit with an editor and we figure out how to piece the story together. This process takes a lot of focus and time. For instance, for a half-hour show, we may shoot 65 hours of footage and it can take up to three weeks to edit, sometimes working 15-hour days. For a three-minute segment, we'll shoot four to six hours of footage and spend ten to fourteen hours in the editing room.

Because I got my start at MTV, music is critical when it comes to editing my stories. For me, it is the soul of the story. The music I choose helps set the mood and the pace of the editing. Music has the power to evoke so much emotion. Some selections can energize you, some can bring you to tears, and others can make you feel calm. I have thousands of CDs, everything from classical to new age to rock 'n' roll, and I'm always listening for new possibilities I can use. It's exciting bringing my vision to life combining the right music with the images I helped to capture. The combination helps me tell what I hope is an unforgettable story.

Setting Up My Own Company

I was happy working for *MTV Sports,* but I wanted the opportunity to create something bigger. When I was growing up, I was always told I could do anything I set my heart to. I reached a point in my career where I knew I wouldn't be content working for a network or cable station; I wanted something that would give me the freedom to pick and choose the projects I wanted to work on. So while I was still working at *MTV Sports* as a producer, I started my own business, Brisun Productions, as a sideline. Within a year, I realized that to make my business a success, I had to make a full-time commitment to Brisun. So I left MTV to give my company my full attention. It was the hardest decision I've ever had to make.

I created Brisun Productions to produce a variety of cutting-edge programming from sports to documentary presentations. Although our specialty is action-adventure subjects, we also produce features for events like the Breeders Cup (horse racing) as well as independent films and original television broadcasting. For example, we've produced a one-hour magic special called "Extreme Magic II: Live on Tour" and a documentary entitled "Ocracoke-Island Inspirations," which was about the local artists on a small island off North Carolina and the connections they have with each other and their home.

At first it was a challenge to get clients to think of me not only as a producer but also as a business person who could put an entire project together, including producing, directing, and editing. It was also a bigger risk financially because now I was in charge of entire productions and budgets ranging from a few thousand dollars to a few million. Each day was a struggle to generate new business and have enough energy left over to pour into creating my own television projects. But little by little, things began to fall into place.

Having my own business gives me the freedom to develop my own projects as well as work on freelance projects (everything is done under the name Brisun). Now I have three partners involved in the company, and they've really helped Brisun grow. It's our passion to produce great television that makes us stand out from the competition.

When I first realized I wanted a career in television, I didn't know anyone who worked in the field so I was on my own to find a way to reach my destination. There have been many people along the way who have given me wonderful opportunities, guidance, and support. But I believe what really helped my career is the passion I have for telling stories that shows through in the projects I've worked on. No matter what job you pursue, I think the key to becoming successful is enjoying what you do, because it will show in your work. I'm sure enjoying my job, and I'm always looking forward to the next big adventure!

A Behind-the-Scenes Look at the Job

Favorite Part: I love to travel around the world and meet interesting people, people who are famous or just getting by in everyday life, and interview them. But best of all, I love to come home and bring their stories to life for millions of people through television. I also love that each production is unique and I'm always working on something new and different.

Worst Part: The traveling is fun, but when I'm away from home too long, I get homesick. It's hard to plan vacations or holidays or get-togethers with friends because sometimes I'll get an assignment that requires me to pack up and leave on short notice. At the beginning of your career, it's important to make a name for yourself, so you have to expose yourself to as many different projects as possible. That means when someone calls, you take the job, no matter how inconvenient it is to your personal life. And a career as a producer usually means there will be sacrifices, like being away from family and friends. But if you really love it and can't imagine yourself doing anything else, you'll know you've made the right choice.

Hours: My hours vary depending on what I'm working on. When I'm shooting a big assignment, I typically work 18-hour days. Working in the edit room, I can work anywhere between 8 and 20 hours in a single day. I do a lot of traveling for my job and that can take me around the block or around the world. And depending on the project, I can be gone for a day, a week, or two months at a time. Even though it's difficult to be away from home so much, it is fun to be on a beach in Hawaii or traveling through Australia and realize that for me, it's just another day in the office!

Dress Code: When I'm on a shoot or directing for a sports production, there's a lot of action and movement involved so I need to dress casually and comfortably, which means jeans and T-shirts. Baseball caps are great for days when I've only had three hours of sleep and no time to shower!

Work Environment: An interesting part of my job is that my work environment is always changing. When I'm in production, I do all my shooting on location. It's great to wake up and go to work in Pamplona, Spain, or stand with a fisherman in the Sea of Galilee. These are my favorite work days. Sometimes I work with a small crew of four to five people and sometimes I work with a couple hundred, but it's always a very creative, fun, and relaxed environment.

Along with on-location shoots, however, I also have to spend time in an editing office. My company, Brisun Productions, has an office where I do a lot of editing. Occasionally, I work out of different edit facilities called post-production houses, mostly in New York.

Education/Skills: To be a producer, there isn't a set list of educational requirements. A college education with a background in media studies, film and television production, or communication studies is a great way to start. Most career training, however, takes place in the field while you're working. You learn how to use the equipment, like the camera and editing systems, as well as how to hone your skills as a director. The training never ends because the craft and technology are always evolving. I'm always learning something new.

Personal Qualities: First and foremost, you have to be creative and imaginative. Not only is this important to create interesting footage, but you never know what environments and surprises await you. Being easy to get along with helps, too, because there are times when you'll be put in difficult situations and you have to make the most of it. Other important qualities are being organized, patient, and a good listener, as well as the ability to become knowledgeable and take an interest in the subject you're shooting. You should be a people person with the ability to put the person you are interviewing at ease and get him or her in a conversational mode.

Perks and Rewards: Traveling all over the world is a definite advantage. Because of my job, I get to have experiences I normally wouldn't have and meet people from all walks of life. Best of all, I get to share the stories of the amazing people I meet with the world.

HOT TIPS

🔥 Watch and study television and films. Pay attention to the editing, use of music, and cinematography. It's all part of the learning process. If you can watch a show and know what you like and why you like it, you'll be more able to successfully reproduce that yourself.

🔥 If you don't already have one, think about saving up the money to buy a DVD player. If that's not possible, rent or borrow one from a friend. DVDs offer so many added features that are helpful to the aspiring producer, like a director's commentary and behind-the-scenes segments. It's the best type of film school there is!

🔥 Check your television guide for specials about new feature films. Many times when a new movie is released in theaters, they will promote it with a behind-the-scenes look at the making of the movie. Special programs like these will give you an inside glimpse of how movies are made and give you a chance to see if it seems like something you'd like to be involved in.

🔥 Get involved with production now. No matter how old you are, there's something you can do. Use a camcorder or regular camera and begin telling stories with it. The experience will help you develop your skills, and it can be a lot of fun. It may help you decide if telling stories with a camera is something you truly want to do.

🔥 Sign up for a school or community play. Whether you act, work on the set design, assist the director, or help with the costumes, it's all great theatrical experience if you decide on a career in film or TV.

🔥 Learn about the industry. Read books about the entertainment industry and flip through trade magazines like *Entertainment Weekly, Premiere, Daily Variety,* or *Hollywood Reporter* to see what's going on.

WORDS OF WISDOM

I've always been a big believer in the concept that if you can visualize it, you can achieve it. It's important to visualize your dreams and set goals to achieve them, but it's also important to remain open to the paths life leads you down.

Find Out More!

Setting Up Your Shots: Great Camera Moves Every Filmmaker Should Know by Jeremy Vineyard (Studio City, CA: Michael Weise Productions, 1999). This book is a virtual encyclopedia of visual storytelling that will appeal to anyone intrigued by how movies are made. Explores types of shots and camera movements, as well as provides examples of films that use them, illustrating frame-by-frame how the techniques work.

Film and Video Magazine
4533 MacArthur Boulevard, Suite A, PMB 576 • Newport Beach, CA 92660 •
1-800-800-5474, ext. 3210
www.filmandvideomagazine.com
From the moment the cameras start rolling to the final editorial cut, this magazine covers everything a film-lover could want to know about the industry, including insights into Hollywood and the tricks of the trade.

Cinematographer.com
www.Cinematographer.com
A global community that cinematographers can access from anywhere in the world, Cinematographer.com contains timely information on film festivals, awards, new tools, people in the community, and helpful resources.

HOT *Job...*

Classical Musicians

The three of us make up a chamber music trio; Lucia plays the piano, Angella plays the violin, and I (Maria) play the cello. We perform more than 100 concerts a year of both old and new works, but we are most passionate about promoting contemporary classical music. So far, we've recorded three CDs: "Ahn Trio: Villa Lobos, Ravel: Piano Trios," "Ahn Trio: Dvorak, Such, and Shostakovich Piano Trios," and "Ahn Trio: Ahn-Plugged."

Home Base: New York City, New York

Number of Years in the Field: 14

Personal Philosophy: "You only live once so you've got to do what you really want in your life."

Our parents loved classical music and the arts, and ever since we were old enough to walk around, they exposed us to as much of it as they could. They took us to a variety of orchestral concerts, singers' recitals, chamber music recitals, ballets, and art exhibits. When Lucia was 5 years old, she decided she wanted to learn piano. After a whole year of begging, our mom finally gave in and Lucia was able to begin taking lessons.

When Angella and I saw what Lucia was doing, we decided we also wanted to take lessons. Having been lucky enough to have attended many classical music concerts, we were already familiar with several instruments. Angella chose the violin and I decided to try the cello. I didn't really know what it was, but it seemed exotic. Besides, it was bigger than my sister's violin! At first the instruments were like new toys, something we could play with. That's how playing classical music started for us—as a fun hobby.

For the three of us, unlike a lot of musicians, becoming really interested in playing professionally was a gradual process. As children, our music teachers told us we were talented. Because people tend to like things they're good at, it was very natural for us to really, really like what we were doing. When we were around 8 or 9, we began entering all sorts of competitions as a trio, from small local ones to larger national competitions, and we started winning and earning a lot of praise. But even at that point, we never consciously thought about becoming classical musicians.

At the time, we lived in Seoul, Korea, where a lot of our friends had tutors and were studying piano, violin, or some other instrument. Everyone talked about a great school in New York called Juilliard. It was highly regarded as one of the top learning institutions for music. When our family moved to the United States in 1981, we were still in grade school and our mom decided we should audition for this renowned school—luckily, all three of us got in. It was amazing to be around so many talented musicians, and actors and dancers as well.

Juilliard offers a program called precollege, which is like prep school, but only for music. Students attend regular school during the week, and go to Juilliard on Saturdays for condensed, college-level musical training. After a few years of that, the three of us definitely felt that music was what we wanted to do when we grew up. We continued with our music education and all of us received our bachelor's and master's degrees in music from Juilliard.

Pursuing a Music Career

We've been lucky; good things just sort of happened to us. For example, when we selected our instruments as children, our parents had no idea we had the makings of a piano trio (which consists of piano, cello, and violin)—and neither did we! By the time we were in high school, each of us knew that pursuing music—whether as soloists, chamber musicians, or as part of an orchestra—was what we wanted to do. Although we had played together, we never thought about becoming a trio professionally. It wasn't planned, but it worked out!

When we came across music we all liked, we occasionally played together. We began playing as an ensemble more regularly when we got old enough to attend Juilliard full time. In 1995, a record company approached us and said they had heard our demo tape (most serious musicians create these) and were interested in signing us as a trio for their label, which was a major thing. We started performing more concerts as a group and had a lot of fun doing it. The recording contract led to signing with a professional artist manager. From there our career just took off and before we knew it, we were scheduled to give concerts the entire next year as the Ahn Trio. After many months of traveling from one concert hall to another, we all came to the same conclusion: "Hey, this is working!"

Now we totally love it. There is a lot more freedom in terms of the repertoire in a piano trio than in an orchestra, where you have to play what the conductor decides. As a small ensemble, we have our own voice, and that makes the music more satisfying to us.

Playing Classical Music

When people think of classical music, they tend to think of Haydn, Mozart, Brahms, Bach, Tchaikovsky—the old masters. We've realized, however, that the spectrum is so much wider than what you usually hear, or even what you think classical music is all about.

At Juilliard we met many brilliant young composers and were exposed to some really great music, more than just the standard classical stuff. It was an intriguing, exciting experience. We discovered that there are a lot of talented, contemporary classical composers who are influenced by their surroundings just as much as the old masters were by theirs. The difference is that now, thanks to modern communications, a contemporary composer's surroundings include a whole lot more. Now someone in Austria can hear jazz from New York, salsa from Columbia, drum rhythms from Ghana, or folk melodies from Tibet without leaving home.

We've always felt that classical music could be forward and modern. It's really the basis for many popular music forms. Most people don't realize this because it's usually presented in a stiff and formal setting. Classical music is perceived as being more esoteric—for a smaller, elite group of people. We're not saying classical music should be presented in rock concert arenas, but at the same time it makes sense to us that classical concerts could be updated; it's not like we're living in the nineteenth century. So that's what we're trying to do, to present classical music in a more approachable manner.

A good comparison is when an art museum has an exhibit of classical painters. The art museum doesn't mandate what kind of clothes museum-goers must wear or demand silence in the museum. They use space and lighting to complement the art. People are encouraged to express their appreciation in any reasonable form. This is unlike classical concerts, where the audience must clap only at certain times and dress formally, and where the performers are placed under stark white lights. We don't understand why classical concert formats have traditionally been so rigid. We love presenting our music in a more friendly and inviting way.

In Beethoven and Mozart's time, classical music was the pop music for the educated classes of their era. These artists were the new music makers of their day and every time they wrote a new piece of music, people got really excited. We think that if Mozart was alive now, he would be this really hip, avant-garde guy, doing everything the most modern way possible. We don't think he would try to make things so old fashioned. So in picking our own repertoire, it seemed perfectly natural for us to explore modern classical music as well as the old classical pieces. Good classical music—new or old—rocks! We absolutely love turning people on to it.

Performing on MTV Unplugged

Juilliard has a wonderful program for helping its students make extra money by playing mini-concerts at different events around the city. People looking for musicians call the school and hire students to perform at their functions, which can be anything from a wedding to a recording session to a major party.

In 1997, we were contacted by Juilliard (we had already graduated, but if they're short on currently enrolled students they'll call alumni) and asked if we were available to sit in for an *MTV Unplugged* session with Bryan Adams. It sounded like a good opportunity so we thought, "Why not?" The *Unplugged* sessions feature musicians performing without amplifiers; the idea is to emphasize the music instead of the sets or any kind of amplified sound. These days, a lot of pop and rock musicians choose to use a string section. It adds richness to the music and makes it more interesting by creating additional layers of sound. For Bryan Adams's *Unplugged* session, the string section added color and beauty to his songs.

The session turned out to be a lot of fun, and Bryan Adams was really nice; we could tell he really respected the students from Juilliard. While it was no big deal to us—we had done a lot of things that meant more to us (such as the record contract)—our appearance caused quite a stir in the classical music world. It just goes to show the power of the media, and of popular music versus classical music. The fact that we were classical musicians, performing on MTV in the string section for a rock 'n' roll musician really drew attention.

What amazed us about the experience was the size of the production. There were more people working on this production than there were performers! Classical music recording sessions are so much smaller, just the performers and a set that looks like a concert hall. It was an eye-opener. We felt it would be so great if we could draw that kind of attention from young audiences with the music *we* play. Then it dawned on us . . . why couldn't we? It's all in how it's presented, so why not present classical music in a modern, alternative format—our own version of *MTV Unplugged?*

Even before we appeared on MTV, we had been thinking about how we could present classical music—and particularly more modern classical music—in such a way that more people would be interested in it. We wanted to draw people to our concerts who normally wouldn't come. That's how our CD "Ahn-Plugged" came about. It's a progressive and creative approach to new classical music. We had wanted to do an album like this for a long time and were so excited to finally record it!

We love presenting things in a new way, kind of like taking an old story and giving it a creative, modern twist. A good way to understand what our music is all about is to think about a classic play or some other type of artistic expression being performed in today's modern style. For example, there have been several film adaptations of Shakespeare's work for the modern audience (such as the recent version of *Romeo and Juliet* starring Leonardo DiCaprio and Claire Danes, set in the present day in a mythical metropolis, Verona Beach). While the movies are based on classic Shakespearian plays, the writers tell the stories in a new light, making them fresh and fun. That's what we are trying to do—present the old masterpieces and the more modern compositions in our own unique style.

Playing Together

When we were growing up, we hated being referred to as one of "the Ahns." It was especially hard in school, because we all attended the same one and are so close in age—two of us are twins with the remaining sister just two years younger. The three of us didn't like hanging out together either; we wanted our own friends and our own space. We needed a chance to be individuals before we could become a trio, and we were able to do that.

Once we started working together, we became better friends. It has brought us much closer. We talk constantly! We've found our trio works because we're family. We don't think we could do this with other people because we have to spend so much time together. We've found ourselves stuck in airports with our flight delayed overnight, and in remote places with nothing to do but sit and wait. Lucky for us we're not only sisters, but also such good friends that we can just hang out and have a great time.

Working together also keeps us in line. If one of us develops a bad attitude, the other two immediately put her in her place! We've also learned how to give each other space and privacy, and to respect one another professionally. Obviously when we're working together, we have to be respectful and not behave in the annoying way sisters sometimes can.

Performing as a trio also means we never get lonely. Having friends who perform as soloists, we know how tough it can be to travel alone all the time. Even though we all live separately, we actually choose to hang out together a lot of times when we're in town and not actually working. We like to explore the unique shops in our neighborhood, go running in Central Park, visit art galleries, and go out to eat.

Being on the road can be pretty grueling and the pace is nonstop. On a pop concert tour, the artists generally perform the same program and travel from one city to the next, making a circle of the United States. Their destinations make sense from a logistical standpoint. Unfortunately, it doesn't work that way in the world of classical music. Because classical musicians don't generally perform at big stadiums or have the massive

Maria, Angella, and Lucia (left to right) take their act to the street.

following that pop stars do, we're constantly zig-zagging across the United States, sometimes even leaving the country in the middle of a tour to perform in Europe or Asia. We have to perform wherever our manager books us. At least we have it easier than pop performers in one respect . . . we only need to travel with our instruments and music, we don't have all that extra equipment for the stage.

In addition to our all-over-the-place schedule, each concert is different since the program is put together depending on who has booked us. Classical music presenters have a definite idea of what kind of music they want for a concert. We may be hired to play contemporary pieces from our "Ahn-Plugged" CD in one venue and the next day we may fly across the country to perform pieces from classical masters like Ravel or Dvorak.

Most of the time we travel by air, but sometimes we play in towns without airports, so we end up driving. Because none of us love to drive, we try to do it as little as possible. How much we travel per week varies. Sometimes we arrive at a venue the day before and have the entire day of the performance to leisurely rehearse and rest. This is optimal because it allows us to work many hours without distractions (at home, we constantly have to take phone calls!). We have the time to really get to know the acoustics of the performance hall. Lucia, the pianist, really loves this because she has plenty of time to get used to the piano.

The hard days are when we have to travel and perform on the same day. It's especially challenging when we've spent the entire day at some airport because of flight delays, wondering if we'll even make it on time for the concert. What is truly amazing is what happens without fail *every* single time this occurs. We walk out on stage, are greeted warmly by the audience, start playing, and suddenly the grueling day disappears and we become totally immersed in the music.

In addition to playing concerts, we're also involved in community outreach programs. In many of the cities where we perform, we offer music workshops at public schools. We play and teach students about composers and our instruments and it gives us the opportunity to expose children to live classical music. They get to ask us questions, so it's a great exchange of music and words. In most cases, they've never seen or heard anything like our presentation. The kids usually enjoy the music and we feed off their excitement . . . if we can give them a sense of how much we enjoy playing, then we're happy. Hopefully we can spark interest where before there was none, or maybe motivate someone to keep practicing their own instrument.

The tour schedule definitely gets tiring, but we've learned to adjust to this kind of lifestyle to make the job work. We used to postpone things we needed to do at home until we got back in town. Then we realized that the small amount of time we're actually home isn't enough to get much done. So now, even when we're on tour, we try to take care of personal matters (like paying bills and returning calls) while we're on the road.

Whether we're on the road or recording CDs, our biggest goal is to expand our audience to include people who wouldn't normally attend a classical music concert. We're thrilled to see babies, kids, and people wearing jeans and sporting tattoos in the audience. All we care about is that everyone is having a good time listening to the music. And if people want to dance in the aisles, great!

Almost on a daily basis, all three of us feel extremely lucky. We wake up and can't believe we're doing exactly what we want to do, and we're making a living at it! How many artists can say that? It's pretty amazing.

One time, we performed a concert in a small town in Michigan. The entire community was really looking forward to our show, and they were so excited to see us. About 700 people attended the recital, and afterward they were thanking us for coming and for bringing something to their town that they don't get enough of. They were genuinely grateful. Imagine what it feels like to share something of yourself and get that kind of positive response. And that's probably the best part of it all . . . sharing with others—and each other—our love of music.

A Behind-the-Scenes Look at the Job

Favorite Part: Chamber music is all about sharing, and the fact that we can share music with each other, as sisters, onstage, while we're sharing music with the audience, is the greatest part of our job. It's such an incredible, intimate feeling. The whole process is fun, and while there are different levels of gratification, the music is the biggest part—the constant motivation and stimulation, and that we can share it.

Least Favorite Part: Not having enough time to do what we want to do. We're constantly pressured for time, but this teaches us how to manage our time better and not waste it. Having so little time for friends back home is also hard. Sometimes we feel really guilty especially when one of us forgets a friend's birthday.

Hours: We don't have a set schedule, but when we're home, we practice as many hours as we can. On the road, we fit in whatever time is available at the concert hall where we're playing so we can become familiar with the acoustics and performance spaces. We also practice individually in our hotel rooms, except for Lucia—she doesn't have as much freedom in terms of practicing. Because she needs a piano, her practice time has to be set up with the concert presenters. We all have to work with the hours available.

Dress Code: On a "girls" level, we love that we get to dress up and wear pretty clothes and shoes. I think all our "regular job" friends are a little envious that we have a reason to buy glamorous things to wear onstage. We like to wear things that you'd wear to a party. Some performers are really formal in terms of wardrobe, but for the three of us it's all about practicality and comfort. We don't wear anything that requires ironing because then we'd have to iron each time we unpack. We used to pick outfits that complimented each other, but since we have similar taste, it almost looks better when we try *not* to match.

Work Environment: Lucia's apartment is our studio; we practice there when we're in town, which isn't very often. When she was looking for a new apartment we had to make sure it was big enough for her grand piano to fit, and have enough space for us to rehearse (Angella and I often rehearse together on the strings, working out intonations, bowings, and all the technical things). We each practice individually, too. Eventually we'd like to have a larger, working studio where we can rehearse together, but because living in New York City is very expensive, that won't happen for a while.

Education/Skills: Taking lessons, in a classroom or privately, and diligent practice will help you learn to play your instrument. An undergraduate degree from a college or university with a major in music will help you train for a professional career as a musician. You'll be able to take classes in music theory, ear training, composition, orchestra, conducting, and learn to understand and interpret the subtleties of music. A master's or doctoral degree in music will give you advanced training in these subjects and allow you to teach music in a college or university.

Personal Qualities: Besides having talent, to be a professional musician you must be determined and dedicated, have stage presence and poise, and be willing to work hard. Auditions can be anxiety provoking so you have to be able to play under pressure. Because you'll face rejection, you need the confidence to keep practicing and studying to prepare for the next audition.

If you're a solo artist or part of a small group like we are (as opposed to being part of an orchestra), you also need to have some business sense. Because we're a trio, we get to spread out the responsibilities, with each of us handling what best suits our personality. I tend to be the "creative director" of the group, Angella the "spokesperson," and Lucia the "administrator." Because our job requires us to be self-motivated (we don't have set hours), we all take turns making sure everything gets done. As performers, we create our own schedules, so we've got to be responsible.

Perks and Rewards: Being a classical musician isn't about glamour; it's hard work. But playing our music for an audience and seeing the look on their faces when they embrace the performance makes the hard work worth the effort—it's the most amazing reward you could imagine.

HOT TIPS

- 🔥 Choose a musical instrument that you personally enjoy and try to get as good as you can. You have to be willing to put in long hours of practice to become a professional musician.

- 🔥 Expose yourself to the arts as much as you can. Attend a ballet, go to the museum, or listen to a singer's recital. Being an artist is all about taking everything in, the old and the new, and reinterpreting it.

§ If you don't already play an instrument and you want to learn, the best place to start is to check if your school has a music department. If so, talk to the head of the department about how to get started. If your school doesn't have a music department, look in the phone book under "music schools" or "music lessons" and set up an appointment to speak with a teacher about lessons.

§ Join the school orchestra, band, or other music program; the more practice you can get, the better musician you will become. You may also want to see if there are any church or community orchestras you can join.

§ Attend performances of orchestras, chamber music groups, or other types of musical concerts in your community such as jazz, pop, swing, rap, R&B, country, or gospel to broaden your musical horizons.

§ If you don't play an instrument, but still would like to pursue a career in music, consider becoming a recording engineer, a music agent, or a music publicist. A lot of jobs in the music world do not involve playing an instrument.

WORDS OF WISDOM

Do things because you really want to; never compromise and settle for less. What's the point of doing something because you think you're *supposed* to do it? Have fun with everything you do, then decide if that's what you'd like to pursue as a career. There are so many different jobs in music—playing in an orchestra or a chamber group, teaching, composing, producing—the important thing is to figure out what aspect of music feeds your soul. Feel free to try things until you discover what you really like.

Find Out More!

Career Opportunities in the Music Industry by Shelly Field (New York: Checkmark Books, 2000). Many career opportunities in the music industry are covered in this book, including recording, radio, and television. Also find out what it's like to work for an orchestra or opera, or at the business end of music.

The Ahn Trio
www.ahntrio.com
Log onto this site to find out more about these progressive musicians. Included are beautiful photos, biographies, updates about new projects, and tour information.

The Juilliard School
www.juilliard.edu
Learn about the prestigious Juilliard School of Music, Dance, and Drama. Information is available about their precollege Saturday program, their college and graduate programs, the history of the school, admission requirements, tuition, and more.

HOT *Job...*

Stuntwoman

During a film or television show, it's my job to perform the action for an actress to keep her safe and unharmed. Sometimes the things I have to do are fun and sometimes they're dangerous, but no matter what I do, it's always something I am trained and prepared for. Looking like I'm out of control yet knowing I am actually in control is an unbelievable adrenaline rush.

Home Base: Los Angeles, California

Number of Years in the Field: 7

Personal Philosophy: "Whatever I am today, it is all because of the mercy and kindness God has shown me."

If I said I "fell into" my career, you'd probably laugh. But that's the truth. I never planned on becoming a stuntwoman. Up until 1992, I had never been involved in anything remotely athletic. I was just living day by day without sense of purpose—and making some poor choices.

Parents often work hard to instill in their children a sense of confidence and self-worth—it's something any child or teen should be able to look to their parents for. But I didn't have that. My parents were struggling with their own issues and didn't have the time or the capability to invest in me. I felt like I didn't matter, that I wasn't important or worthy of their attention and neither were the things I was thinking or feeling. I spent my childhood and teenage years believing that if I couldn't gain my parents' attention and love, then no one else in this world would love me either. I felt empty, without a sense of hope . . . and those feelings led to despair.

In an effort to dull the pain in my heart of sadness and loneliness, I began using alcohol to ease the pain. By the time I was 18, I was drinking with friends on the weekends, and by 21, I had started using drugs and became more and more lost, with no interest in my future. The alcohol and drugs anaesthetized the feelings that were drowning me, even if the numbing only lasted for a short time. I was in so much pain, I mistook the temporary relief of getting high for real help.

What started out as a desire to feel free of pain turned into a vicious downward spiral. Not only did I have the poor self-esteem that led to my drug use in the first place, I also felt horrible about *doing* drugs—so I started doing *more* drugs to cover the feelings of guilt. Before I knew it, I couldn't stop the terrible cycle because getting high to solve my problems had become a habit. At the time, I didn't have a clue who I was. I didn't have a shred of self-confidence or self-esteem; I was desperately searching for answers to questions but I didn't know where to look for the answers. Who was I? Why was I here? What would I become? Who could help me? If there really was a God somewhere out there, how could this be happening to me?

Finally, when things were looking pretty bleak, my life took a major turn. I had been to church as a child but the services never really impressed me. I couldn't figure out why the love I kept hearing about in sermons never seemed to show in people's behavior when they weren't in church. Then when I was a young adult, a dear friend reached out to me, helping me realize that the way a person begins to change is through her heart. Since then, my faith has been my strength and has kept me grounded. It's helped me think about myself and others in a whole new way, to make better choices—including giving up drugs and alcohol—and has opened the door to many new possibilities for my life.

Finding My Path

One weekend in the fall of 1992, some friends and I took a weekend trip to Lake Havasu in Arizona; the guy I was dating was competing in the Jet Ski World Finals and we wanted to cheer him on. As I watched the riders whiz by on the water, I turned to a friend standing next to me and said, "You know . . . I could do that." "Sure you could," he responded. But I didn't just mean I could learn to ride jet skis; I meant I could race and be world-class competitive.

I don't know exactly what made me feel so certain that this was something I could master—it was just a really strong feeling that overtook me. Up until that point, I had never done anything athletic. When I was a kid, anytime I mustered up the confidence to try something new, the response was, "Who do you think you are?" But when I announced that I thought I could ride jet skis, it was the first time in my life I felt like I could succeed at something—and that someone agreed with me. Just hearing another human being say they thought I could do it was all I needed. So right then I decided to go for it and become a jet-ski racer.

I decided to win and set new records in the sport. And to the amazement of people who knew me, I did just that.

After that weekend at the Jet Ski World Finals, I started working toward my new goal. By good fortune, I was given a jet ski by a friend, and I set aside time three days a week to practice riding. I had no idea what my physical capabilities were, but as it turned out, I was more athletic than I realized, so with lots of practice and proper training, I quickly learned more advanced riding skills. First, I set out to become familiar with the machine—what it felt like to ride at different speeds, to turn left and right, and to fall. I wanted to be good right away, but I soon learned that it takes time to acquire new skills. So in addition to learning to jet ski, I had to learn to be patient during the learning process itself. Steely grit and sheer determination is what kept me going.

From the beginning, though, I enjoyed my newfound sport and began to discover things about myself. I had spent most of my life without ever really thinking about myself in a positive way, but as I began to experience success and see myself as an athlete, I started making the kinds of choices an athlete would. I started to eat right, exercise, and train my body to be stronger and quicker for my sport. And I knew that to be a better racer, I would have to adjust my thought patterns—retrain my thinking about myself, my potential, my worth, and my capabilities. Excellence became my new goal. But I wasn't competing with or comparing myself to others; I was competing with myself, to improve my *own* time and performance. With my newly discovered faith and confidence, I knew I could keep my focus.

By 1993, I was racing full time and earning money from sponsors and competitions—it had become my job. In May of '93, I won my first World Cup Championship, and in June, I set what would be my first of three Slalom World Records—and it was only my first year on the National Tour! In 1994, after only one year of competing on the Factory Thunderjet Team, I was asked to become a team rider for Kawasaki, one of the largest manufacturers of jet skis. (Jet-ski racing is similar to car racing in that companies sponsor racers.) Being a factory team rider for Kawasaki meant they sponsored me to race on their behalf.

It wasn't long before I was known in the personal watercraft industry for my accomplishments as a jet-ski racer. Being part of the team also helped me become known in the entertainment industry for my expertise in the sport, which is what launched my career as a stuntwoman. I was asked to do a commercial for Kawasaki and after that I performed my first stunt job as a double for actress Linda Hamilton on the film *Dante's Peak*. More offers started coming in and my new path was laid.

Joining the Stunt Community

The stunt community is a very tight knit group, very protective of each other and the work they do. Stunt professionals like to maintain a sense of mystery, the "Wow! How did they do that?!" reaction moviegoers have when they see some action sequences. If only a select few know how to pull off those stunts, it's easier to sustain the mystery. You need to be tenacious to enter this community. What really helps is having a specialty, something you're really good at that makes you stand out.

The things today's stunt people are asked to do are a lot different from what they were years ago. We don't just jump off horses, bite the dust, and take it to the body like they did in the old westerns. Because the level of difficulty of stunts has increased so much, one person isn't able to master all of the different areas of stunt work. Stunt people specialize in different areas, such as gymnastics, martial arts, equestrian skills, bicycle motocross, or extreme skateboarding. Each person is highly trained in one particular area or a combination of areas, which allows for more intense, on-the-edge performances.

I'm a personal watercraft specialist. In addition to jet skiing, I can also water ski and drive speedboats. Together with three other women I met through the Stunt Women's Association (our professional organization), we formed a water specialty group called S.W.I.M., which stands for Stunt Women in Motion. A group of stuntmen who are water specialists formed a group called Frogmen, so we figured why not create a women's group? One of the women in S.W.I.M. is a world-class swivel water skier, one is

Terri performs a ramp jump for the television show V.I.P.

a scuba diving master (she "tags" sharks for a hobby!), and the third is a high dive artist. We work together to get referrals for jobs in our particular areas of expertise.

Even though having a specialty in this business is a must, it's also valuable to become well-rounded. This is accomplished when people of differing specialties share their expertise with one another. The call for water work can be limited, so it helps to be able to do other things, too. For example, I was able to apply personal watercraft racing dynamics to working with cars and am now able to perform various stunt driving and other automobile work.

Taking the Risk

Even though personal watercraft and car work are my main areas of expertise, I'm not limited to working with vehicles. Like most stunt professionals, I have been taught many of the basic tricks of my trade and double for other types of stunts, including giving reactions when taking hits or punches, throwing punches, jumping out of the way of oncoming cars, and falling off cliffs or buildings. As a stuntwoman, it's my job to take all the risk of injury away from an actress. If her character has to fall down a flight of stairs, the actress will do the scene leading up to it, and then I would step in and actually take the fall. At the bottom of the staircase I crawl away and the actress replaces me and picks up from the scene where the fall ended.

Even though I don't do any acting myself, a stunt person needs to have some understanding of acting and movement to make the illusion work. The audience can't know that a switch has been made so I have to study the behavior, posture, gait, and other traits of the character portrayed by the actress I'm doubling for so I can mirror her actions. For example, there's a completely different posture for a strong, self-assured woman than for one who has been beaten down, either physically or emotionally. So when I'm working on a movie, I like to stay close behind the camera the entire time, even if I'm not needed on the set. That way I can pick up on mannerisms and behaviors being portrayed by the actress, so I can make the change seem as flawless as possible when I take over.

Another skill that's needed to be successful in stunt work is becoming very aware how your own body works in order to emulate how a person physically reacts to real falls, punches, and the like. It really helps to have a background in an activity or sport that improves your body awareness. A lot of stunt people are former acrobats, gymnasts, divers, or dancers, so they have an excellent sense of how the body moves. It takes a lot of awareness—as well as strength and skill—to be able to pull off a fall or a reaction from a punch and make it look like there was actual contact. There's a technique to everything we do. Mastering those skills not only makes you better at your job, but also protects you and those around you from getting hurt in the process.

An Experience to Remember

It's been a privilege to work on so many incredible movies, but the most memorable experience by far was working on the Academy Award–winning film *Titanic. Titanic* was a fictional love story that was set on the nonfictional massive luxury liner that struck an iceberg and sank in the North Atlantic in April 1912. Everything about *Titanic* was huge—it was the most expensive movie ever made and it had the highest ever box-office grosses for its time. The production was done on a lavish scale as well—four big sound stages were constructed in Mexico where the film was shot and an 8.5-acre, 17-million-gallon exterior tank was built to hold the 775-foot long replica of the *Titanic* ship that was needed for the movie. The shoot took three years and more than 150 stunt people worked on the film—I was employed for six months. It was a tremendous experience in every sense of the word.

I performed a lot of different stunts during the course of that movie. I wasn't doubling for an actress but was playing different women of different social classes as each of them drowned. I was a first-class passenger, a middle-class passenger, a woman in steerage (which was the lower deck where the poor people traveled and became trapped when the ship started sinking). I must have died 100 times in that movie!

At one point in the movie, during the sinking of the ship, the boat splits in half leaving one end shooting straight up out of the water. Viewers watched people sliding down the deck of the ship, hanging from the railings high in the air, and plummeting into the icy water below. To shoot this scene, the back end of the boat was separated and placed on a hydraulic device, which provided the mechanical strength needed to move the massive parts of the ship. The effect was created by lifting the end of the boat and causing it to rise out of the water, then sink straight down. The hydraulics enabled the special effects crew to stop the boat at various angles in order to get the shots they needed.

As the boat tipped upward, we began to lose footing at about 12 degrees of slant (and it went all the way to 180 degrees—completely vertical). We were doing stunt work in early 1900s costumes, complete with bustles, layers of clothing, and lace-up shoes—*and* wearing bulky life vests (which made it easier and safer to slide down the deck when the boat tipped up). For one stunt I did a cherry drop, which means I performed a short fall from the railing to a smokestack. A rope was attached to a harness under my costume and was digitally erased during the editing process. All around me people were falling from the top railing to a catch made beneath us, some bouncing off pieces of equipment on deck, smokestacks, and each other. It was a pretty crazy ordeal with so many people doing stunt work at the same time. Filming the nighttime sequence of the ship's back end tipping took about three weeks, and filming the complete sinking of the ship took between six and eight months.

Working on this film was the most fun I've ever had, but it also provided the most uncomfortable moment to date in my career. During the scene where the end of the boat was lifted by the hydraulics and became vertical, we had a major mishap. At the time there were 70 to 80 stunt professionals, some cabled to the railing, and we were straight up and down. Suddenly we heard a snap—the safety chain, which insured that the huge back portion of the ship could be returned to its original position after rising up to a 90-degree angle, broke. You could feel the reverberation of the chain as it bounced back to the boat, and it was obvious that something was wrong. The whole boat started swaying back and forth, and you could hear its massive weight creaking and moaning as it moved. It was very frightening—I've never heard metal moan like that. The ship was huge (it was built 90 percent to scale) so we were approximately 40 to 50 feet in the air and people were clinging to anything they could find to hang onto. I was near one of the ship's stairways and stayed tucked behind it during the ordeal. We were stuck up there for almost two hours before the crew was able to bring us down.

Being part of something that was as enormous as that film was an incredible experience. Director James Cameron took a story that's part of our nation's history and re-created it with passion and detail. During production we had a sense of how grand *Titanic* was going to be, but when I saw the finished product, it was bigger than I had imagined. Words can't describe how it felt to sit in the theater and see such a magnificent production that you were a part of unfold on the screen.

Stunt Professional vs. Daredevil

Stunt work is very intense. Naturally it's physically demanding; I leave work completely spent, which is a feeling I really like. To me it means I've put in a good day and given everything I've got while I'm on the job. But it's mentally difficult, too. When I'm driving, for example, the shot may call for the car to be out of control, but I have to be *in* control. I have to be aware of where the cameras and crew are at all times. People's lives are at stake— people who are there doing their own behind-the-scenes jobs working with lighting, cameras, or safety. That's why mental focus is critical.

As a stunt person, you're keenly aware of everything that's going on every second and also the importance of safety. You choose to take that risk for the love of what you're doing. Most people wouldn't want to do this for a living because of the constant danger and pressure, but then I could never do a desk job because I just couldn't sit still that long! What I do is pretty unusual, but part of what I love is the adrenaline rush from doing something that's not totally predictable, but having the ability and training to pull it off.

Stunt people have a very different mentality, where it's okay to be on the edge. Every day on the set is full of risk, but that's a choice we make. Still, there's a big difference between being a stunt person and being a "daredevil." A daredevil is the kind of person who goes out and tries to jump a motorcycle over 50 burning cars just because someone else jumped over 49. That's not a stunt to me. That's doing something death defying to get attention.

A professional stunt person doesn't think that way. For every stunt I do, I've been trained to perform it and the reason I'm doing it is to contribute to making a successful movie. I have confidence in my training and in the skill level I've achieved to make a stunt work. Stunt people create an *illusion* of danger. If a scene called for jumping 50 cars, I would jump just the number of cars needed for camera angles and editing to make it look like there were 50 cars there and still be reasonably safe.

Taking risks is an obvious part of my life. In stunt work, those risks are calculated and evaluated very carefully. In my personal life, I haven't always been so cautious. But my experience and faith have taught me to examine the risks I take now. I've been involved in a lot of stunts during my career and it's been an exciting ride. I may not perform stunt work forever and I believe there are other hot jobs that await me! I plan to continue to follow my faith with determination . . . and whatever I am, it is because of God's mercy and kindness.

A Behind-the-Scenes Look at the Job

Favorite Part: The adrenaline rush I get right before doing a stunt is unbelievably exciting. I come so close to danger but I'm always controlling every move I make. When the day is done, it feels good to be paid for doing what I enjoy. I love being able to do something that's serious but also so much fun.

Least Favorite Part: Even though I love every aspect of my job, it's difficult to be away from my children, which is what happens when I'm on location. Sometimes I'm away for extended periods of time, and that's really hard on me.

Hours: My call to arrive at the set is always different, but it's usually sometime between 5 A.M. and 8 A.M. Depending on what I'm doing that day (for example, doubling for a certain actress), production has to allow enough time for me to get dressed, get my hair and makeup done, and be on the set on time. The day is over when the last shot is done. I'm technically under contract to stay until I'm released for the day so I don't get to leave until the camera has "shot me out," meaning my scene is complete. The longest I've ever worked was a 16-hour day, but the average workday is 10 to 12 hours.

Dress Code: What I wear depends on the type of film or show I'm doing and whether I'm doubling for an actress. I generally wear whatever costume the wardrobe department designs for the show and puts in my trailer. Sometimes it's cut a bit larger or baggier to accommodate the pads, harnesses, or other safety gear I may need to perform my stunts. During *Titanic,* I had on sweats, a dry suit (a skin-tight, water resistant suit sealed up around my neck, ankles and wrists to protect me from cold, dirty water), and my costume over my padding. For car crashes I wear shin guards, kneepads, a five-point harness (straps over my shoulders and across my lap and a lap belt), a mouthpiece, and a helmet if necessary; sometimes all this protective gear isn't needed.

Work Environment: The atmosphere on a set is basically the same regardless of what I'm doing—different departments have a head person and everyone works together so the movie-making process is pleasant and safe. Sets can be large or small, but it's always very obvious where the action or filming is taking place; there are tons of lights, cords, equipment, and people congregated in that spot. The environment during stunt work, however, can go from one extreme to another. It can be cold, dark, and wet, like during *Titanic,* or sunny and beautiful, like when I did a jet-ski ramp jump on the water in Long Beach, California, for the TV show *V.I.P.*

When I'm not needed on the set, I hang out in the Honey Wagon, which is like a motor home provided by the production company. Usually I'll have my own motor home assigned to me, but occasionally I'll share one with several other stuntwomen. It has all the comforts of home and is a nice private area where we can read, sleep, play cards, or just hang out.

Education/Skills: No particular educational background is required to become a stuntwoman, but having basic athletic skills is a definite plus. The training that helps most in this line of work is martial arts for discipline of body, gymnastics or tumbling for grace of movement, and trampoline skills for good air sense. Any other type of skill or specialty training that sets you apart from everyone else—skydiving, scuba diving, extreme skateboarding—is good, too.

Personal Qualities: If I had to choose one personality trait to best suit this industry it would be flexibility. You have to be the type of person who is comfortable with change and uncertainty. Every day on the set brings something new. You may set up a shot first thing in the morning, then not get to it for hours. Or by the time your shot is up, the lighting may have changed, it's either too windy or not windy enough, the streets are too wet or too dry, or whatever happened in the last shot causes the start mark of your shot to be moved (meaning the spot where you set up to begin the stunt). It also helps to be the type of person who doesn't mind getting a bump, bruise, or cut now and then.

Perks and Rewards: I can't imagine any bigger reward than getting paid to do what I love!

HOT TIPS

🔥 If there is a sport or an activity you're involved in, stay with it. Don't ever let yourself think there's nothing more to learn. You can always learn more and hone your skills, and bring things to the next level.

🔥 Sign up for a dance or martial arts class. You'll become more coordinated, limber, and increase your body awareness.

🔥 Train yourself to carefully watch the action scenes in movies or television shows. Based on how the scene is shot, see if you can figure out how things are done and where the cameras are. Ask yourself, "How did they get that shot?"

🔥 If you don't already exercise, start a fitness program to strengthen your muscles, condition your heart, and make your muscles limber. Whether you're jet skiing, cliff diving, or even falling down a flight of stairs, being a stuntwoman requires you to be active and fit.

WORDS OF WISDOM

When preparation meets opportunity, that *is* success. Take the time to get to know yourself. Figure out who you are and what you stand for. In today's fast-paced world it's imperative that you know *you*. Define yourself *and* your boundaries. Personally, I learned to know me through the art of journaling. I was able to slow down and really listen to what I was thinking. Whether you journal or not, listen to what you think! Your thoughts will determine your choices. Take a few quiet moments to listen: What are you saying to yourself? What are your dreams? Thoughts? Attitudes? Goals? Discovering your true self will help to ground you and prepare you.

Find Out More!

So You Wanna Be a Stuntman: The Official Stuntman's Guidebook by Mark Aisbett (Blaine, WA: Lifedrivers, 1999). This is the official guide for aspiring stunt performers. Includes tips on getting into the industry and information about salaries and the employment market.

Stunt Performers: Life Before the Camera (Extreme Careers) by Cherie Turner (New York: Rosen Publishing Group, 2001). This book takes a look behind-the-scenes to provide a taste of the stunt performer's life. Find out what they do, the risks they run, and why they love their profession.

Stunt Women's Association of Motion Pictures, Inc.
(818) 762-0907
www.stuntwomen.com
This organization is involved in fundraising and networking to keep its members in front of the camera. Their Web site introduces women actively working in the stunt industry. View photos, lists of stunt performances, and special skills that they possess. Browse through the doubles catalog to see what stars they most resemble.

HOT *Job...*

Design Director

for Nike Kids Footwear

The textbook description of my job is to set the creative direction for the Nike Kids Footwear line, manage a group of six designers, and function as a leader for the category of kids' footwear. Translation: I need to be creative and motivating in order to help fire up the imaginations of my designers so that we can create a fresh look for each new season.

Home Base: Portland, Oregon

Number of Years in the Field: 10

Personal Philosophy: "If you set your mind on something and focus on it, you can do anything. There are no limits."

Picasso once said, "Every child is an artist. The problem is how to remain an artist once he or she grows up." With so many schools eliminating art programs due to budget cutbacks, it's hard to cultivate a child's natural sense of wonder and expose him or her to possibilities when it comes to the arts. But finding a creative outlet, whether it's sculpting, acting, or anything else you like to do, is essential for self-expression. Don't deny yourself that!

As a kid, I was always painting or drawing and I took a lot of art classes in grade school and high school. But when it came time to decide on a career direction and choose a college, it never dawned on me to study art. After all, who makes a living doing art? Luckily, I had a great art teacher in high school. She wanted to know what I planned to do when I graduated and asked me when I was going to put my art portfolio together. When I replied that I wasn't planning on putting together a portfolio because I was going to pursue an engineering degree, her response was definite: "You love art and you've got talent. Go for your dreams." At the time, I had no idea I could make a living as a designer.

But when my teacher brought in recruiters from different art schools who showed our class different projects their students were working on, I realized I had to go to art school.

I chose the Rhode Island School of Design where I majored in industrial design. I graduated in May 1991 and worked for two other footwear companies before being hired by Nike in January 1997. I never in a million years thought I'd be working at Nike. The Swoosh logo is everywhere. Even though I'd worked for other shoe companies, I've always viewed working for Nike as the ultimate "hot job." I never thought I would get here; it was similar to making it to the Emerald City like Dorothy in *The Wizard of Oz*. But here I am, and it's better than I imagined!

Everything about my job is amazing. I have a tremendous amount of freedom as a designer, I get to travel all over the world, and I've been given the challenge of remaining socially and environmentally responsible while creating cool footwear for kids. What could be better?

Being a Shoe Designer

The process of creating a new line of shoes begins when the marketing team gives us (the design team) their report detailing what types of shoes need to be created for the upcoming season. For example, we may be asked to design a cross-trainer, aqua socks, sandals, and hiking boots. The report gives us basic guidelines, like how much the shoe will retail for, what our profit margin needs to be (how much money we need to make from it); what kind of technology it will include, like "Zoom Air" or "Total Air" (which add extra cushioning and support); and what kind of materials to use, such as leather or mesh. Once I have an understanding of the line, I divide the work up among my design team and we get started.

When I'm trying to envision a concept for a shoe, I come up with an idea and then put it on paper. I do research by shopping, looking in magazines, and flipping through books in Nike's extensive design library. A lot of times I'll develop a great design with my first sketch, but then I'll doubt myself, thinking I didn't work hard enough and that it should be more difficult. I'll sketch a lot more designs, but I usually end up coming back to my first idea. I'm starting to realize that I need to trust my instincts; I've been doing this job for a while so sometimes it *should* come easy.

Once a preliminary sketch is done and I have a visual of what the shoe will look like, it's time to get down to the mechanics of shoe making. The first thing I do is determine what the toe character of the design will be (such as a rounded or square toe) and then find a last (which is a three-dimensional mold of a foot) that determines the shape of the shoe. From there, I make a rough sketch of the shoe by hand and scan it into my computer. Next, I create line art, which is a more precise drawing of what the shoe will look like, using specialized computer software. Then I add the stitching, eyelets, laces, and all the other little details.

I also design what the tread pattern will look like on the outsole, which is the bottom of the shoe. The tread is based on what activity the shoe is made for. For instance, on a hiking boot, the tread will be "luggy," which means it will have a chunky surface with lots of variance in the height of the tread pattern, to create traction on different types of terrain, such as slippery, wet, icy, or rocky. Treads on hiking boots are kind of like snow tires for a car—you want them to be stable!

On the other hand, the outsole tread design for a cross-training shoe would be the same height, if not flat, with a combination of waffle and herringbone textures. These kinds of textures allow you to sprint, stop, start, spin, and jump on flat play surfaces like grassy fields, blacktop play-grounds, and hardwood gym floors.

When the line drawing is completed, I print it and color it in with my colored pencils and markers so it looks real. I present it to my team and if everyone likes it, we make a sample, which shows us what the finished shoe will look like.

Together with a pattern engineer, I work to create the upper part of the shoe. The pattern engineer uses a software program to scan my art-work onto a digitized image of a last. From there, a pattern is cut in the sample room and fitted together with material I've selected. When the upper part of the shoe is made, I take it to our model shop where they sculpt the outsole in clay based on the design and dimensions I give them, then a model maker takes the clay model and casts a resin (a natural organic substance) part from it to simulate a rubber outsole. Finally, the model maker combines the upper part of the shoe with the outsole, and I have my sample of the finished product!

Next, my team reviews the sample. They may say, "Wow, we love it," or they may want to make changes and fine-tune it. The sample is also a great tool for the factories where the shoes are made. It gives them a clearer picture of what the finished shoe should look like.

It helps to know basic anatomy when you're designing shoes for kids. I always have to keep in mind that a child's foot is a lot different than an adult's. Children go through a series of growth stages until their feet sta-bilize into their adult size. Because their feet are always changing, it's important to know a little about the structure of their feet and be able to use that knowledge when you begin designing a shoe. For instance, through the infant, baby, and toddler years, the child's foot is very fat and is comprised mainly of soft tissue because their bones aren't fully developed. For this reason, they need a shoe that's flexible.

I have the opportunity to consult with the Nike Sports Research Lab, which has a team of biomechanists who specialize in how the body works. We bring kids in to test our shoes for performance, function, and durability. Using devices called force plates, we can measure how much pressure they're putting on a shoe, and exactly where the pressure is being placed. With this information, the biomechanists can tell from a scientific standpoint how the shoe can be improved and what type of adjustments are needed, so we can create the highest quality product available.

Connecting with My Customers

It's easy to get caught up in the day-to-day business of making shoes, but I never want to lose sight of the fact that there's a little kid who will eventually wear the product I design. As a group, my design team needs to figure out what kids like and how we can make our designs fit those objectives. It's important for us to get out of the office and connect with kids, so each year I request a travel budget from Nike that I can use to plan trips for my entire design team. These excursions give us a chance to hang out and bond with our target market—kids. The goal is to immerse ourselves in their world; see what they do, everything from what they eat to what they have to say.

One trip we took was to San Diego, where we spent a day at LegoLand and an afternoon drawing with kids at the Boys and Girls Club. We had them come up with their own footwear designs and asked them what they were looking for in a shoe and what kinds of things they wanted to see. Then we went to Las Vegas and stayed at the New York, New York hotel, which is a family-oriented place. The hotel has a roller coaster and an arcade, and batting cages nearby. We always want to maintain a connection to kids, so the whole idea of this trip was to do things they do.

Every year we invite school children to our campus for field trips and I also play host to about 50 girls for the *Ms.* Foundation's annual Take Our Daughters to Work Day. Students come in and we do an educational presentation, teaching them how shoes are designed. Then we draw with them or do collages. There have been times when we've tried to do something different, but all they seem to want to do is draw shoes! I guess when they come to Nike, that's the expectation.

Whenever I spend time with kids, they share a little of their spirit. I always try to give something back, too—whether it's an idea, inspiration, or attention. Spending time like this with kids is a good reality check for me. It's also a great way to find out what they like and what interests them.

I look at my job as an opportunity to play while I work and to connect with people who think that way, too. I go to work and am taken seriously, but inside I feel like I'm always going to be a kid, similar to Tom Hanks in the movie *Big*.

The Creative Process

Quite frequently, I sit with my designers and we have sketch sessions. We hang out in a conference room, play some music, and draw. Someone will come up with a concept and say, "Hey, what do you think of this?" That's usually enough to get the group bouncing ideas off each other.

Pretty soon, everyone's talking back and forth, brainstorming all kinds of ideas. I love collaborating like this; it's really a lot of fun. We have a very open, free-flowing kind of work environment here and I thrive on that.

Getting out of the office for meetings is another way to get our creative energy flowing. We've had meetings in a barn, in my living room, on my boss's deck. One time, we even discussed plans for an upcoming line of shoes on a train. We

Jane in her creative mode.

boarded the Amtrak in Portland and had our meeting while we traveled to Seattle. When we arrived, we ate lunch, shopped at the market, got back on the train, and finished what was on our agenda on the train ride home. When we're in the office, there's always some kind of distraction, like ringing phones and emails, so having off-site meetings gives us a chance to come up with some enterprising ideas.

That's one cool part about being a designer—ideas can come from anything at any time. I get ideas everywhere, especially when I travel. Once I went to New York over the holidays with the color designer from my team. We were in a store that had a wonderful display of Christmas trees and glass ornaments in beautiful iridescent shades of green, blue, pink, and purple. The colors were so beautiful that we thought about designing baby booties that were so precious that people would want to decorate their trees with them! We haven't moved forward with this idea yet, but concepts like these are the seeds that stimulate us to think. In this case, it inspired the marketing group to think of new ways to package and present our baby booties.

But traveling helps in other ways, too. Seeing the world gives me the opportunity to look at new textures and materials, things I don't see at home. I get to go on a lot of development trips where I travel overseas to different Nike factories to make sure the shoes are being made the way I designed them. I've been to a lot of countries in Asia, including Thailand, Korea, Indonesia, and Taiwan, as well as Brazil and countries in Europe. The workers in our contracted factories receive competitive wages, all legally mandated benefits, and many receive free meals, dormitory or subsidized housing, and medical care.

Every country and its culture has so much to offer. In Brazil, for example, I saw streets with black and white mosaic patterns that I thought might look good on the bottom of shoes. I also love going to malls and grocery stores in different countries and looking at the graphics on their packaging, basically taking in everything around me. It's nice to be able to go away and come back feeling rejuvenated, especially when I'm trying to come up with new ideas. I'm always reinventing, trying to improve on my last design.

Environmental Responsibility

One of my biggest challenges lies in trying to come up with a shoe that kids will appreciate while keeping its materials and manufacture environmentally friendly. Nike is always thinking about the future and ways we can improve how we manufacture shoes to benefit the planet. One of the programs the company has initiated is called NEAT (Nike Environmental Action Team). Collection barrels have been placed in select stores where people can donate their old shoes. The shoes are collected and taken to a facility in our Oregon warehouse that grinds them up. The material is then used to make court and play surfaces, such as playgrounds, tumbling mats, horse stables, or anything that needs cushioning. But our goal is to take it a step further. Right now, we're trying to figure out a way to refurbish shoes so they can be used again or donated to charity.

Another way the company has taken action to address environmental concerns is by forming Team Shambala, which is Nike's sustainability program. At Nike, sustainability refers to doing business in a way that doesn't harm the planet. As a designer, I need to be accountable for my output. In other words, I have a responsibility to come up with solutions to minimize the waste that could result from the shoes I design. There's a potential for anything I create to be thrown away and dumped in some landfill, which will eventually have an impact on how much pollution ends up in our lakes and oceans. My job is to design a stylish shoe without depleting or poisoning the earth's natural resources.

I have a lot of respect for the planet and am often in awe of its beauty and design. A lot of inspiration can be derived from the natural world—plants, trees, and animals are all examples of great designs that have evolved over time. Nature is my teacher. At home, I compost everything I can and separate the garbage for recycling. For every new thing I bring into the house, I try to recycle or donate to charity two old things. I also carpool to work to conserve fuel. It's easy to feel helpless and think you can't make a difference in keeping the environment safe and clean, but you can; every small thing you contribute to conservation makes a difference in the world. For me, I think the best way to promote conservation is to lead by example. At work, even if I spot a glass bottle or a piece of paper that someone has placed in the garbage, I take it out and put it in the recycling bin.

I'm one of many team captains for Team Shambala and part of my duty is to educate my coworkers on how we can be a more sustainable company. I've had to do a lot of reading and studying on the subject. One interesting book I read presented examples of companies that were able to save both money and the earth's resources by coming up with smart ways to conduct business. This book highlighted a city in Brazil called Curitiba. Curitiba was once impoverished, overpopulated, and polluted. What's amazing about this city, however, is that instead of continuing to decline, it was able to turn itself around and become a model of modern urban planning. Leaders in Curitiba have been great problem solvers and have been able to look at the needs of their citizens and find simple solutions that are good for both people *and* the environment.

A good example of Curitiba's renewal is the Green Exchange Program. In many of the poorest sections of town, the city dump trucks can't get in to pick up trash because the roads aren't accessible to large vehicles. In these areas, trash piled up and became a serious problem and health risk. So the city came up with a great solution. Now they send a smaller truck to these areas to collect the garbage. When the truck arrives, the driver rings a bell and people bring their bags of trash right up to the truck. In exchange, they receive tokens they can use for food or other necessities. So the trash issue was resolved and people benefited from the plan.

More Inspiration from Brazil

I recently planned a trip to Brazil because some shoes I had designed for the Argentinean and Brazilian markets were being manufactured there. My whole design team went and, as long as we were there, I decided to check out the city of Curitiba since I had read so much about it. I contacted the city's Institute of Urban Planning and was eventually put in touch with the Superintendent of Sport and Leisure. We were taken to all sorts of sporting events around the city that kids were involved in, giving us firsthand interaction with our consumer.

There aren't any socioeconomic limits in Curitiba with regard to sports. Sports facilities are easily accessible and open to everyone, rich or poor. It's an accepted fact there that for a child to have a better life and sense of well-being, they need to be active. It was amazing, like an inspiring Nike ad brought to life. The children are treated like a precious resource. For me, it was an unexpected, magical surprise that so much was being done for kids and sports.

What inspired me most was when we went to a park where there was a 3,000-meter race going on. Ten-year-old girls and boys were running, and there was quite a crowd, with lots of enthusiastic energy. We watched and cheered as the children ran their race. When I looked closer, I noticed that many kids were running barefoot. They couldn't afford to buy shoes.

At that moment, it hit me: I wanted to be available to these kids, to create something they could have . . . not an elite product only the wealthy or privileged could afford. Nike is a huge corporation, a global brand, and I felt like we needed to be more far-reaching and responsible.

The insight gained on that trip transformed my thinking and helped me realize several things. First, kids in Brazil and everywhere need an affordable shoe for running and playing and for sports. To address that need, my design team has teamed up with the marketing team to work on developing specific business plans around children and their need for affordable footwear. Second, Curitiba is a socially responsible city and we, as a company, need to be, too. We can't just be about making cool shoes. We have to make an impact on the world as a whole with the way we do business—it's our responsibility to society and to the environment.

I definitely have a great job. It's melded my love of design and drawing with my environmental respect and efforts. The sustainability group at Nike will continue to explore, develop, and implement policies that allow us to manufacture shoes and apparel in a way that reduces our impact on the environment. My challenge now, as a designer and as a consumer, is to continue to look for ways to do everything I can to protect the earth's resources. Whether I am designing a cool pair of athletic shoes or washing the dishes at home, it's my responsibility to take action and find ways to contribute to a better way of life for people and the environment by minimizing waste. It's up to each individual to do his or her part because every little bit helps.

A Behind-the-Scenes Look at the Job

Favorite Part: My boss is a wonderful mentor; she is very nurturing and encouraging. I have been given the freedom to do whatever I want as a designer, and if I encounter a limit, I challenge it, which is encouraged at Nike. I feel that anything is possible here, and there is so much potential to do a lot of great things.

Least Favorite Part: Nike is a huge company (there are about 5,000 employees in Beaverton, Oregon, and more than 25,000 globally) so it's easy to get overwhelmed by the size. I try to maintain more of an entrepreneurial attitude by pretending we're still a small company and remembering that Nike's founder, Phil Knight, started out really small by selling shoes out of the back of his car.

Hours: Twenty-four hours a day! I usually roll into the office by 9 or 9:30 in the morning and stay until 7 P.M. Since my days are so busy, I come up with a lot of ideas in the evenings at home when I have quiet time to draw. Basically, I'm always "on," with ideas popping into my head all hours of the day.

Dress Code: There isn't a dress code at Nike but wearing jeans is the most casual I get. I like to look professional for meetings, so I'll wear business casual, which is nice pants and a blouse.

Work Environment: The Nike campus is beautifully landscaped. There are creeks with wildlife, little bridges, a Japanese garden, even a lake in the middle of the campus with bronze sculptures of people fishing and sitting on a park bench. The setting is very natural, but the buildings are modern.

I work in an office on the fourth floor of the Mia Hamm building (named after the 1999 World Cup soccer team captain), which is so big it looks like an airplane hangar! The campus has two fully equipped fitness centers with classes in everything from yoga to cardio-kickboxing. I schedule at least two classes into my calendar each week because working out is great for blowing off steam. There's also a soccer field, a mini-football field, the Michael Johnson running track (made out of 50,000 pairs of recycled Nike shoes) and the Lance Armstrong Center, which has a pool and a climbing wall.

Education/Skills: Drawing skills are essential for becoming a designer. Art or design school—or a liberal arts or community college with an art program—is the best place to get started. Art school will teach you how to work with different materials, like wood and metal. There's a kind of "Zen" intuition to knowing how materials move and work and bend and join; it's like materials have their own spirit. How they move depends on how you cut them. A good analogy is your hair. There are bad haircuts and there are good haircuts. A good stylist, like a good artist, knows how your hair moves, grows, and falls when it is cut and shaped a certain way. Hair can be cut to be spiky or curly or blunt. The same goes for wood and metal. You just have to get to know what you are working with.

Artists need a portfolio, which is a big book filled with samples of your best art and design work. You'll need a portfolio to bring on job interviews to show employers and clients what kind of talent you have. A great way to build a portfolio is by filling it with the best projects you've worked on in school (junior or undergraduate college, university art program, or art school). Another way to add to your portfolio is to include work you created during an internship.

Personal Qualities: To be a good designer, it's important to cultivate your own creative identity. In the workplace, personalities can be strong and competitive. You need to develop confidence so that your creativity isn't inhibited. When you know who you are and believe in your abilities, nobody can ever take that away from you. Because half the job is being able to express your ideas, people skills are important, too. Once you come up with an idea, if you want people to share your vision, you must be able to communicate it in a way that excites them and makes them want to be a part of the project.

Perks and Rewards: A great perk I have is inexpensive access to the workout facilities, which includes full gyms and exercise classes all day long. I can basically structure my day around my workouts if I want to. You also get great deals on Nike shoes and gear (like workout wear, hats, watches, eyewear, and bags)!

HOT TIPS

🔥 Getting into a good college or art school is competitive, so the best thing you can do now is to be a good student with a wide array of interests and good grades.

🔥 If it's available, sign up for an art class, such as sketching, drawing, or painting at school. If not, find an art class at a community center to work on your artistic skills.

🔥 Buy an inexpensive sketchbook and fill it with your own designs, drawings, and ideas for practice and experiment with different mediums. Keeping old sketchbooks gives you perspective on how much you have changed and what you have learned. I still have sketchbooks from when I was 7 years old! My sketchbooks are like a running story of ideas going on in my head.

🔥 Keep a journal or file of favorite magazine clippings—nature, fashion, sculpture, people, or whatever moves you—and put them in a notebook or tack them to a bulletin board. Collecting designs that strike your interest is one way to help you figure out what you like and don't like and will give you inspiration to create your own masterpieces.

🔥 Find a creative outlet to feed your soul ... dance, music, photography, acting, painting ... anything that allows you to express yourself because creative expression is important for a designer or an artist. It's fun and it gets you to think outside the box.

🔥 Visit a museum, go to a library or bookstore, surf the Internet, and look through art books to find artists, architects, or designers who inspire you.

🔥 Take advantage of computer classes at school whenever you can. Many design firms and visual artists use computers as a design tool.

WORDS OF WISDOM

I have a theory that people who are in touch with their creativity live long and fulfilling lives. Many famous and not-so-famous artists and designers work well past the age of retirement because as they age, they get better and better at their craft. They are constantly expressing what's in their heart, because that's where creativity lives. Remember that creativity is not limited to artists and designers; it is as expansive as writing in a journal, nurturing a garden, working on a car, dancing, cooking, or decorating your bedroom. Everyone has creative talent, you just have to experiment with different mediums to find what touches your soul.

Find Out More!

Becoming a Graphic Designer: A Guide to Careers in Design by Steven Heller and Teresa Fernandes (New York: John Wiley & Sons, 1999). A complete guide to today's graphic design careers, this book includes information on opportunities in print, television and film graphics, advertising, and Web design. Also provides tips for preparing personal portfolios and practical advice from leading graphic designers.

The Complete Sketching Book by John Hamilton (London: Studio Vista, 1998). This book offers beginners essential techniques for sketching, then builds students' confidence through exercises in lighting, perspective, still life, and outdoor scenes.

Dream/Girl Magazine: The Arts Magazine for Girls
P.O. Box 97365 • Raleigh, NC 27624
www.dgarts.com
Dedicated to "encouraging creative genius in girls," this magazine explores creativity in art, music, writing, and other mediums. Contests, ideas, and advice help toward expanding individual creative expression.

Nike
goddess.nike.com/nikegoddess/index.jhtml
Dedicated to the spirit that makes every woman an athlete, this Nike Web site is just for women. There's information on sports, fitness and fun, inspirational stories, tips on meeting challenges and finding adventure. If you would like to take a virtual tour of a Nike factory, go to *www.nikebiz.com.*

Dawn Turner Trice

HOT *Job...*

Reporter/ Columnist

Chicago Tribune
newspaper

I have two jobs at the *Chicago Tribune*—one as a writer of a weekly column that runs each Monday, and the other as a reporter doing longer stories that take more time to put together. As a journalist I feel it is my job to illuminate the issue I'm writing about by using people and their experiences to personalize the bigger picture. I love "people stories" and I try to focus on smaller, individual struggles and victories within each piece that I write.

Home Base: Chicago, Illinois

Number of Years in the Field: 13

Personal Philosophy: "Keep going, even in the face of adversity. If you can get through it, you'll be able to see the other side."

I've always loved reading. As a child growing up in Chicago, I also loved listening to the stories that my family told, especially at get-togethers. My sister and I used to hide under the kitchen table and eavesdrop, often trying to swallow back our laughter as we listened to the adults talking away. While we didn't understand all that we heard, we did know that when the adults lowered their voices and leaned forward as they spoke, whatever was being discussed took on a whole new meaning. We also knew that before long, our mother would catch us under that table, and then smile as she pulled us out saying, "You all are the nosiest kids God ever gave breath to."

Some of what I overheard definitely wasn't meant for my ears, and I don't dare repeat it! But most of the stories I heard were fond remembrances from my parents' childhoods, of growing up in the Ida B. Wells housing projects on Chicago's south side during the 1940s and 1950s. Those neighborhoods were nice places back then and the memories they shared were rich with humor and character.

205

One story that I remember hearing was about my mother. She had been a very spirited and lively little girl. The neighbors who sat on their porches and watched as she ran about would help keep her in line: "Hey, you shouldn't be over there, girl. Now you get back over here!" One neighbor in particular kept an eye on my mother, and she noticed that my mom ate pickles and peppermint sticks for lunch every day. This woman began inviting my mother over to her house where she would fix hot dogs and canned soup for her. Momma often told me how tired she got of that soup!

As a child, I was fascinated by that story. As an adult, I'm awed by that caring woman who felt the need and reached out to tend to a little girl in the community, even though it wasn't her biological child. And she probably did it without thinking twice. Those types of stories, as well as others I overheard from my family, instilled in me a tremendous sense of community. The things they reminisced about weren't all fun, though. I also overheard tales about some of the tougher issues my parents dealt with growing up, such as the political structure at the time, difficulties the family faced moving to Chicago from the South (Mississippi), and the restrictions imposed on African Americans mandating that they only live in certain parts of the city, areas which were collectively called "The Black Belt." But when I think of the times I spent under the kitchen table, I'll always recall the fondness with which my parents spoke of those days. Eavesdropping on their real-life stories helped shaped my life. What I do now as a reporter is a product of all that rich experience. And I still like to listen.

Getting Started

In addition to a love for reading and listening to stories, I was also always really interested in science. So when I began college, I started out as a pre-med major, taking lots of math and science courses. But midway through school, I came to a realization and thought, "I don't really want to do this. I want to write."

In many lower- or middle-class African-American families, parents have aspirations that their kids will go into a profession that will allow them to leap to a higher social standing. So when I changed my major to journalism, my family was a bit distraught. They thought I wouldn't make any money as a journalist and they were worried. It's very rare that someone leaves college and goes right to a *Chicago Tribune* or a *New York Times*, which are considered the journalistic big leagues. Most graduates go off and start at a weekly newspaper, barely making more than minimum wage.

I suppose when I decided to go into journalism, I was young enough not to have the sense to be afraid. I never thought in terms of the future implications of what I was doing, that I could be making a long-term mistake. All I knew was that I wanted to follow my passion—to listen to the voices of other people and use my creativity to tell their stories.

Right after college I attended a National Association of Black Journalists convention, an annual event that hosts a job fair. Aside from my educational experience and a few internships I held during my last year in school—one for New York University and one at the *Chicago Sun Times*—I had very little experience under my belt. But the job recruiters I met at the convention were still willing to take a chance on me; I got several job offers. I guess they figured that I had some level of talent and they could mold me to fit their style. I also think it was during a time when a lot of news groups were trying to put together more diverse staffs.

One of the recruiters I talked to offered a proposition worth considering: "You live in Chicago . . . if you spend a couple of years in Orlando at the *Sentinel* (a paper owned by the *Chicago Tribune*'s parent company, The Tribune Company), then you could transfer to the *Chicago Tribune*."

So I began my career in Orlando in 1987, starting out in the newsroom as a reporter and moved up to become an editor. I was lucky in that the *Orlando Sentinel* is considered a midsize paper so, unlike most new grads, I didn't have to start at a small weekly paper and work my way up. The fact that I did so well coming out of school allayed my fears that journalism wouldn't pay well. After awhile, even though I liked Florida in the warmer months, I started to miss Chicago's snowy winters and became really homesick. In 1988, I left Orlando to return to Chicago for an editor position at the *Tribune*.

Writing and Reporting

In June 2001, after 13 years of reporting and editing at the *Tribune*, the Metropolitan editor called me into his office and asked me to consider writing a column. My initial response was a humble, "Thank you," because I didn't think I had anything to say in that format. I worried about how exposed I would feel sharing my opinions with millions of people, not only on topics I already had an opinion on, but also on others I had never given much thought about. I finally warmed to the idea, and my first column appeared in print on July 9, 2001.

My job at the *Tribune* is twofold—columnist and reporter. Each requires a different type of writing. As a reporter, I have to be very objective. In a news story I write what I see and tell the facts. As a columnist, however, it's my job to give my opinion about what I see. That's the biggest difference; my opinion has absolutely no place in an objective news story.

Most of the ideas for my column I get from the news. When I see something that catches my attention, I try to take a different angle on it and go from there. Some of the things I've written about include changes at Chicago's O'Hare Airport; my all-time favorite book, *To Kill a Mockingbird;* and the city's ever-evolving neighborhoods and the everyday people who inhabit them.

When I am reporting, I write longer, more project-type stories. I don't write daily, which means I don't go chasing after breaking stories about fires or bank robberies. Instead I cover stories about Chicago, a city with a great hodgepodge of neighborhoods and people. I've written about a number of topics from the city's colorful aldermen (members of the municipal government) to feisty nuns in housing projects. I'm lucky that I've come up with a lot of my own ideas for the stories I've written. One of the things that helps me with that is leaving the office, getting into the company car and driving around—being visible to the community. I like to get out and talk to people. Sometimes I'll be talking to someone in a neighborhood and they'll mention something that catches my attention and I'll ask them to tell me more about it. I feel that I'm blessed with a knack for spotting a good story; I know one when I hear one. I also get story ideas from reading neighborhood newspapers, looking for things that seem interesting. Frequently, neighborhood papers don't have the time to devote or the resources available to put someone on a story that takes two or three weeks of research and writing. So if I find an issue that seems to need more in-depth exploration, I look into it.

When I begin working on a story, the first thing I do is look in the *Tribune's* computer archive system to see if we've already covered the topic. I have access to every story the newspaper has done since 1985. I use past stories to get some background information, and then I start calling people. I use the Internet very little in my research—mostly just to get sources; I never pull anything directly from what I find there. I also never pull anything out of a story that's already been written because it would be necessary for me to check all those sources and facts again, which would create a lot more work. It's possible that the original reporter may have quoted an inaccurate fact, and it doesn't help to perpetuate inaccurate information.

When writing a news story, I quote sources when I need to, use facts I've collected as background, and then cull or sift out the information I want to use. My researching style is to "over report," which means I tend to gather much more information than I actually need. In fact, it's not unusual for me to have entire sections of a story I've researched that never see the light of day. An average story takes about a week and a half to two weeks to complete.

The hallmark of this trade is the reporting. But the newspaper business has been losing readers in recent decades due to the simple fact that a lot of people are getting their news elsewhere, like from TV or the Internet. Because of this, there's been a trend of trying to hire people based more on their writing skills than their reporting skills. Many newspapers now seem to be looking for storytellers—people who can write the news in a story fashion, hoping that will keep the interest of their readers—as opposed to reporters. While good writing is important, that's not what real reporting is about. Being a reporter is about getting out there, asking questions, checking facts, and making sure you have all the right information. If you don't have the facts, you can't write around what isn't there. I've seen people try to do that and it doesn't work. It's like dressing up a hole; it may be dressed up, but it's still a hole. As far as I'm concerned, no amount of good writing makes up for shoddy reporting.

A Memorable Story

In 2001, I did a Father's Day story about a man named Daniel Carmickle who had struggled with Chicago's Department of Children and Family Services (DCFS) for two years in order to get custody of his daughter, Alexis. She had been in the social welfare system since she was 2 months old because her mother was a drug addict. The mother had already lost several other children to the child welfare system. Alexis, her youngest child, was monitored from birth and, because of the continued substance abuse, was removed from the home. Even though Daniel lived there and didn't use drugs, he was considered part of the problem because he knew the mother was using drugs and failed to remove Alexis himself. For this reason, the child was taken from him as well.

Daniel was young, African American, and very tough looking—many people's stereotype of a thug. But what he looked like on the outside didn't represent who he was on the inside. A lot of fathers don't bother showing up, but Daniel voluntarily went through every hoop the DCFS put in front of him to get his daughter back. In the end, he was successful.

The story I wrote didn't focus on all the red tape that Daniel dealt with, but instead took a close look at the metamorphosis he went through in the process. He initially went in to fight for his daughter by yelling at everybody, by being really gruff and surly. But when it counted, he was able to do what needed to be done in the way it needed to be done. It was his personal journey that was significant to me and that's what I chose to write about. He could have dropped out at any point, but he didn't. He was even randomly tested for drug use throughout the two-year process. Whenever someone at DCFS called him, he had to urinate in a cup to prove he wasn't taking drugs. He never tested positive. The story was about the changes he had to make and his willingness to do whatever it took to reunite his family.

This piece not only had a big impact on my readers, but also on me. The story made me rethink the way I view people and how forgiving I am of past mistakes. We tend to look at people and think we know them, but most of the time we really don't. There was a time, if somebody ticked me off, I'd say, "That's it—I'm done with you." But as I get older, I realize that most people deserve to have their past taken into account; they're a product of what they've been through. That doesn't mean you should simply forgive them for everything, no questions asked, but if you have a better understanding of where they've come from you can better understand who they are and why they do what they do.

In the end, the story had a wonderful point. Daniel will never be the type of person who puts on a suit and tie and carries a briefcase. He would say to me, "Look at me. Do I look like the type of person you want to mess with?" (Of course the answer was no!) But he also was not just what he appeared to be. Daniel Carmickle turned out to be one of the most intelligent people I've ever spoken to. I had never met anybody like him before. Writing these types of stories allows me to meet and represent people who others have dismissed at first glance as unintelligent and with nothing to say. I've been able to write about amazing people who we otherwise would never get to hear from because they aren't usually given a platform from which to speak.

Another memorable story I worked on was the Ryan Harris story. She was an 11-year-old girl who was raped and murdered. The story garnered national attention when two young boys, a 7-year-old and 6-year-old, were initially arrested for the crime. The authorities realized these boys couldn't produce semen, so they were exonerated.

For my story, I talked to Ryan's mother. It was the first time she fully told her story; what it was like to have her child missing for so many hours and then for her body to be found. It's a person's worst nightmare. This was one of those stories that I couldn't leave at the office. Having a little girl of my own made it especially difficult and made for some bad dreams.

Despite how difficult it was, though, I don't regret writing the story. As strange as it sounds, I actually feel grateful. I had been an editor for so many years, with an office and a staff of my own, and I lived and worked in the suburbs. I was a girl from the city, but because I had been away from it for so long, I was very wary about going back. To write this story I needed to go to Englewood (where Ryan died), one of the toughest neighborhoods in Chicago.

Writing stories that deal with urban issues forces me to deal with my own fears, those things that make me uncomfortable. I realize a lot of people—myself included—are content to drive up their manicured drive-ways, pull into their safe garages, watch the news on television and say, "Oooh, that's awful. But it didn't happen here, thank goodness." It's like we've created protective fences around ourselves and our hearts; if it doesn't happen in our backyard, we may feel bad for a second, but then we move on. The Ryan Harris story really took me out of my comfort zone, and I needed that.

The Job of Putting Words to Paper

I find it so funny when people say to me, "You're a natural talent." To me, nothing is natural about it. Writing is absolutely the most grueling thing in my life. I do believe that I have the sensibilities to write well, and that part may come naturally. I have this knack for picking up on certain things when people are talking, even if they're rambling on in all different directions. It's like a light bulb goes off for me. I tend to know when something works, and how to make it fit into the story I'm writing. But I'm very insecure when I sit in front of the computer, face-to-face with a blank screen. Even though I've been at this for quite some time, I still become filled with fear, worry, and dread—and probably always will. Sometimes I think I'd rather walk down a dark alley than face a blank computer screen!

Perhaps the oddest thing is that I do much better when I'm working with a deadline. I think it's because I know the job has to get done and I can see through to the other side of it. When I don't have a deadline, I tend to procrastinate. I'll do anything to avoid the task at hand. For instance, I have this wonderful Boggle CD game that I love—my vocabulary is really great thanks to that game! I sit in front of the computer and all I want to do is play Boggle! I'll play for an hour then tell myself that I'll start writing the next day. If I don't have a deadline, I absolutely have no self-control. But when I *do* have a deadline, I can be very disciplined. When something has to get done and there is a due date, I get the job done.

For instance, once I knew I was going out of town with my family and I had to turn in my column early, on the Friday before we left. When I turned in the column, my editor didn't like it. He called me at home around 7 that night and said, "Can I have something else?" Considering we were leaving in two days, it wasn't what I wanted to hear. But I did it. I sat down and typed it out. The first column took me two days to complete, but the revision was completed in a matter of hours. I received more responses from my readers on that column, one that I didn't have time to agonize over, than any other that I've written so far.

The Next Stage

There was a time in my life when I felt like I had it all together; my husband and I got married right after we graduated from college, bought a nice house, and amassed a lot of the material things that one strives for in life. I had a wonderful family, a couple of published books, and a great job at the *Tribune* as an editor. But I still didn't feel complete. Something definitely was missing for me. I felt I was lacking the fulfillment that comes from making a contribution to the world. I wanted to be able to say I was doing something that made a difference.

Writing an opinion column and sharing my views with the readers has served to fulfill that need to a certain extent. Some people would argue that I'm only tackling issues with words, that there's a distance there. They would say I'm not really in the trenches. My answer to them is, I'm a lot closer than I was a few years ago and the words I write have the capability of touching so many.

Is this my dream job? It might be, but I feel hesitant to say for sure. If I did, I'd feel like I was saying that I'd made it, and that's far from being the case. There are still things I aspire to; for example, I've already written a couple of novels, and I'd really like to write one more. After that, I want to try writing nonfiction books. It feels good knowing I'm using the ability that was given to me, something that I've worked hard to develop. In that respect, I'm on the right career track. But I still want to be open to all that life has to offer. I feel a lot of pieces are coming together in my life, and I know that there are still things out there for me that I can't even begin to imagine. And I can't wait.

A Behind-the-Scenes Look at the Job

Favorite Part: Telling people's stories is the best part of my job—they're as complex and varied as the people who tell them. Issues and situations are never simply black and white, and the shades in between are no longer simply gradations of gray. They're more like a rainbow. And the voices? They comprise a symphony. I love meeting people and listening to what they have to say.

Least Favorite Part: The challenging process of the actual writing is by far my least favorite thing. You'd think it would get easier after all these years, but it doesn't! Sometimes summoning the energy, or the muse, or whatever it takes to get going in the face of a blank computer screen is really difficult.

Hours: My hours vary, but I normally start around 10 A.M. I generally try to get out of the office by 6 or 7 P.M., but often I'll come home and sit in front of the computer and work some more. Technology is certainly on my side; I'll email my story home and then I can continue to work on it after my daughter goes to sleep. There isn't really a cut-off time for me, though, because I'm constantly thinking about whatever story I'm working on.

Dress Code: Everyone dresses very casually in the newsroom; there isn't really a dress code (except we can't wear shorts). I can even wear blue jeans if I want to. It's great because I can run the gamut of my closet! If I have to go out of the office to interview or meet with someone, I try to look professional. Sometimes that means I'll wear a suit, or maybe a nice pair of slacks and a blouse. But if I'm just out and about in the community, I tend to dress pretty casually.

Work Environment: I work in a newsroom, which has rows and rows of cubicles and lots of people around. It can be very chatty and noisy at times, so you really have to learn to focus to get your work done. People are constantly talking on the phone, and you can hear exactly what everyone is saying! That's one of the reasons I like to email my stories home and work on them there.

I feel very lucky because I work two days in the *Tribune's* Southwest Suburban Bureau, in Tinley Park, and three days in the downtown Chicago office. The Tinley office is also set up like a newsroom but with far fewer people in that office. The biggest advantage to my schedule is that I'm much closer to home when I'm in the suburban office, so I can spend more time with my daughter.

When I'm focused on writing my column I tend to stay in the office a little more, but I prefer to spend about half my time inside and half outside. I really like to get out, even when the weather's bad, because I feel kind of cloistered in the office. I don't like doing interviews on the phone; I always prefer to meet with someone in person.

Education/Skills: A college degree, especially in journalism, is almost a necessity now if you want to work as a news reporter. Most journalists at the *Tribune* have formal journalism training, although a handful don't even have college degrees—but they're the exception, not the rule and are very, very talented.

As far as skills, either you need to have wonderful dexterity to take copious notes quickly and accurately, or you have to get a tape recorder. Normally I take everything down, nod a lot, and direct the questions. One of the things I love about interviewing is letting the subject "go." You can't bombard them with question after question just because you have a list of things you want to ask. The person being interviewed should dictate where the interview—and subsequently the story—will go.

You have to know a little bit about body language, too. If you watch closely during an interview you can tell when people want you to back off without saying it in so many words. You have to be able to hone in on things that may not otherwise be said.

Personal Qualities: To be a reporter—even if you're not an investigative reporter or covering a hectic beat like City Hall—you have to be aggressive and outgoing. You must be comfortable talking to people in order to get them to tell you what you need to know. Some people won't say anything, and it's your job to draw them out.

At the same time you have to be a good listener—you listen far more than you talk. If you really listen to people, you'll be able to hear "between the lines"—and learn things you would have missed if you weren't listening closely.

Perks and Rewards: What other job allows you to just leave the office in the middle of the day and hang outside in the great weather and mine the community for stories? For me, getting out there and meeting people is the best reward I could imagine.

HOT TIPS

- Write for your school newspaper, especially in college. It's a great way to practice your reporting and writing skills as well as learn what it takes to put a paper together on every level.

- Research the parent companies of different newspapers you enjoy reading or are interested in. You can find this information at the library, on the Internet, or by calling the editorial department at the paper.

- Internships are a great way to learn about the news business, get experience, and make contacts.

- Find something you're passionate about and act on it. If a cause is important to you, volunteer to help, contact an organization, or look into local activities that support it. Developing an activist spirit may make you more aggressive in going after a story, as well as giving you an edge or voice about particular issues.

- Read often, and read everything you can get your hands on. Read Russian novels, journals, biographies . . . materials you wouldn't ordinarily pick up. And read not so much for the enjoyment, but to learn about writing styles and how people approach different things.

WORDS OF WISDOM

If you decide you want to choose this path, the best advice I can give is to find your voice, your own style. This can be very challenging, because often we want to use somebody else's voice. When you work for a newspaper you have to adopt its style to a certain extent, but you can still find your own way of approaching things, then work to hone it. Having the confidence early on to listen to your own voice and apply it within your writing is just tremendous. The sky's the limit for the person who can do that.

All of this is just hard work, and there's nothing wrong with that. Along with working hard, you need discipline. I may love to procrastinate, but when I have to get something done, I can do it. That's discipline. I believe that even if you're not the brightest, if you're disciplined, work hard, and have the tenacity, you can make up for it.

I've never *not* done something because I was afraid to do it. If I'm afraid, I jump into it so that fear isn't an issue. It's good to be a little apprehensive sometimes, but try not to get caught up in fears to the point that they stop you from doing what you want to do.

Find Out More!

Careers for Bookworms and Other Literary Types by Marjorie Eberts and Margaret Gisler (Chicago: VGM Career Horizons, 1995). There are so many things you can do with the written word—work on a newspaper or magazine, in book publishing, at a library or bookstore, as a proofreader, as a story analyst for a film company, or as a segment producer for a TV show. They're all covered in this book.

Careers in Journalism by Jan Goldberg (Chicago: VGM Career Horizons, 2000). For those who share a love of words, you'll find information on careers ranging from newspaper reporter, working for a magazine, technical and business writing, to writing books, both fiction and nonfiction. An historical overview of the journalism field is also included.

The Elements of Style by William Strunk Jr. and E.B. White (Needham Heights, MA: Allyn & Bacon, 2000). This classic reference book is a must for anyone interested in writing. It provides rules for clear and concise writing and use of proper grammar, punctuation, and context.

Chicago Tribune
www.chicagotribune.com
Find out the latest on world events and read articles by Dawn Turner Trice.

HOT *Job...*

Director

*Girls on the Move
(a special event of
Outward Bound)*

As an Outward Bound instructor, I work outdoors and guide people (adults and teens) on adventure expeditions. It's instantly gratifying to see people change as they face their fears and do things they never thought were possible. Coming up with the idea for "Girls on the Move," a bike ride across the country, proposing it to Outward Bound headquarters, and having it accepted was a dream come true. The ride helped raise awareness of issues facing girls today as well as reasons why we need to celebrate being female.

Home Base: Eugene, Oregon

Number of Years in the Field: 10

Personal Philosophy: "Never give up on what you know is possible."

I remember riding my hot pink Schwinn down a hill—freedom on two wheels and a flowered banana seat. I love thinking of those days as the days of pink: a pink bicycle, a pink canopy bed, and pink dresses. I was like a lot of girls and enjoyed so many different things, from lifting my legs onto bicycle handlebars as my dress blew in the wind to using my mother's curling iron to style my doll's hair. The days of my girlhood felt as wild and free as my imagination. Loud, happy, and imaginative, I was a child of no restrictions—free to play, free to express myself, free to imagine possibilities.

I don't remember a significant event happening that made me go from feeling completely free to being easily inhibited. It seems like one day I was wearing little girl clothes and singing in the back of the bus—and the next day, I was developing breasts and wearing a training bra. (In sixth grade, my new and unwanted nickname, "Mother Brassiere," made for great entertainment for the kids in the lunch line at school. What made it more horrifying were the girls joining in the laughter as the boys snapped my back bra strap.) On the outside, my life didn't look much different; I still went to slumber parties, swam once in a while, and shopped with my friends at the mall. On the inside, however, I felt silenced, embarrassed of what I might say, horrified to be noticed.

In eighth grade, I began to feel more confidence. I would have my mother wake me two and a half hours before school started so I could work on my appearance, which included plugging in three curling irons to create perfect, long-feathered curls. I envisioned myself as Farrah Fawcett, the mega-celebrity of the time and the woman my male classmates worshipped. I would leave for school with a bottle of hairspray tucked between peach-colored folders in my black backpack (no longer pink). I was a cheerleader, had a good figure, and the cutest boy in class took notice.

In ninth grade, however, I began to discover my true identity—one that wasn't about my appearance. I discovered sports. I played volleyball and basketball and ran track, and by the end of the year, I was a different person—I had found myself. I continued playing sports all through school. My life now revolved around older teammates who were my best friends and women athletes who served as role models. As I discovered my physical strength on the court, my emotional strength increased dramatically off the court. Once again, a confident and sassy girl sat in my place at the dinner table.

After high school, I went to a large university and joined a sorority where the goal was for each sister (sorority member) to look good and adhere to the reputation of our house. My personal qualities, who I was on the inside, no longer seemed to matter. It was one house, one identity. On the surface, I thought joining a sorority would be fun and give me a sense of belonging. But at a deeper level, it became destructive to the strong person I had become. My sense of self plummeted. I was consumed with my looks, reverted back to using three curling irons to do my hair, and to keep my figure perfect, I started forcing myself to throw up.

Throwing up was a way I thought I could control my naturally curvy body type. One time I ate too much and I thought sticking my fingers down my throat would be a quick, one-time solution to the guilt I felt. But that one time led to another and then another. I became scared and embarrassed. I was ashamed because I knew I was too smart and too together to be doing something like that. I thought bulimia was something that happened to other girls in magazine stories I had read, not to me. I had a pretty face, was funny, athletic, and intelligent. In my head, the only thing that made me not perfect was my body. I thought if I could get that under control, I *would* be perfect. At the urging of my parents, I came home for the summer and the long difficult process of healing began.

Most eating disorders are as much psychological as they are physio-logical. I started to realize that I had fallen victim to something I didn't even believe in, an ever-changing definition of what it means to be female in the United States. I was bombarded with messages from the media, men, the sorority, and my peers that a woman's worth was dependent on her physical appearance. Those messages of needing to have a perfect appearance played a negative role in how I defined myself. I had joined those girls who spend too much time primping in front of the bathroom mirror, discussing who had a good body, who was pretty, and whose "look" we should be striving to imitate. The message of trying to be the perfect-looking woman was so loud, I forgot to look inside myself for *my own* def-inition of what it means to be female.

This is where my path veered in a different direction and brought me to where I am now. This new path was no longer defined by how I thought society wanted me to act or look, but by what I wanted, what my spirit needed to be alive and free.

Joining Outward Bound

I went back to college in the fall and continued my education. Right after graduation, I was searching for a job, not sure what I wanted to do. I con-sidered joining the Peace Corps because I wanted to help others. I was a runner, and often while running, I would think things over and some-times pray and ask for guidance. On one of those occasions I thought about something a recruiter for the Peace Corps had said to me, that since I like the outdoors so much, I might like working for Outward Bound, the largest nonprofit adventure-based organization in the world.

At that very moment I had a very strong urge to call them, and as soon as I got home from my run, I called the Human Resources Director for the regional branch of Outward Bound and told her I was looking for a job. "You're not going to believe this," she said. "I need to hire one more woman for our river program, but you only have 24 hours to get here." Luckily, the training site was in the same state I was in, and the follow-ing morning I drove there. For the next three weeks I trained to become an instructor.

As an Outward Bound instructor, I have the responsibility to care for the physical and emotional well-being of participants as they hang from the side of a rock cliff, swim in white water rapids, or navigate their way through an expedition. These challenges often show humanity in its rawest form. I've seen people join a group of strangers, leave behind their preconceptions about who they're suppose to be and give themselves a chance to find their true identities. It's as if they are able to become who they really are inside.

An Outward Bound experience will change most people at some level. Students shed their fears and allow themselves to realize new possibilities in their lives. In every course I've been on, there's this magical moment where people begin unpeeling themselves—they start getting real about who they are and what they want out of life.

I remember on one course there was a quiet, timid 14-year-old girl named Sarah. She said nothing for the first 13 days of her Outward Bound experience. There were strong, enthusiastic, male students and less motivated, quiet, female students on this particular expedition. The division of personalities based on gender was the strongest I'd seen as an instructor.

On day 14 our group made a unique decision within the given norms of Outward Bound: to divide the group into single-gender patrols. Six girls and two female instructors would climb a mountain range called the Three Sisters of Central Oregon and the boys and their instructors were to go on their own expedition. This was how Sarah finished the last six days of her course and her transformation after the boys left was instantaneous. On the trail, she was enthusiastic and confident and by nightfall, she was at the front of the line, leading the girls to camp.

On day 20 of our 23-day journey, I pointed my finger to the South Sister, looked at that group of 14-year-old girls and said, "Tomorrow at this time you will have led us to the top of that mountain." We awoke at 4 A.M. to start our long hike to the peak. As the sunrise came up over the top, we realized that something was wrong with Sarah. She was limping and using a wooden stick to help her walk. We stopped the group and asked her what was wrong. "I have blisters on my foot," she said, then asked to continue the hike. Seven hours later, the top of South Sister was engulfed in screams of jubilation with the exception of Sarah. She quietly cried and whispered, "This is the greatest moment of my life."

Arriving at camp 18 hours later Sarah said, "I think I may have broken my foot." "What?" I replied in surprise. She continued, "Last night I went to get water and fell down. I heard something crack." I looked at her in wonder. I asked Sarah why she hadn't told us earlier. She replied, "My entire life, every person has told me all the things I can't do. My brothers and father bet that I wouldn't finish this course because I'm a girl. I had to do this for myself . . . I had to climb that mountain."

We immediately evacuated Sarah from the wilderness to a nearby hospital. She had broken her foot in two places, but she came back to our final celebration at the end of the course with crutches and an enormous smile. This situation brought up larger questions like, what is the magic of single-gender groups? What would cause a girl to go to such lengths to prove her strength? What enabled these girls to become so much more outspoken and alive on this 21-day course? More specifically, what would cause a girl like Sarah to go to such lengths to prove her strength?

Thinking about the answers to these questions raised some of the big issues facing girls today, such as loss of self-confidence and not feeling like they have a voice; and this is what led to the creation of the "Girls on the Move" bike ride. This insight came while I was running on a dirt road in North Carolina where I was working as an Outward Bound instructor. I envisioned an event that would enable communities to celebrate the power of girls and women. Even though I had no idea how this event would take shape, I knew girls like Sarah needed organizations like Outward Bound and I knew they needed strong role models. I brought the concept of celebrating girls to a small group of women at an Outward Bound conference, and within minutes the potential of the idea grew. Ultimately, it became a 3,865-mile cross-country bike ride from Portland, Oregon, to New York City. We saw the 10-week event as a way to unite women of all ages in a demonstration of physical, mental, and emotional health and to celebrate the power of being a girl!

Once the idea was set in motion, we determined that there would be several key purposes to the ride. The ride would:

- raise awareness of the issues facing girls and women today

- celebrate the strength of being female

- increase self-esteem for girls and women nationwide by promoting challenging growth experiences that would instill confidence and a feeling of connectedness

- raise scholarship funds for girls across the country to participate in Outward Bound programs

Creating the Dream

Early during the creation of Girls on the Move, there was a moment when I realized there was no turning back; this idea *had* to become a reality. A woman at an Outward Bound conference approached me and said,

"If you do this, I will take my daughters out of school and go with you." In that instant, as I looked at her, I knew that Girls on the Move would attract thousands of people. This event was not only needed; it was definitely going to happen.

When Girls on the Move began, I didn't know everything I would have to do to make it happen, but that was okay. It took three years to get the event off the ground. During that time, I wrote the proposal, put together a budget, hired 16 people, created a marketing campaign to promote the ride, developed a curriculum for school visits, and raised money for the ride.

We wanted to assemble a core group of women who would ride the entire coast-to-coast route from Portland to New York City. Our goal was to find women who would be positive role models for girls and who had a story of their own to tell. We searched out organizations, Web sites, schools, universities, and adventure cycling magazines for women who shared our vision of wanting to help girls feel empowered. Our dream was to put together a diverse group who would be able to talk about their lives, including their struggles and their achievements, and inspire girls along the route with their stories.

We received more than 200 applications and conducted extensive interviews before we ended up with our final team of 65 women. The core group of 21 would ride the whole way; the rest were broken up into three groups, each of which would ride a leg of the journey—one from Portland to Denver, another from Denver to Chicago, and the final group from Chicago to New York. The women ranged in age from 17 to 72 and came from all areas of life. One woman had overcome an eating disorder, another was a kidney transplant survivor, and yet another had survived breast cancer. There was also a woman who had fled Nazi Germany. One of the most inspiring participants was a woman who had been disabled after a car accident that left her with a spinal injury, but who went on to become one of the most successful athletes in the world, competing and winning medals in the Boston Marathon and the Olympics. She pushed a handcycle across the country for Girls on the Move.

My mom, BJ, was also one of the riders. When I was 5, my mom, my 3-year-old brother, and I were in a car accident. Tragically, my brother died. My mom was in a coma for three days and not expected to live. After six months of excruciating rehabilitation, she came home and eventually went back to her job as a teacher. As a teacher, she saw firsthand the problem of low self-esteem among girls as well as the positive impact physical activity had on improving how girls feel about themselves.

My mom is a huge believer in looking to yourself to find your own strength. She used to tell me that to compare myself to my teenage friends was to give my life and spirit away, and that physical appearance is the shine that comes from within. When I battled bulimia, my mom was instrumental in my recovery by constantly reassuring me and reminding me of these lessons. The values both my mom and dad instilled in me when I was growing up really became the core concept of Girls on the Move. Today, both my parents are my inspiration. When the opportunity to ride with Girls on the Move came along, my mom trained hard for the event so that she could be part of the celebration to help girls become strong women. She was eager to join this group of amazing women that became the team that would ride across the country to promote the mission of Girls on the Move.

Overseeing the Journey of Celebration

The cross-country ride began in September 2000. Sometimes I rode with the team, but for the most part I was stationed in the mobile office (which was a motor home that followed the group), so I could coordinate the ride as well as the activities that would take place at each stop. Most days we were up by 6 A.M., ate breakfast, and got on the road, averaging 55 to 70 miles a day. In the evenings, we were usually off the road by 5 P.M., when we would have a potluck dinner with the Girl Scouts in the communities we visited, followed by a service project, such as picking up trash or visiting with specific community members.

Whenever we rode into a new city, our team spent one or two days visiting private and public schools where we'd have

Robyn and her mom on the road with Girls on the Move.

big rallies to talk about the need for events like Girls on the Move. We'd show the students clips from the road and discuss how far women have come and why we need to celebrate. Within the communities we'd team up with organizations like the YWCA or the Girl Scouts for events to promote the healthy development of girls. These "Education Days" and "Community Workshops" were designed to raise awareness of important issues for girls—such as self-esteem, body image, and building confidence—and to give girls a chance to connect with the riders.

In five of the cities we visited, we hosted a Girls' Festival, which was a four- to six-hour entertainment event. At the center of each Festival was a main stage where celebrities shared their messages of inspiration. Some of those who appeared were Olympic gold medal gymnast Dominique Dawes and swimmer Summer Sanders; Stacy Allison, the first American woman to climb Mount Everest; and plus-size supermodel Kelly Repassy, who spoke about body image. Motown singers the "R" Angels also performed and spoke about how they got started in their careers. In each city, we featured local performers as well, including dance groups and folk musicians.

In addition to the entertainment and speakers, a challenge course was set up at each Festival where girls could get a feel for what it's like to participate in an Outward Bound adventure. The challenge course was a huge obstacle course allowing girls to test their strength and endurance through a series of demanding physical activities.

We also created a Girls' Expo at the events, with booths and exhibits sponsored by organizations that had something positive to offer girls and women. Information about health and fitness, self-defense, and community arts programs were available, as well as literature about our partnering organizations, including the Girl Scouts, the YWCA, and Girls Incorporated. Attendees of the events also had the opportunity to look at our Achievement Walls, with photographs of and memorabilia from female role models in sports, music, movies, and politics. It took three large moving trucks to carry all of our equipment from one stop to the next!

On the last day of the ride, we rode into the World Financial Center in New York City. Television journalist Deborah Norville greeted us there with Kristine Lily from the U.S. women's soccer team. We also saw the Statue of Liberty across the water, which was a really neat moment, because when we first started developing Girls on the Move, we made up a little chant, "To the Big Girl!" and would repeat it as a way to get everyone excited about the ride. I was able to ride in the last couple of miles with my mom, which, for me, was an emotional part of the journey.

Overcome by a combination of dreamlike disbelief and pure joy, I pinched myself as a reminder that what was happening was real. My entire family was there and I looked over at my mom and saw that she was crying. Our final Girls' Festival was held in Central Park. When it was all over, everything felt surreal; I wasn't really aware of what was happening.

I've always known that there was a need for something like Girls on the Move, that it's important to have programs that target girls and give them ways to develop better self-esteem, show them how to achieve their goals, and teach them that their dreams can come true. After completing the first ride, I realized there is still so much work to do to help girls realize their full potential and celebrate their successes and that this will be my calling for the rest of my life. I saw so many eyes and faces of women along the route light up when we came into town, and they'd say, "You know, I needed something like this 20 years ago." They, and the young girls who would tell us how important our message was, only strengthened my belief in Girls on the Move. It's now part of my life.

A Behind-the-Scenes Look at the Job

Favorite Part: It was great working with such interesting women during Girls on the Move—women who were developing their own leadership and voice, either on a bicycle, at their jobs back home, or within the group on the road. All of us had so much in common, yet we learned so much more from our differences. The best part of all about creating Girls on the Move, though, was seeing my dream become a reality and doing something to help others in the process.

As an Outward Bound instructor, I love watching people tackle things they thought would be impossible, like paddling through a stretch of white water, climbing a mountain, or rappelling down a rock.

Least Favorite Part: Not being able to eat sushi or big salads when I'm on an Outward Bound expedition! Also, in all the facets of my job, I work long hours, so there isn't much time left over for myself. When you've never done something before, like when I was organizing Girls on the Move, it's really hard to budget your time. You have no idea how long things take or exactly how to get them done. But in the long run, I learned a lot and fulfilled a dream.

Hours: Outward Bound instructors typically teach courses for 21 days and during that time work all day, every day. Most of the time we get a week off between courses and the busiest season is from May to September.

My typical day in the office planning the Girls on the Move ride was between 10 and 12 hours. And those hours were just that—office time. I was either writing letters, meeting with staff members, making telephone calls, or returning emails. On the ride itself, I put in 16-hour days. Those hours consisted of planning time, riding or driving (depending on the day), and time in the evenings talking with the team or participating in community service events.

Dress Code: When I'm teaching courses, I wear hiking boots, shorts, T-shirts, and warm layers (like a pullover fleece and a jacket) that I can take off as I warm up. For meetings in our New York office during the planning stages of Girls on the Move, I would wear a suit, complete with briefcase in hand. During the ride, I was either dressed in a rider uniform or casual jeans and a blouse, depending on what I was doing that day. If I was speaking onstage at one of our Festivals, I tried to dress with a little flair, to celebrate: a nice sweater, pants, and a funky hat.

Work Environment: The expeditions I have been on as an instructor have taken me to many scenic and beautiful locations, such as the Cascades in Washington, the Sierra Nevada mountains in California, the Appalachian mountains in North Carolina, volcanoes in Mexico, and the Deschutes and Rogue rivers in Oregon.

On the road for Girls on the Move, the motorhome was my office, and every drawer in the place was labeled. Big plastic containers of files were everywhere, and a computer, printer, and copier that ran off the generator were sitting on the kitchen table. I would sit at the table with my seatbelt on checking my email while the office manager drove us to our next destination.

Education/Skills: You don't need a degree to work for Outward Bound, just personal and professional experience in the outdoors, with some type of teaching experience. A typical Outward Bound instructor has taught wilderness skills at either a camp or school. Most know how to rock climb and set up climbing stations, read a map, and paddle a canoe or raft from having spent personal time in the wilderness.

Personal Qualities: One of the most important qualities in an Outward Bound instructor is compassion. You need to understand that everyone comes from a different place, and it can be hard to read people sometimes. You must be both empathetic and encouraging as people struggle physically and emotionally, and you need to be a good listener to connect with students. Sometimes we talk on a very real and raw level, and if I am open to discussion, my students usually are, too.

You also need to be the outdoorsy type. The ability to connect with nature, reach out to people, and help them discover their strengths is what this job is all about.

Perks and Rewards: It's gratifying to see people change, to see them start a personal journey of self-discovery. As an Outward Bound instructor and working on Girls on the Move, I've seen people face their fears and do things they never thought would be possible. It's a powerful feeling.

HOT TIPS

◊ Study the history of the women's movement. Learn about the obstacles women have overcome, how they did it, and the people who led it. There's always something you can do to promote the celebration of being female, such as participating in walks or runs that promote women's health, speaking up in school, and pursuing your dream, no matter what or how big it may be.

◊ Talk to your friends about the issues girls face and discuss what you can do about it. Recognizing the barriers, issues, and concerns related specifically to females is an important first step to working for and with girls and women.

◊ Take time to get to know yourself; keep a journal of your dreams, fears, and thoughts. This is key. It's easy to be pulled into pressures and expectations. Knowing who you really are helps keep you grounded and assists you in making decisions that are right for you.

◊ Get as much outdoor experience as you can. Learn how to camp, read a map, cook food outdoors, and tie knots. It's not only valuable experience, it's fun! Gain white water sports experience, like canoeing, kayaking, or river rafting. Join a hiking group, take an introductory rock-climbing class, go biking and swimming. Do whatever gets you out there!

◊ Join the Girls Scouts, YWCA, 4-H, or any other group that can give you the opportunity to learn outdoor skills.

◊ Become or stay physically active.

◊ Consider becoming a youth summer camp counselor. You'll gain valuable communication, leadership, and outdoor skills. The experience may also help you determine if being (and leading) in the outdoors is truly your passion.

WORDS OF WISDOM

Believe that you can do anything you put your mind to. There will always be people who say you can't achieve your dream, so you've got to surround yourself with people who believe in you and your dreams. Work hard, follow your thoughts, and share your ideas—you may surprise yourself.

Find Out More!

 Leading Out: Mountaineering Stories of Adventurous Women edited by Rachel De Silva (Seattle: Seal Press, 1998). This book is comprised of inspiring stories of women who climb mountains. Whether new to the idea of rock climbing and mountaineering or a practiced climber, readers experience the physical and emotional challenges faced by 25 of the best women climbers in the world.

 Outside Magazine
P.O. Box 7785 • Red Oak, IA 51591 • 1-800-678-1131
www.outsidemag.com
This magazine for the outdoor enthusiast has feature articles that will inspire the adventurer in anyone! Included is a directory of products and services for active travelers, product and book reviews, training tips, and more.

 Outward Bound USA
1-888-88-BOUND (1-888-882-6863)
www.outwardbound.org
Outward Bound is a nonprofit organization dedicated to wilderness education. International in focus, Outward Bound has over 50 years of experience conducting outdoor adventures, making it the largest and oldest organization of its kind. The Web site is filled with information about the many exciting courses offered, including the location, cost, and enrollment information for each.

Afterword

What It's Like to Have (and Lose) Your Dream Job

—by Pam Drucker

If you look up the word *dream* in the dictionary, you'll find it defined as an illusion or fantasy—as in not real. And if you look up the word *job*, the definition will read something like "a regular position of hire." I spent the past four years of my life at my dream job, and while it was a regular position of hire, it definitely wasn't an illusion. It was the most real experience of my life.

I worked at *Jump*, a former magazine with a slogan that ran on the cover of each issue: "For Girls Who Dare to Be Real." When Lori Berger was named Editor-in-Chief, she brought me over from *Sassy* magazine where I was working as an intern. Lori opened a big door for me. Establishing a mentor connection with someone who can teach you can really enrich your learning experience. I don't think I'd be exaggerating to say that, without Lori, I might have had a long-term career in the hot dog business, which is what I was doing when I met her, in addition to interning.

I was 21, still in college, and not a great writer, but I was eager. Not only did I love the *Jump* philosophy, I was a *Jump* girl. I was into sports and fitness, which was clearly part of the *Jump* philosophy, and I was also strong and daring—I took risks, believed in myself, and most of all, embraced my so-called failures so that I could learn how to succeed in my own way. Daring to be real was about being the best *you* you could possibly be, and I had that concept down flat.

My enthusiasm paid off, because I continued to climb up the masthead (which is kind of like the credits at the end of a movie, only in a magazine it's the editors' names and titles and it's usually found at the beginning of most magazines), a certain proof of legitimacy in the magazine world. I made it all the way to Senior Associate Editor. But more importantly, I had so much fun! Think of your favorite class in school; now imagine being able to take it all day long. That was what my life was like at *Jump*.

Because I was the only girl on staff who was really athletic, my niche at the magazine became sports and fitness. Eventually, I was given the title of Sports and Fitness Editor. Having this on my business card entitled me to tag along on some really cool sports press trips with companies like Nike and Reebok, receive more free sporting gear than you can fathom, and run my very own sports and fitness column that appeared monthly (not to mention that I got to interview some fascinating people). All in all, this job pushed every creative button in my body.

So you can see why I never anticipated an end. I thought that this was it. At 24, I had attained what most people search for their whole life: a "hot job" that I loved. It's not that I thought I'd be at *Jump* for the rest of my life—I just didn't ever think about leaving. I was happy where I was, so why change a good thing?

But almost four years after I started, my relationship with *Jump* was over. And I wasn't even dumped in person—I received the news over the phone that *Jump* was folding. I was shocked, bummed out, confused, angry, and above all, scared. How does one move on from a dream job?

I didn't want to work for another magazine even though that was my field of expertise. I decided to take some time to think about it. Instead of sending out a million résumés, I put out the word to a few contacts that I would be available for freelance work (a girl's got to pay her rent). But for the most part, I needed some time to figure out what I wanted to do next.

And this is where I actually get to my point: *The fact is, it's possible to have more than one hot job in a lifetime.* I was so comfortable in my previous job that I really didn't have to push myself to see beyond it. Once it was over, I had to reinvent myself to figure out what I wanted in a career. While I was an editor at *Jump*, I always had an untapped affinity for sales and marketing. But I never let myself explore it, because number one, I didn't have to, and number two, why walk away from a good thing? But when I lost my job, I started thinking about sales and marketing.

When the ex-publisher from *Jump* presented me with the opportunity to join her sales staff at another publication, I was very intrigued, yet I struggled with the idea. I made a list of pros and cons. I interviewed everyone who has ever known me . . . family, friends, random cab drivers—basically anyone who would listen—about what it would mean to change my career and whether or not it was possible to do it. Aside from a few discouraging remarks, the people who knew me best seemed to agree with my instincts to go for it.

So I did. And now I'm in a new dream job and on a new path. It's scary, interesting, fun, challenging, and exciting. But I realize that with every change in life, you learn something new about yourself. Change forces you to grow as a person, and, in the end, the things you learn about yourself and the world are more rewarding than any paycheck you'll ever receive.

Pam Drucker
Account Manager, Primedia Publications

Pam interned at *Sassy* magazine for over two years and held various editorial positions at *Jump* magazine for four. She has freelanced for magazines such as *Glamour, Cosmopolitan, Shape, Mademoiselle,* and *Seventeen.* Pam currently lives in New York City and has a hot job working as Account Manager for Primedia Publications, selling ad space for their youth entertainment group—*Tiger Beat, Teen Beat,* and *Bop* magazines—and she's loving every bit of it!

PART 2

*. . . and how you can
go for it, too!*

Preparing for
Your Hot Job

Your Future Is Up to You

After reading about the amazing women in Part 1, you were no doubt fascinated by their diverse experiences and journeys. You may have noticed similarities, too, for despite the fact that their careers range from the depths of the earth (Egyptologist Jennifer Wegner) to the farthest reaches of the sky (space plasma physicist Claudia Alexander), these women share commonalties that go beyond their careers—they all hold visions of their futures, confidence in their ability to reach their goals, and courage to go after what they want.

Their stories also illustrate that you may not always know exactly where you're headed when you embark on your career path. Maureen Holohan, who never achieved her dream of playing basketball at the professional level, was forced to suddenly shift gears and discovered a new dream that she *did* achieve. Claudia Alexander started out studying to become an engineer—only to discover a love of science. Like them, you too may switch plans, goals, and dreams midstream—and that's okay. It's natural to change your mind several times before you find what really feeds your soul.

That's what makes life interesting and challenging—dreaming a dream, putting your faith in your own ability, being courageous enough to move forward despite the obstacles, and having the flexibility to change as your dreams do. These women prove that even the highest aspirations can be achieved. Whether you're focusing on a short-term or long-term goal, something that seems likely or unlikely, something that will be difficult or easy to pursue, you have to know what it takes to get started on your journey and how to keep moving forward, regardless of the bumps in the road.

The Keys to Success

There are many ways to unlock the door to your future. Some of the tools you need exist within you right now. It may be something as simple as being really good at following instructions or having an aptitude for science. There are qualities you may not discover within you for quite some time, which will emerge only after you've been put on the spot. For example, you may never have had to speak in front of a large group, when suddenly you're assigned an oral report. While butterflies dance in your stomach, you give your presentation without faltering and receive a warm reception from the class, which makes you think, "Hey, I didn't think I had the courage it takes to do that . . . but I guess I did!"

There are specific qualities and skills you can start to develop right as you take the initial steps toward pursuing that hot job. No matter what your aspirations are, five key traits are essential to your success: imagination, confidence, willingness to take risks, courage, and determination. These traits are not only the keys to your future career; they're also the keys to unlocking the potential to meet whatever goals you may have.

Key #1: IMAGINATION

Imagination is the origin of all inspiration . . . it's what gives you the ability to dream big dreams. Looking beyond what is around you, beyond today, and envisioning things you've never tried—or that have never even existed before—is the sign of an open, imaginative mind.

Without imagination things would stay the same forever. We'd be without airplanes, space exploration, the Internet, even electricity . . . the list is endless. We wouldn't have music or any of the arts and our clothes would be something just to cover our bodies. The future is uncharted territory within your imagination, and it's up to you to use yours to create a blueprint of what that future can become.

Developing your imagination is like working on a muscle; in order to build it up and make it stronger, you have to use it. Robyn Reed had no idea what she was in for when she first imagined an event called Girls on the Move. It was a flash in her mind, surfacing when she was relaxed and in tune with herself on a peaceful country road. But her idea was all encompassing; she imagined no limits on how helpful and important this event could be to girls and women across the country. When the idea came to fruition and Girls on the Move was complete, the reality of what it had become exceeded even her own expectations. Her life, as well as those of the people involved, had been forever changed.

Like Robyn, you may find that your imagination soars when you allow yourself time away from others, time for yourself. While you may find your life filled with school, sports, chores, friends, family, and a hundred other daily activities, try setting aside some quiet time to exercise your imagination. When you allow yourself to slow down, you give your mind the opportunity to go wild with possibilities and ideas. When your thoughts are cluttered with to-do lists, homework assignments, and a mental transcript of the last fight you had with your best friend, it can be difficult to let your imagination take flight. So try this: sit and do nothing for at least five minutes each day. If you're soothed by soft music or nature sounds, turn on the CD player. Allow whatever images you want to enter your mind to do so. Is there something in particular you would like to imagine a solution or possibility for? Focus on that for five minutes and see where your thoughts lead you. Or maybe there's nothing in particular that you want to focus on . . . that's okay, too. Many of the ideas that flash through your mind are flashes of imagination, and it's possible something exceptional will surface once you've had some practice slowing down and letting your mind go.

Perhaps you're the type of person who has no trouble daydreaming and can easily imagine all sorts of things. Great! Why not jot down some of those inspirations? Putting your ideas in writing means you can look them over at your leisure, and you can put them to good use when the time is right. In your imagination there are no limits, and creating a vision of a limitless future may be just the motivation you need to achieve your dreams.

Imagination is . . .

- the ability to dream big dreams

- creating a vision of how you'd like things to be

- believing that all things are possible

- finding a way to use obstacles to your advantage

- not putting limits on your potential

- figuring out how to turn "no" into "yes!"

Think About It!

Give yourself permission to daydream; keep a journal of your imaginings. Make a promise to yourself to turn at least one dream into reality. Start by talking to someone you trust. Their excitement and support of your idea may be just what you need to make it happen!

Key #2: CONFIDENCE

Confidence is having a realistic expectation that you can reach your goals or accomplish a task. The ride may be bumpy and you may come face-to-face with obstacles, but you know in your gut that you have the ability to reach your destination.

If you don't believe in your abilities, you'll have a difficult time achieving your goals. Regardless of what your aspirations may be, you can't get to the finish line without self-confidence. Olympic champion figure skater Tara Lipinski went to the 1998 Olympics with enough confidence to fill the entire stadium. When she headed to Nagano, Japan, she had one goal and that was to come home with a gold medal. Tara knew the competition would be fierce, but she believed she could win. Only 15 years old, she skated the best program of her life and was able to achieve her dream of Olympic gold. Had she stepped on the ice doubting her ability to win, another skater would have claimed that medal.

One of the best ways you gain confidence is by experiencing success. When you reach a goal or complete a task, it gives you the confidence to set and accomplish more difficult challenges. For example, the first time you snowboard, it can be nerve-wracking, but you strap the board to your boots, bend your knees, and summon the courage to surf down the bunny slope, shaky knees and all. When you get to the bottom, despite a spill or two (or three or four), you feel exhilarated, proud, and in awe of your feat. Now that you know you can handle the beginner's hill, you feel more confident to tackle a run that's slightly more challenging. Each time you make it down the hill, you feel more secure and your confidence level increases.

Confidence is also gained by looking back on things you've already accomplished and acknowledging what it took to achieve them. You may not think you've done much, but if you take some time to think about where you were a year ago—or even a month ago—you may be surprised. Facing challenges, moving forward, and taking on responsibility are all part of growing up. Chances are you've done things that you (and others) never thought you could, and that should make you feel pretty good!

If you ever feel your confidence wavering or you begin to question your ability to handle something, sit down and make a list of things you've achieved in the last several weeks or months. They don't have to be earth-shattering accomplishments; just acknowledge the everyday successes you've had, whether in school, at home, with your friends, or in overcoming personal obstacles. As you write, you'll probably start remembering more and more. And the longer your list becomes, the bigger boost it will be to your confidence. Take some time to celebrate where you are and where you've been . . . that way you can truly appreciate where you're going.

As with anything important in your life, always share your thoughts and feelings with people you trust—your parents, friends, a teacher, or a counselor. Sometimes just saying something out loud will give you the confidence you need to move forward.

Confidence is . . .

- knowing that you have what it takes to reach your goals

- a willingness to tackle new challenges

- having faith that even things that seem beyond your reach now will someday be attainable

- a commitment to keep going, even when times get tough

- believing that you can do practically anything you set your mind to

- recognizing that your talents and skills are special

- putting one foot in front of the other and going for it

- knowing you can make mistakes and learn from them, without seeing them as a sign of failure

Think About It!

Is there an area of your life where you lack confidence? If so, what is it? What steps can you take to improve your level of confidence? Write these steps down and take the first one today.

Key #3: WILLINGNESS TO TAKE RISKS

Risks are challenges that force you to step out of your comfort zone. When you take a risk, you're taking a chance on something that has an unknown outcome. Taking healthy risks—ones that require you to face unfamiliar challenges and conquer them without putting yourself in unreasonable harm—will fill your life with never-ending surprises and satisfaction. For one person, enrolling in an advanced-placement English class is taking a huge risk. For another, it's entering a 5K race to fight breast cancer. Whatever the risk, it will send you soaring higher, and ultimately, make you stronger. Most people feel safest when they do what everyone else is doing, but always being a follower doesn't challenge you to stretch your wings and fly. Trying something new, putting yourself out there does.

When you take unhealthy risks, like getting into a sexual relationship before you're ready or experimenting with drugs, you're taking chances with your health, your future, and your life. How do you know a risk is unhealthy? Ask yourself: What are the consequences of the action or decision? Does it put you or someone else in danger? Is it illegal or against your morals? If you can't live with the consequences, it's a risk not worth taking.

J.K. Rowling, author of the Harry Potter book series about a young boy with magical powers, took a risk when she wrote her first book and submitted it for publication. No one thought today's kids would want to read about wizards and magic. Although she was rejected several times, she persisted and found an agent who sold her first manuscript to a major publisher. All of the Harry Potter books have become a huge success, making the *New York Times* best-seller list, receiving international critical acclaim, and selling millions of copies. The first book in the series, *Harry Potter and the Sorcerer's Stone,* was made into one of the top grossing films ever. It takes guts and self-confidence to open yourself up for rejection when you share your talents with the world. Whether you want to be a writer, an athlete, a scientist, or an entrepreneur, you never know how your efforts will be perceived—but the leap you take will help you learn and grow. For J.K. Rowling, the risk she took made her a legend in the publishing world.

It can be scary to take a risk, but that's how you move forward in life—by taking the chance that you might fail and learning from the outcome, no matter what it is. How do you know when something you're thinking about doing feels risky? It makes your palms sweat, your heart pound, and your stomach do somersaults. Your body is telling you that you're afraid of doing something you've never done, afraid of failing, afraid of making a mistake or looking foolish. If what you're considering isn't going to harm you or someone else, taking that chance can be a positive experience, despite the fear. Even if you do fail, you can learn from it and develop the confidence to try something else. Taking risks helps you learn and grow. If you never try anything new you might be stuck in the same place indefinitely.

Being a risk taker is . . .

- doing something despite a fear of failing

- being honest about your feelings, wants, and needs

- enjoying your individuality

- going for a goal even though it seems out of your reach

- challenging yourself, either physically or mentally

- trying something new or different

Think About It!

Have you ever had something wonderful result from your willingness to take a risk? If so, how did you feel afterward? Have you taken an unhealthy risk and later regretted it? What did you learn? Is there a healthy risk you're thinking about taking? What, if anything, is stopping you? Here's a simple exercise to help with indecision. Take a sheet of paper, make two columns, and label them "Pros" and "Cons." Using what you learned in the imagining exercise (page 235), let your mind go and write down everything you think of about why you should or shouldn't take a certain risk. One list may be so much longer than the other that your decision is obvious, or the shorter list might have more crucial factors on it than the longer list and you'll know in your gut the way to go.

Key #4: COURAGE

Courage is about facing your fears and moving forward in spite of them. Look around you and you'll see how people demonstrate courage every day and on many different levels. A child who is being treated for a serious illness bravely undergoes the painful procedures that provide hope for recovery. A girl raises her hand and offers an idea or an opinion that is different from what her classmates have expressed. A teenager says "no" to drinking and driving in the face of great pressure from peers. Firefighters, police, and rescue workers risk their lives to help anyone in need.

Learning to confront your fears and do the right thing is how you grow as a person. If it were easy to stand up for your beliefs and do what you know is right, you wouldn't need courage! Everyone feels nervous when they're confronted with situations that are unfamiliar. Going to a new school, starting your first job, interviewing for college or a specialty training program, telling a friend you don't like something they've done or said—these can all be scary things to deal with. But when you face your fears with grace and confidence, you'll know for yourself the true meaning of courage.

When we think of courage we usually think of someone like Rosa Parks, who in 1955 in Montgomery, Alabama, refused to give up her bus seat to a white passenger and was arrested and put in jail. This single act of defiance eventually led to the Civil Rights Act of 1964, which states that all Americans, regardless of race, nationality, or religion, must be given equal treatment under the law.

But being courageous doesn't always mean doing something as socially significant as Rosa Parks did. Courage comes in all shapes and sizes and reflects each person's situation and life challenges. Perhaps you look forward to a dissection in your biology class, but your friend and lab partner is scared beyond belief. Completing the dissection wouldn't require courage for you, but it would be a courageous act for your friend. But if you and that same friend went rock climbing, she might scamper up a steep cliff without hesitation, while you might have to muster all the courage at your disposal to take the first step.

Key #2, confidence, is about believing in your abilities. Courage is about putting that confidence to the test by taking action in a situation that you're nervous about or where the outcome is uncertain. It's normal to feel afraid when you're facing something new. But if you move forward despite being fearful, then you're demonstrating courage. For some people, being daring and courageous in just about any situation seems to come easily. They're the ones who instantly raise their hands the moment a teacher poses a question to the class, the ones who boldly march up to a group of people they don't know and introduce themselves. But there might be other aspects of their lives when they're not as courageous, or perhaps they really work hard at overcoming their fears and worries because the results are worth it. Remember that for most of us, building and demonstrating courage is an ongoing process.

As with the other key traits, there are things you can do to build courage. Start with a small task you would like to accomplish, something that presents you with a low level of fear. After you succeed in that task, start another one that presents a slightly higher level of fear, and so on. If there's a larger issue you'd like to tackle, break it down into manageable parts. For instance, you see a notice on the job board at school for a part-time job at a doctor's office, and you know it would be a great way to learn about the medical profession (the hot job of your dreams) while earning some money. But you're scared to go for an interview, because you don't have any experience and this would be your first job. Keep telling yourself that you have to start somewhere and you'll never know if you don't show up. Replacing negative statements that are repeating themselves in your head with positive, empowering ones is important for your self-esteem, as well as your courage. Ask a friend or family member to practice doing a mock interview with you; rehearse things to say about yourself and answer potential questions so you feel more at ease. Each step you take—out the door of your house, inside the medical office, into the interview room— is a courageous step. Keep putting one foot in front of the other until you get where you need to go. Even if you don't get the job, you combated your fears and tackled something with courage. The next time you are confronted with a situation you're afraid of, you'll have more courage, confidence, and experience.

Courage is . . .

- standing up for yourself and others

- owning and applying your strengths when facing a difficult situation

- doing the right thing, especially when the wrong thing would be easier or more fun

- standing apart from the crowd

- confronting your problems and asking for help

- facing adversity and coming up with a plan to get through it

- a willingness to make mistakes

- taking a step toward your goal

Think About It!

What's the most courageous thing you've ever done? How did you feel when you did it? What about afterward? Was there a time when your courage failed you? What happened? Knowing what you know now, what would you do differently?

Key #5: DETERMINATION

Determination is about staying committed to your dreams, even in the face of obstacles or setbacks. To reach a goal, you need determination to stay on track. There will be times when you'll hit a roadblock and you'll face a decision: give up or find a way to keep going. If you give up, you'll never reach your destination. If you hang in there and find a way to get around the hurdles, you'll be on your way.

For Debbi Fields, founder of Mrs. Fields cookies, it took determination to build her famous cookie empire. She went from bank to bank trying to get money to open her first store, but was continually turned down for a loan. Debbi refused to give up, and someone finally took a chance on her and gave her the money. When she opened her store, however, the lines of customers she had been hoping for didn't show up. By mid-afternoon of opening day, she hadn't sold a single cookie. Undeterred, she put the cookies on a tray and hit the streets, handing out samples. Once people tasted how good the cookies were, she directed them to her store to buy more. Had she given up, you wouldn't find her cookies all over the world!

You can work on determination by breaking goals into smaller steps when you feel overwhelmed, by having backup plans when you hit an obstacle, and by reevaluating your goals and your progress from time to time. To help you stay determined, make sure you share your goals with people who will be supportive of your efforts, like your parents, teachers, friends, neighbors, or spiritual leader. Nothing kills a dream faster than negativity. Suppose you've always been fascinated with space and your dream is to attend the Air Force Academy, become a pilot, and eventually command a space shuttle. It's an ambitious goal, but definitely attainable. Lieutenant Colonel Eileen Collins proved that when she became the first female Space Shuttle Commander aboard the Space Shuttle *Columbia*.

What happens if you tell someone your dream of space exploration and he or she counters it with all kinds of reasons why you shouldn't waste your time? "The Air Force Academy is too competitive," "Not very many women make it into the NASA program," or "Even if you do get in, you'll probably never fly in space anyway because budgets are always being cut." This kind of negative thinking can make you second-guess your decision, doubt your ability to succeed, and undermine your determination. So make a point to surround yourself with people who want you to succeed, will encourage you, will help you, and will celebrate your accomplishments with you. When you're faced with reactions that are less than positive, determination can help you stand your ground and refuse to let go of your dream.

Determination is . . .

- going for a goal even when some people doubt you

- coming back and trying harder at something you've failed at before

- persisting with your goals despite the obstacles

- revising your plans as needed to adjust to changes and challenges

- never giving up

Think About It!

Name at least one thing you've achieved because you were determined to go for it. Do you know or admire someone who has demonstrated determination in his or her life? What did this person face and what did he or she do to persevere? How can this person's determination serve as a role model for your own life?

* * * * *

With the five keys to success—imagination, confidence, willingness to take risks, courage, and determination—firmly in hand, you're in a great position to start climbing the stairway to your dreams. Even if you need to work on one or more of the traits, knowing you have to do so and doing something about it will help you reach your goals in ways you never imagined. Now it's time to get moving! The rest of Part 2 is designed to help you follow the three main steps you'll need to take to someday find the hot job that's waiting for you:

- Know Yourself

- Set Goals

- Move Ahead

Find Out More!

The Girls' Guide to Life: How to Take Charge of the Issues That Affect You by Catherine Dee (Boston: Little, Brown and Co., 1997). This interactive book touches on many different areas important in developing determination and confidence, key attributes in achieving goals. Learn how to be a strong person, to speak up and become more effective as a student, to get involved in the community, and to help show the world what women are made of.

Girls Who Rocked the World: Heroines from Sacagawea to Sheryl Swoopes by Amelie Welden (Hillsboro, OR: Beyond Words Publishing, 1998). Throughout history amazing young women have been making a difference in the world. This book tells the story of 33 incredible teens from the past and present whose accomplishments set them apart and left a lasting impression on the lives of others.

Girls Who Rocked the World 2: Heroines from Harriet Tubman to Mia Hamm by Michelle Roehm (Hillsboro, OR: Beyond Words Publishing, 2000). This sequel includes more stories of amazing girls throughout history who had the courage to fight for their beliefs and started making waves before they'd reached their 20s.

The 7 Habits of Highly Effective Teens: The Ultimate Teenage Success Guide by Sean Covey (New York: Simon & Schuster, 1998). This step-by-step guide will help teens improve self-image, build friendships, resist peer pressure, achieve goals, and get along with their parents.

What Teens Need to Succeed: Proven, Practical Ways to Shape Your Own Future by Peter L. Benson, Ph.D., Judy Galbraith, M.A., and Pamela Espeland (Minneapolis: Free Spirit Publishing, 1998). This book emphasizes the importance of assertiveness and taking positive action in becoming strong, confident, and better at making healthy choices. Learn the importance of internal and external assets, including values, a strong identity, good time management, and a strong support system.

Know Yourself

Great! You're inspired, motivated, ready to make a move, but how can you figure out what you want to do in your life if you don't know what your interests and talents are or what makes you happy? We hope this book will help steer you to a hot job, but it can't decide what that hot job is. *You* can! While you may not think you know it, all of the answers are already within you. Figuring out what you enjoy, what you're good at, and who you are will lead you to choose a career path. And one of the best ways to start the discovery process is to write in a journal.

Women throughout history have kept journals as a way to chronicle their dreams, life journeys, and career paths—as well as help them deal with personal issues. Explorer and educator Ann Bancroft, the first woman to cross the ice to both the North and South Poles, often used journals to record her amazing adventures. Beginning in November 2000, Liv Arnesen, another daring female explorer, and Ann embarked on the journey of a lifetime—to ski together across Antarctica. During this mission they recorded the details, triumphs, and heartaches of their historic expedition in journal entries on a Web site. For nearly 100 days these two women braved the elements to complete their journey, and they took along anyone who was interested by sharing their experience through journaling online.

Many of the women in this book have kept journals. Terri Cadiente used journaling to help work through the pain of her youth and learn about her true self. Maureen Holohan and Laura Hogg used journals to write down everything from mundane events to their innermost thoughts, feelings, and frustrations. Jane Pallera kept an art journal. These women all used journaling as a tool to self-discovery, which in turn helped them become confident enough to tackle their challenging and exciting careers. For these women and others who journal, writing down their thoughts is a way to get to know themselves to the very core . . . to discover what's important to them and gain new insight that will help them to live their dreams.

Keeping a journal gives you the opportunity to explore career options, but beyond this, it also allows you to record your thoughts and feelings about *everything* that matters to you, including your friendships, family issues, worries, hopes, fears, dreams, and opinions. There are so many great reasons to journal. One of the following may encourage you to try it:

• It's like having a best friend who is always there for you and won't criticize you or drift into space halfway through your sentence.

- A journal gives you a safe place to address the things you don't feel like talking about with another living soul. Whether it's issues concerning sex or drugs, worrying about getting into college, or feeling annoyed because your best friend has been getting on your nerves, a journal is a safe haven where you can talk about anything without worrying about negative repercussions.

- Putting your thoughts on paper clears your mind of all the excess stuff swirling around in there. When you have a lot on your mind and stress is building up, writing things down can ease the load. If you've been feeling like you've got too much on your plate lately, once you make a list of what you need to do, you may discover your responsibilities don't look so overwhelming. Seeing things on paper puts everything into perspective, which might make you feel a whole lot better.

- Your journal is a celebration of you! Every entry is about you: your thoughts, your opinions, your joy, your pain, your dreams, your words.

- Keeping a journal improves your writing and communication skills, which are essential to success. The ability to express yourself clearly is essential to reaching many goals. You'll never succeed as a professional basketball player if you can't explain a play to your teammates and you won't make it as a famous fashion designer if you don't know how to articulate your vision to a pattern-maker.

- Taking a few moments to write in your journal gives you the chance to tune out from the world for a bit of alone time. Everyone needs time away from the craziness of the day, to wind down and breathe a sigh of, "Okay, I got through it. Now what?" This is your license to indulge yourself with thoughts about the day, including what was great about it and what wasn't so great.

- Chronicling your thoughts and feelings provides you with a personal timeline. You can go back later and read old entries to see how much you've grown, how things have changed, and how you've been able to meet and exceed challenges.

- When you can't seem to make a decision or are at a loss for a solution to a problem, sometimes writing it down will lead you to the answer you're seeking. Putting things on paper is a way to take the chaos out of your head, making the entire picture seem a lot clearer. When your mind is free of clutter, it's much easier to sort things out.

Journals come in all different shapes, colors, and sizes. You can buy one that will guide you with daily questions to answer and topics to ponder, or you can simply purchase a blank notebook with or without lined pages and fill it up however you choose. This latter option is good because it gives you the freedom to be as bold and creative as you dare, and really, that's the whole point of keeping a journal. This isn't the place to hold back, it's the place to let loose.

There are no rules when it comes to writing in your journal. You can write every day or when the mood strikes. You can choose a special place to work on your entries, like on your bed or under a tree, or you can jot down your thoughts wherever you happen to be when you feel like putting pen to paper. You can use a favorite pen, a pencil, markers, or even a box of colorful crayons. You can write as little or as much as you desire; 10 pages or a single word. And you can write *whatever* you feel like writing. There are no restrictions! Your journal is meant to be private, for your eyes only, so you should feel free to express whatever's on your mind.

Let your journaling routine and style fit your needs. Writing in a journal isn't meant to be a chore. It's meant to be just the opposite, something to look forward to. Once you get started, it might become one of the best parts of your day, a time when you can be alone with your thoughts and sort through the day's events. This is the time when you can take a deep breath, exhale, and let it all out on paper. If writing in it every day stresses you out and makes you feel guilty when you don't, then everyday writing isn't for you. Instead, write in it when the mood strikes. If you've always wanted a special diary, then get one! If you're worried because writing never has been your thing, you might be surprised. Without the restrictions of academic writing (such as perfect spelling, grammar, and paragraph structure) you might find that writing actually *is* your thing. Journaling is all about you—whatever feels right.

Once you get into the groove of writing in a journal, your words will flow more naturally. More than likely, your thoughts will pour out so fast that your hand will have a tough time keeping up with them. Until you get to this point, however, here are a few ideas to get you started so you don't have to stare at a blank page.

Lists

At the top of a blank page in your journal, write down one of the following headings. Underneath it, list everything you can think of that pertains to that list. Use a single word, phrases, or draw pictures!

- Stuff I'd Buy if I Won the Lottery

- What I Like About Myself

- My Special Talents

- I Am Grateful for . . .

- Things I'd Like to Accomplish This Year

- Things I'm Afraid Of

- Places I'd Like to Visit

- My Responsibilities

- What I'm Good At

- Things I'd Like to Change About Myself

- I'm Happiest When . . .

- Things That Stress Me Out

- Things That Make Me Laugh Out Loud

- Careers I'd Like to Consider

- What I'd Change in the World

- Things I'd Like to Do in the Future

- My Favorite _____ (colors, books, movies, CDs, travel spots, sports, ice-cream flavors, school subjects, TV shows, magazines, radio stations, people, restaurants, animals, flowers, and so on)

Questions

Ask yourself a question and see where your answers take you! Try these to get started:

- What is it about your favorite song that moves you?

- If you could meet anyone in the world, who would it be and what would you say to him or her?

- How have you been supportive of your best friend recently?

- Who's had the biggest influence on you this year and why?

- If you could get paid for doing anything on earth, what would it be?

- If you were deserted on an island but could have five things sent to you from home, what would they be and why?

- What do you and your mom have in common? What do you and your dad have in common?

- When you consider the next few years of your life, what scares you the most?

- What's been the happiest moment in your life so far?

- What's the biggest mistake you've ever made and what did you learn from it?

- How are you different from your friends?

- Have you ever stood up for someone when they've been wronged or put down by one of your friends?

- How would you describe the kind of person you are?

- If you could do anything on your next birthday, what would it be?

- How has your faith made a difference in your life?

- When you're feeling down, what usually cheers you up?

- What's the biggest risk you've ever taken and was it worth it?

- How has a particular movie or book influenced you?

- If you were elected the first female President of the United States, what would do to make this country a better place for women?

Daily Activities

Simply jot down key words or phrases that pertain to the day's activities. You can include the big stuff, like having an argument with your mom or dad, as well as the more mundane, like a dentist appointment. Include descriptions of what you ate, who you talked to, what you learned at school, and how you felt. Answer all of the five Ws: Who, What, When, Where, and Why. Make it lively and consider including some specific details like what you wore or the texture of the food you ate. This kind of journal entry is similar to what you'd write in an appointment calendar, just a bit more descriptive and colorful.

Letter Writing

Another way to explore your thoughts and feelings is to write a letter. Feel free to spill your guts—it's not meant to be mailed, just another way for you to take a load off your mind. Try one of these ideas:

- Write a letter to your mom or dad and tell them something you'd like them to know but haven't been able to open up about.

- Write a letter to someone at school who's been causing you grief and let them know how their actions have hurt or annoyed you.

- Write a letter to someone in your family (brother, sister, grandmother) and tell them how much you appreciate them.

- Choose a hot job and write a letter to your future employer explaining why you'd be perfect for the position. If you want to become an Academy Award–winning movie director, write a letter to Steven Spielberg explaining your vision for a feature film you'd like to direct. If becoming a flight attendant is your dream, write to one of the airline carriers detailing why you'd be a good candidate for their training program.

- Write a letter to your principal and let him or her know what your school could use in order to create a better learning environment.

- Write a letter to yourself as if you were writing to a dear friend. Tell yourself what's been going on in your life, what's new, and what your plans are for the upcoming months.

- Write a letter to yourself, only pretend you are going to seal it and read it 25 years from now. Include all of the goals and dreams you hope to accomplish by then, such as college graduation, marriage, a house of your own, a cool career, travel, or children.

- Write a letter to yourself from somebody else's point of view. What words of advice would someone in your dream field tell you? If you're currently at odds with someone (a friend, teacher, or parent, perhaps) what do you imagine they would say to you?

Doodles

Write a single word or phrase anywhere on the page and doodle all around it, anything that comes to mind. The word or phrase can be anything that pops into your head. For example, it could be something you've been looking forward to, such as "summer vacation." Next, fill the page with anything you feel like drawing or scribbling, such as a picture of a pool, the beach, a hotel, a campground, a basketball court, a pile of novels, ice-cream cones, a bathing suit, inline skates, the sun's rays, and so on. Here are some other "doodle" words and phrases to consider using:

- Final exams
- Interests
- Joy
- College
- Heart's Desire
- Spirit
- Sports
- Career
- Motivation
- Road Block
- Challenges

- Fitness
- Responsibility
- Independence
- Work
- Love
- Fears
- To Do
- Make It Happen
- Play
- Time to Shine
- I Can

Photographs

Take a favorite photograph of yourself and paste it on a page in your journal. Underneath your photo, write the date it was taken along with a fun caption describing the essence of the picture. Next, take a pen or marker and fill the page with words that describe who you are. Are you fun to be with, shy, optimistic? Are you motivated, stubborn, curious? List as many descriptive and feelings words as you can, words that describe you in general or words that are specific to the particular photo you pasted in.

Another option is to find a picture of someone you admire and paste it in your journal. Write his or her name and who he or she is next to it. Now fill the page with words that describe why you admire this person. Is this person intelligent? A leader? Resourceful? Courageous? Noble? Kind? Friendly? Spiritual? Generous? Supportive? Witty? Moral? Athletic? Does this person stand up for his or her beliefs? Have a positive attitude? Has he or she achieved greatness in spite of obstacles or personal odds? Is he or she striving to better humanity?

You can also look for a picture of someone who has the kind of career you imagine yourself having in the future. Now fill up the page with words you feel best describe the job. For example, if your dream is to become an MTV VJ, find a picture of a VJ in a magazine or draw one and surround it with words like Cool, CDs, Hip Outfits, Famous Recording Artists, Backstage Passes, Grammy's, Autographs, Concerts, Interviews.

Collages

Cut out pictures and words from magazines of things you like or things you dream about and paste them in your journal. The pictures you include can be random, like one of the bands you adore, a field of flowers in full bloom, an airplane on its way to Paris. Or you can create a collage around a central theme, such as:

- **How I See Myself in the Next Few Years.** These pictures may include things that symbolize different events like studying at college, living by the ocean or in a dorm, working at your first job, driving a car, studying abroad, meeting your first love, joining the Peace Corps, planning your wedding, or having a lot of friends.

- **My Hot Job.** Cut out pictures that represent a career you'd like to have. For example, if you've been considering becoming a wedding coordinator, fill a page of your journal with pictures of bridal gowns, bridesmaids' dresses, cakes, rings, churches, hotels, limos, place settings, restaurants, brides and grooms, menus, formal parties, bands, and honeymoon destinations like Hawaii and Mexico.

- **People I Admire.** Include anyone and everyone that you look up to. Perhaps it's your mom who works hard to support you, a missionary like Mother Teresa, a teacher, a world leader, a scientist, an actress, or a poet. When you're finished, the faces on this collage will probably mirror the values and characteristics that are important to you, the wonderful qualities in a person that make you take notice.

* * * * *

Got a pen? Get to work and unleash what's on your mind! Once you get started, you'll find that writing in a journal is an amazing process of discovery. Putting pen to paper is nourishing for the soul and a great way to learn about *you*—including your likes and dislikes, fears, dreams, and most personal thoughts and feelings. Finding yourself can lead to all sorts of revelations—everything from what makes your heart want to burst with excitement to the hot job that seems like it was tailor-made to match your talents and personality. You have so much to gain and nothing to lose when you embark on the road to journaling. Have fun and embrace the many discoveries along the way.

Find Out More!

The Creative Journal for Teens: Making Friends with Yourself by Lucia Capacchione (Franklin Lakes, NJ: New Page Books, 2001). A resource for discovering yourself through journal writing, this book gives you creative ways to achieve your goals. The journaling techniques will strengthen your identity and improve your confidence.

It's My Life! A Power Journal for Teens: A Workout for Your Mind by Tian Dayton (Deerfield Beach, FL: Health Communications, 2000). A hands-on workbook that guides you on a journey of self-exploration. Emphasizing the importance of having a healthy relationship with yourself, the book encourages you to examine your internal feelings and motivations with a new perspective. Understanding these aspects of yourself can help determine what you want from your future job and relationships. This knowledge empowers you to make good decisions, take positive action, and take charge of your life.

Life Strategies for Teens by Jay McGraw (New York: Simon & Schuster, 2000). A straightforward guide from a fellow teen that empowers you to take positive action in your life, this book discusses potential problems and attitudes that can inhibit your healthy development toward adulthood. Emphasizing that life changes with action, the book asks you to take a close look at your life, acknowledging both positive and negative aspects. Also check out the companion book *Life Strategies for Teens Workbook: Exercises and Self-Help Tests to Help You Change Your Life.*

Set Goals

Right now, your life is full of possibilities. Picture a huge blank scrapbook with your name engraved on the cover. What kind of memories, achievements, and milestones would you like to fill it with? Photos from your African safari? The Pulitzer Prize for a book penned by yours truly? Your face on the cover of *Time* magazine because you developed a cure for a deadly disease? Give it some thought, stretch your imagination—go crazy even! You have your entire life in front of you so don't put a limit on your dreams.

If you can envision it, chances are you can achieve it. If you can believe it, you can be it. But the question is, how do you get started? The answer: set goals and design a plan of action to reach them. One of the best reasons to set goals is that they'll take you where you want to go. To make your dreams come true, whether you want to go to college or become a rock star, goals are a necessary part of the equation. Setting and achieving goals will give you:

- purpose and direction
- a take-charge attitude
- a plan for action

- a sense of accomplishment
- a reason to celebrate
- the desire to challenge yourself with new goals

Setting goals has no downside and you just might unleash the potential to accomplish the great things you're capable of. When you decide on something you'd like to achieve and are ready to go for it, here are a few tips that will make it easier.

Get It In Writing

Putting your goal on paper makes it much more real. It's like making a written promise to yourself. And if it's important enough to write down, it should be important enough to take seriously.

A good way to record your goals is by using a journal or writing log. You can use your daily journal or create a special one designated for this purpose. The ideas you've just learned for journaling can get your pen flowing for goal-setting ideas as well. Collages, lists, and questions are all useful for helping you to develop clear, measurable, attainable goals. Put headings on pages such as "Personal Best" for personal goals, "School

Successes" for things you'd like to accomplish in school, or "Hot Job" to set up a plan for researching the career of your choice. Personalize the pages with doodles, photos, song lyrics, or quotes to inspire you and make it your own. Date your entries and put a completion date on each goal. That way you can review your progress, revise your plans, and continue setting new and improved goals.

Get Personal

Your goals are personal and reflect who you are. They are what your heart desires, not what your teacher, parent, or best friend has decided for you. If you choose a goal to make someone *else* proud or excited, you'll have trouble staying motivated. And when you're not all that crazy about the end result, it's difficult to stay focused on the work it will take to get there. There's nothing wrong with asking for the opinion or advice of someone you trust, but the goal you choose must be something that's important to *you*, something that *you'll* be proud of.

Get Specific

When you're deciding on a goal (or making a list of them) be specific about what you want. For example, saying, "I'd like to get better grades," is too vague. Achieving this goal leaves too much room for interpretation. Does this mean you need to improve your grades in all your classes or just some? Is going from a C- to a C okay, or does it need to go up a full grade? How long do you have to complete this goal? A goal that's more defined is saying you'd like to raise your grade in algebra from a C- to a B+ by the end of the quarter. Once your goal is clear, the steps you need to take to reach it are easier to map out. For instance, if you really did want to bring your algebra grade up to a B+, you could:

- talk to your teacher about suggestions for improving your grade
- find a tutor
- commit to studying an extra 45 minutes a day
- create a study group

Setting specific goals also gives you a way to chart your progress, so you can see how you're doing. If you simply say your goal is to get better grades, how do you know when you've achieved your goal or if you've been truly successful? When you say you want to earn a B+ in algebra by the end of the quarter, your success can easily be measured.

Don't Get Overwhelmed

Every dream-come-true began with a small step. The long-term goals you set for yourself are reached by taking many small steps—by setting short-term goals. Goals aren't reached overnight; it takes a lot of time and effort on your part to see them through. Overnight success doesn't happen even in Hollywood. Most actresses spend years working at their craft and face tons of rejections before they work regularly, much less reach celebrity stardom. If you research your favorite actress, chances are you'll discover that her journey began with small steps, whether it was signing up for her first acting class or auditioning for her first role.

No matter what your long-term goal may be, creating a plan with lots of small steps can make getting there seem less overwhelming. Suppose your dream job is to become a pediatrician. There are many small steps you can start taking now that will lead you in the right direction. For instance:

- Improve your study skills; excellent grades will be important from now until the time you graduate from medical school

- Take as many math and science classes as you can fit into your schedule

- Spend time with children to see if you enjoy interacting with them; volunteer to help in the childcare center at your place of worship or offer your services to a busy mom in your neighborhood

- Talk to your high school counselor about colleges and universities with good pre-med programs

- Start researching scholarships and their requirements

- Volunteer at a hospital or ask your doctor if you can spend a day with him or her to see if you like the medical environment

- Read books about the medical profession and what it's like to become a doctor

Get Real

Seeing the realization of your goals can be a long process. Some people spend their entire lives in pursuit of that ultimate dream, while others are fortunate to achieve success in their journey rather early, enabling them to seek out new challenges to tackle. But even if reaching your goal takes longer than you expect, the process of reaching it can be one filled with learning, growth, fun, and fulfillment. It all depends on how you choose to look at it. And who knows—that added anticipation may make reaching your final destination that much sweeter!

Should you fall short of your goals it's important to remember that it's not a reflection of who you are as a person. Sometimes what we aspire to is a little too large to grasp, or perhaps it wasn't something that was meant to be (in other words, you may discover you are better off without it!). Maybe you simply need to reexamine your approach and redefine smaller, more manageable steps in the process. Regardless of the outcome, whatever you achieve during the pursuit is still worthy of celebration, and you should always appreciate and commend yourself for the attempt.

Just as it takes courage and determination to continue pursuing a goal when you encounter obstacles, it takes those same qualities to rise to the challenge of letting go when you realize it's not going to happen. Courage helps you face that loss with grace, dignity, and inner resolve, while determination pushes you to take another risk or try something new, knowing in your heart that there's still a dream out there with your name on it. No matter what you decide to do—keep trying, let go, or change your plans— feel good about your decision. Who you are and who you've become during your journey can't be taken away from you. It's your choice to put the strength, new outlook, and lessons you've learned to positive use for the next challenges you will face.

When you're reaching that point of no return, when things look far too difficult and your dream seems out of reach, don't feel that you have to shoulder the burden alone. A trusted friend, teacher, mentor, coach, clergy member, parent, or sibling can be there for you to share your feelings of frustration, disappointment, wonder . . . whatever's on your mind. If your goal involves something related to school or your future career, consider turning to your school counselor or a college advisor. Not only does it take a load off to unburden your feelings, he or she may have some advice or insight that will open up a whole new realm of possibility for you. No matter what, you're never alone . . . whether it comes to celebrating a victory or accepting defeat.

Celebrate

The journey is just as important as the destination, so take time along the way to acknowledge the small steps you've accomplished. Didn't get the internship but you made it through the interview? Why not treat yourself to a small reward? Bake your favorite cookies, write a special thank-you note to someone who's been supportive of your efforts, or buy something small you've been saving for. Did you find a mentor and job shadow her for a day? Pamper yourself with a home spa night, have a movie night with your best friends, or pick some flowers from your yard and place them in a vase in your bedroom. Whatever the accomplishment, be proud of yourself. Every step counts and every one is worth a celebration!

* * * * *

Putting your dreams on paper and coming up with a plan to achieve them is one of the best tools to ensure that you get what you want out of life. It's important that the goals you set are personally meaningful and worth striving for. Once you've identified a goal and charted a plan of action to reach it, think of the steps to get there as an exciting adventure. Stay focused, motivated, flexible, and open to new challenges along the way. Reaching a goal is a great accomplishment and a reward in itself, but the best part is knowing that you have some control over your future when you take responsibility for it!

Find Out More!

 Any Girl Can Rule the World by Susan M. Brooks (Minneapolis: Fairview Press, 1998). This book is filled with ideas to help girls take charge of their lives. It contains resources, stories, and advice on setting goals, taking action, and using your voice to make a difference.

Hands On! 33 More Things Every Girl Should Know: Skills for Living Your Life from 33 Extraordinary Women edited by Suzanne Harper (New York: Crown Publishers, 2001). This is a book for teens who want to challenge themselves and prepare for the future. Stories, essays, and comics from 33 successful women in diverse fields provide practical advice for attaining goals and show what is possible with a little passion and effort.

Teens Can Make It Happen: Nine Steps to Success by Stedman Graham (New York: Simon & Schuster, 2000). Readers are guided to know themselves better so they can use their strengths and desires to make plans and achieve their visions. Graham drives home the point that we are not our circumstances, we are our possibilities.

What Do You Really Want? How to Set a Goal and Go for It! A Guide for Teens by Beverly K. Bachel (Minneapolis: Free Spirit Publishing, 2001). This book is a treasure chest of ideas and insights into setting and achieving goals. You'll learn how to assemble a Goal Tracker journal, and you'll discover how important clearly defined goals and a positive attitude are to successfully fulfilling your dreams.

Move Ahead

There's a saying that if you don't figure out what you want to do with your life, someone else will. No young woman wants to fall into the latter scenario, but even if you're comfortable with who you are and know your strengths and interests, how *exactly* do you figure out what you want to do?

Beyond questioning yourself, journaling, giving yourself time to think, and setting goals, there are lots of other ways to sort out the thousands of possibilities available to you. Some of them take a lot of time and energy, others take just a little. Some require significant planning, others don't. As you read this chapter, jot down ideas that come to you. Write about possible mentors, internships, and volunteer experiences you could pursue. Write down the names of people or job titles you'd like to read more about. Don't limit yourself to our ideas; come up with your own. Just as your career options are limitless, so are the routes that will get you there.

Stay in School

There's power in education. When you have knowledge, your future possibilities multiply *exponentially*. Having a solid background in the basics—reading, writing, math, science, and computers—is essential to success regardless of what path you choose to follow. The benefits of a good education will last you a lifetime; conversely, without an education, you'll have fewer opportunities, lower pay, less rewarding work, and a higher rate of unemployment. What you learn in school will give you the foundation to build your life upon, so soak up all that you can.

Sticking it out in school can sometimes be tough, especially if your classes are too difficult or too boring, or if other responsibilities in your life are pulling you in lots of different directions. Don't give up! Before you take drastic measures such as quitting school, reach out for help. Meet with your teachers and tell them about the difficulties you're having. They might be willing to spend extra time with you before or after school. Or talk to a counselor or an advisor; he or she may have information about tutoring that can help bring you up to speed. You may find that someone in your community, a family member, or fellow or former students can provide the help you need to clear the hurdles in your way.

You also can try changing your class schedule so your enthusiasm is re-ignited. Discuss your hopes for the future with your counselor. He or she can suggest courses you might find more interesting or manageable that still fulfill graduation requirements. In some instances, a counselor may suggest a different school for you. More and more specialty high schools are popping up—for example, schools that focus on the arts, technology, or science, or vocational high schools, business high schools, and many others. They aren't right for everyone, but one may be right for you.

Talking with a favorite teacher or school counselor may help you realize that the things you're learning in your classes have long-range importance, too. For example, trigonometry may seem like a foreign language, but if your ultimate goal is to become an architect, it's probably a prerequisite for the specialty training program or upper-division class you'll eventually need to take. You may not understand why you have to take an art class when your plan is to become an auto mechanic, but your counselor can point out that drawing figures and diagrams to explain the inner workings of a car is both standard and beneficial. Sometimes knowing that the classes you're taking *do* have a purpose can make all the difference in the world.

Opening up to your parents or a sympathetic friend or relative is another thing that can help when school seems difficult. It can be tough juggling all your responsibilities at home (like watching a younger sibling, taking care of the yard, or handling chores like cooking and cleaning), finding time to study, going to sports practice, thinking about your future, and finding some time to hang out with friends or relax. Sharing your concerns, frustrations, and feelings can help put things in perspective. Your confidants might be able to offer helpful suggestions. Improving your time management skills, lessening the load of things you're trying to do, or simply vocalizing your frustration could make it easier to handle the demands you're facing.

Lastly, remember that finishing high school is really a short-term goal in the overall scheme of things. Earning your diploma is a major step toward anything you may want for the future and it will be over before you know it (actually, you'll probably be left wondering where the time went!). School is a place to learn, make new friends, meet challenges, have fun, play sports, join clubs, develop social and team-building skills, have your questions answered, and prepare for higher education, such as college or trade school. When you look back in 10 years, you'll be glad you stuck it out.

Meet with Your School Counselor

A convenient resource to help you figure out where you want to go in life is your high school counselor. Make an appointment to discuss ideas or goals you may have about your future career. Guidance counselors have access to information about college and university programs, trade and technical schools, scholarships, internships, potential mentors, and leads on part-time jobs. They can also help you plan which classes to take and which extracurricular activities will best optimize your chances of getting into the college or trade school of your choice.

A school counselor can also help prepare a résumé. A résumé is a wonderful chance to pat yourself on the back and celebrate your accomplishments; it lists your academic achievements and experiences, job history, involvement in clubs and community service projects, extracurricular activities, hobbies, interests, and skills—everything about you that would be of interest to a potential employer, college, or vocational admissions representative. If you've never composed a résumé, it can seem a bit intimidating, so turn to your school counselor for help with drafting a personal history you can be proud of.

Open Your Mind

The steps you take when you're trying to figure out your future don't have to be big. In fact, inspiration can happen in the comfort of your own neighborhood, school, or home. Try the following suggestions and your future may open wider and quicker than you had ever imagined.

One way to discover what path you'd like to follow is by trying new things. It's never too early to open your mind to all of the amazing possibilities the world has to offer. Experience life. Explore as much as you can. Discover your talents. Learn a new skill. Volunteer at a charitable organization. Become a detective and find the answers to things you've been curious about. How good of an athlete do I need to be to try out for the track team? Where can I learn to play the guitar? How are feature films made? What does the future hold for our space program? As a woman, what new ground can I break? No matter what you choose to do, set your sights high, and get ready to soar in the direction your heart leads you.

Read, Read, Read

Books open up a world of knowledge. Whether it's a fictional tale or a factual account, there's always something to be gained from turning the page. And you never know where newfound information will lead you. You may be so uplifted by an inspiring story, you can hardly contain your enthusiasm. A subject you'd never thought about may pique your curiosity. Or you may find the solution to a problem that's been bothering you. Reading about the experiences of women who have traveled a path similar to one you are considering might give you the motivation to take that first step. The lessons you can learn from the successes and shortcomings of women like Sally Ride, the first woman in space, or Shannon Faulkner, the first woman admitted to the Citadel Academy (Military College of South Carolina), are invaluable. Take their advice and example and use it to fine-tune your own goals and ideas. Allow their words and wisdom to give you the strength and conviction to reach for the stars.

Helpful reading isn't limited to books; magazines and newspapers are great for finding short, quick, up-to-the-minute news and information. What's hot, what's not, breaking stories, global issues, interviews, human-interest stories, fashion, entertainment, fitness, food, computers, the Web, sports, architecture, medicine, and just about any other topic you can imagine can be found in a magazine or newspaper. Check out the bookstore, library, or newsstand to see how many different types of magazines and newspapers are available. Peruse to your heart's delight!

Surf the World Wide Web

The Internet is an electronic universe loaded with a wealth of information that didn't exist when your parents were thinking about careers. It provides a fast and fun way to learn about any topic you can think of. There are sites that will educate you, sites where you can chat with other teens who have similar issues and concerns, sites to help you with your homework, and sites to learn about careers. This information super-highway can also lead you to organizations that will help with everything from applying for college scholarships to finding help for eating disorders.

If you're already tech-savvy, you know the drill. If you're new to the Web, be bold and log on (you may be able to gain access at your local library or school). To get started, log onto one of the many helpful Web sites listed throughout this book. Or type a keyword in a search engine and see where it takes you. If you need help, check in with a tech-savvy friend or your school or local librarian.

A word of caution: Not all Web sites are created equal and not all are appropriate for young people to view. Although a lot of valuable information is on the Net, there is also inappropriate material as well. Your parents or teacher may have guidelines or restrictions they'd like you to follow when you surf. Talk to them before you explore.

Get Real-World Experience

Books, magazines, and Web sites are great learning tools, but there's no substitute for real-world experience. The only way to know for sure what you like or what you're good at is to get out in the world and try things. You've got to put yourself out there to make your dreams a reality. Get involved. Join a school club, participate in student government, volunteer, try out for a sports team, play an instrument, apply for a part-time job, or lend a hand at your place of worship. Activities like these will help you develop confidence, improve your interpersonal skills, and they look good on college applications and résumés, too. Live life to the fullest!

Make a list of the things that are important to you in a job or career, both now and in the future. Use your list to help determine if a particular job has what you're looking for. You may find that you're willing to compromise on certain things, but not on others. You might also find that your priorities change over time. Here are some ideas to get you going:

- Salary range

- Work setting—indoor vs. outdoor, formal vs. informal, office vs. nonoffice

- Flexible hours

- Evenings or weekends off

- Working on your own vs. being in a group work environment

- Fun

- Travel

- Creative freedom

- Close supervision vs. autonomy

- Protecting or helping the environment

- Making a contribution to society

Use this list as a starting point for your search, and make adjustments to it as you learn more and have new experiences.

Volunteer

Offer your time and services to those who need it. It's good for the spirit, it gives you a chance to contribute to the community, it's a fun way to meet new people (including mentors), and it looks good on college and job applications. Giving your time freely demonstrates that you're willing to work for something you believe in. Volunteering is also an ideal way to explore potential careers. Spending time in a hospital, for example, may help you decide if becoming a nurse is something you really want to pursue. It may also give you something entirely new to think about, such as becoming a physical therapist or a doctor—or you may decide the medical profession is not right for you.

There are many different organizations that could use your special talents and skills. Here are some places in your community that may need a volunteer like you.

If you like being around people, consider volunteering at:

- a place of worship
- a nursing home
- a childcare center
- a retirement center
- a day camp
- an elementary school
- the Boys and Girls Club
- the YMCA/YWCA
- the Girl Scouts of America
- a hospital
- a recreation or community center

If you like animals, consider volunteering at:

- a veterinary clinic
- an animal shelter
- a zoo
- an aquarium
- a ranch/farm
- an equestrian center
- an animal training facility
- a grooming salon

If you love being outdoors, consider volunteering at:

- a botanical society
- a national or local park
- a ranger station
- a beach or other environmental clean-up area
- the conservation corps
- an environmental organization
- an outdoor education facility
- a nature center

If working to better humanity is your calling, consider volunteering at:

- a place of worship
- a food bank
- a homeless shelter
- a hospital or clinic
- a blood drive
- a community recycling center
- a political fundraising event
- a childcare center

Find a Mentor

A mentor is someone who can offer you guidance in some or all facets of your life. A mentor is someone who can teach you, provide emotional support, help you with moral dilemmas, help you meet challenges and tackle obstacles, offer advice, guide you with personal decisions, and impart wisdom. A mentor is someone you can turn to when you need help. Many exceptional people have benefited from mentor relationships, for example, Michelle Kwan from coach Frank Carroll, Oprah Winfrey from poet and author Maya Angelou, and Helen Keller from teacher Annie Sullivan.

If you'd like to find someone to serve as a mentor to you, you can pursue several routes. One is to consider somebody who's had a big influence on your life. This person can be anyone who you feel would make a good role model, such as a teacher, a relative, a spiritual leader, a friend of your parents, a senior citizen, an older student, a coach, a neighbor, or anyone else that has the time to offer you direction and encouragement.

Another way to find a mentor is through organizations such as the Boys and Girls Club or the Big Brother, Big Sister program. They offer support in all kinds of ways to those who need it. You can also find mentors by networking. Talk with your friends, neighbors, and relatives. Do they know people who have similar interests as you or work in a field you want to pursue? Don't be afraid to ask, something good could come of it.

You don't have to limit yourself to a mentor who you'll work with directly. A mentor can be anyone—someone you've read about whose actions have inspired you, such as Golda Meir, who served the people of Israel as their Prime Minister, or Mother Teresa, who tirelessly took care of the ill and poor of Calcutta, India. He or she could be an actor who donates a lot of time, a sports celebrity who is top in his or her game, or a famous musician who overcame all kinds of obstacles.

If you're interested in hooking up with a mentor, you need to be ready to take action. Once you identify someone who qualifies, you have to summon your courage to talk to him or her. Tell your potential mentor about yourself—your hopes, dreams, and goals for the future. Explain what his or her experience or knowledge means to you, and ask if you could spend some time together, or simply call or email from time to time. You may even request to job shadow him or her at work. Most people are flattered to have someone interested in what they have to offer, and chances are your potential mentor will be, too.

If the person you admire is out of reach (someone famous or deceased), become a student of that person. Read all you can about him or her, surf the Web, and share thoughts and ideas with others who know or knew of the person. Learn everything you can about your mentor including his or her life philosophy, motivations, inspirations, achievements, struggles, and strategies for dealing with obstacles. Whether you have direct contact or not, immerse yourself in what your mentor has to offer, such as lessons, advice, and past experiences. Let your mentor's words and deeds help motivate you in your own quest.

Network

Networking is all about talking to people who can point you in the right direction on your career path, and it's an incredibly valuable skill. Put the word out to anyone you can think of—relatives, friends, classmates, teachers, neighbors—that you're interested in learning about a particular career or topic. They may know someone who knows someone and before you know it, you've started your own network of connections.

Networking can definitely improve your communication skills, which are essential to both asking the right questions and successfully "selling" yourself. Asking someone to tell you about their job takes courage and confidence. The more practice you have at posing questions, the better you'll become at selecting the right ones to ask—those that will lead to valuable answers. Refer back to your career priorities checklist (see page 262) and ask about things like hours, perks and rewards, daily pressures, and job availability or outlook for the future. Also ask about some of the not-so-fun realities of the job. Every job has its drudgeries, and it's helpful to have a balanced picture in order to make a good decision.

If conversations with your network contact go well, ask if you can spend time observing him or her on the job. Being in a work environment is a good way to find out what really goes on in that line of work. You may find a career that you thought sounded like fun isn't at all what you imagined. Or you could get an even bigger jolt of excitement than you had before.

Find an Internship

An internship offers you the opportunity to go beyond what's offered in a classroom setting or what's on paper to learn something about a particular job, business, or organization—a "learn-and-work" situation. Not only is the experience you gain incredibly valuable, it might save you a lot of time and trouble later when you're making a major decision about the career path you want to take. Interning allows you to explore a career and find out if it is something you are interested in pursuing further.

The benefits of an internship include:

- hands-on experience in a real work environment

- the chance to learn the ins and outs of a business or organization

- an opportunity to see if you like working in a specific field or setting

- contact with people who could become mentors, references, or future employers

- getting your foot in the door . . . and maybe putting you a few steps ahead of other candidates if you apply for a permanent position later

- learning about things you wouldn't ordinarily learn at school or from a textbook

- improved confidence in your skills and abilities

Interns don't simply observe, they have actual tasks and responsibilities. Some internships can be very challenging, like working on a political campaign or in a hospital laboratory. Others may have you doing things that regular employees don't have time for (for example, filing, photocopying, and mail sorting). Though your responsibilities may seem small, everything you do will teach you about the field and contribute to the project you're working on. Once you feel you've mastered the duties you've been given and are ready for bigger challenges, talk to your supervisor; there's no doubt he or she can come up with more for you to do! The best way to ensure that you're going to have the experience you're looking for is by doing a lot of research and asking questions before you interview or accept a position. But remember, even the most menial tasks may be a necessary part of a particular job, and getting a handle on those types of tasks early could make you more qualified when a regular, full-time or part-time position opens up.

So how do you know if an internship is right for you? Requirements in terms of previous experience, educational background, and hours vary from program to program, so it's important that you do your research. However, your enthusiasm, willingness to learn, and positive attitude are the best qualifications. While some internships do offer a small salary (called a stipend), most don't. The length of time you're required to stay varies as well, but the majority last for at least one semester (and many qualify for school credit). Use the ideas for possible volunteering options on page 263 and the lists you made on page 247 to give you a clearer picture of the type of internship you're looking for. Your school guidance counselor or the career center at a local college or university can also help you find something in an area that interests you. If you're curious about a particular field or organization, do some research of your own. Go to a library or bookstore and check out the internship directories (see also the "Find Out More!" section on page 270). Call information, check your local phone book, or surf the Internet to find a company, an association, or a cause you would like to become involved with. Tell them you're interested in an internship; if they have a program in place, get more information. If they don't, they may still be interested in you if you tell them your goals. Put your enthusiasm to work!

Become an Apprentice

An apprenticeship is very similar to an internship. The main difference is that apprentices generally get paid to learn a trade or craft by working side-by-side with a master craftsperson, technician, or supervisor. The U.S. Department of Labor sponsors youth programs for students under 18 years old in addition to regular apprenticeships (state and local employment agencies also sponsor these). Apprenticeships can be found in many different fields, including cooking, design, contracting, construction, computer programming, and many more. Some positions also require you to attend classes at a trade school, vocational school, or community college at the same time.

Searching for a job as an apprentice is similar to trying to land an internship or volunteer position—it's important that you do your research. Decide what type of work you want to do and then research your apprenticeship possibilities. Call around, write, or look on the Internet. Talk with your guidance counselor or search your local library. The benefits of an apprenticeship are similar to an internship—with the added bonus of being paid while you work. It's possible that as you progress through your training your pay will increase, too. When you complete your apprenticeship, you may be granted a certificate of Occupational Proficiency or some other official certification of your new level of competency. If you don't plan to attend a four-year college, this type of experience can give you a head start into a better paying career.

Get a Job

If earning money is a high priority, a part-time job—after school, on the weekends, or during school breaks—is another option. You'll gain valuable work experience and job skills, whether they're general (like working with customers or making a schedule for other employees) or specific to your career goal (such as interacting with kids or choosing merchandise for a new display). As you begin your search for employment, remember that it's possible to find a part-time job you truly enjoy. Consider the options previously mentioned for volunteering, internships, and apprenticeships. The same businesses or organizations may have an opening that fits your schedule and pay requirements, or perhaps reviewing these options will give you some ideas about other businesses you can approach for a paying job.

Interviewing

Whether you're applying for a paying job, an internship, or a volunteer position, you'll have to go through a type of interview. Some companies have more formal approaches to interviewing, others are very casual. The interview process—talking with the person who does the hiring—is something you'll encounter in many different forms as you make your way to your hot job. Other situations that may require an interview include applying for college, a specialty training program, scholarships, or grants. Because interviews are inevitable, and it's better to be prepared, here are some tips to help you make the best possible impression:

- Be professional—dress appropriately. This means no ratty jeans, shorts, mini skirts, or tennis shoes! Wear something that's slightly nicer than what you would be wearing to work at the job you're applying for. Also, avoid lots of jewelry, makeup, and perfume.

- Be friendly—firmly shake your interviewer's hand, look the person in the eye, smile, and say thank you as you leave.

- Be relaxed—sit up straight, don't cross your arms, and don't do things like wringing your hands, twirling your hair, or biting your fingernails. And definitely NO GUM!

- Be prepared—arrive with your résumé, references (check with anyone you plan to list as a reference to make sure they're okay with being listed), and pad and pen to take notes.

- Be ready—think about possible questions you may be asked before you get there and practice answering them. Some likely questions are: Why do you want this job? Do you have any experience doing this type of work? What motivates you? What are your plans for the future? What are your strengths and weaknesses?

- Be honest and straightforward—both about what you can and can't do.

- Be on time—period!

- Be inquisitive—think about some questions you'd like to ask if given the opportunity: What will I be doing? What are the hours and days I would be working? How will I be trained? If I do well, will I be able to gain more responsibility?

Going on an interview doesn't have to be a terrifying experience. You're bound to be nervous; it can be a little scary to sit with someone you've never met and talk about yourself. The best approach is to be prepared, confident, and enthusiastic. If you don't get the position, move on to another. There are a lot of reasons why people do—and don't—get hired for a job. Just file the experience away in your mind and use it to better approach the next one. If you're comfortable doing it, you might even call the interviewer back at a place where you were turned down and ask for feedback on your interviewing skills.

* * * * *

With the five keys to success—imagination, confidence, willingness to take risks, courage, and determination—firmly in hand, the future is yours for the taking. And as you've read, there are many ways to get there. As you make your way toward your ultimate destination—the hot job that's waiting out there for you—enjoy yourself! Stay well-rounded by getting involved in extracurricular activities that are just for fun. Keep healthy by exercising regularly . . . it's good for your body *and* your mind. Experience all of the wonderful things life has to offer. The more you know and have enjoyed, the better prepared you'll be to make confident decisions about your future.

While it's true you need to have a clue about where you're headed in life, nothing is etched in stone. As you plan for your future, don't obsess about it. Be open to new things, new possibilities, new paths. Don't be afraid to talk to people who have had interesting experiences or whose opinion you trust. The women you have read about in *Cool Women, Hot Jobs* have hopefully piqued your curiosity and inspired you. Now get out there and discover other women who are living their dreams, too—maybe one day a young woman will approach you to let you know what an inspiration you've been to her!

Find Out More!

Ferguson's Guide to Apprenticeship Programs edited by Elizabeth H. Oakes (Chicago: Ferguson, 1998). This resource lists 7,500 programs in 52 job categories, helping teens locate apprenticeships and on-the-job training. Includes profiles of previous participants, application instructions, and advice for evaluating programs based on individual interest.

The Girl Pages: A Handbook of the Best Resources for Strong, Confident, Creative Girls by Charlotte Milholland (New York: Hyperion, 1999). This all-inclusive resource is filled with information to help you develop your interests and skills and discover what you love. Books, Web sites, organizations, and more put you in contact with people who can help you in your quest.

The Internship Bible by Mark Olman and Samer Hamadeh (New York: Random House, 2001). Including more than 100,000 opportunities, this resource provides information and brief descriptions on internships available all over the country.

The Pathfinder: How to Choose or Change Your Career for a Lifetime of Satisfaction and Success by Nicholas Lore (New York: Simon & Schuster, 1998). For beginners about to embark on their career path as well as seasoned professionals considering a job change, this book is designed to help you choose or change your career so you will be satisfied and successful.

Peterson's Summer Jobs for Students 2002 (Princeton, NJ: Peterson's Guides, 2001). Holding a summer job in an enjoyable field, like holding internships and volunteering, can prepare you for the career that you want. This book documents summer jobs across the United States and Canada, detailing specifics like benefits, training, and résumés.

The Teenagers' Guide to School Outside the Box by Rebecca Greene (Minneapolis: Free Spirit Publishing, 2001). This book is for young people who feel "boxed in" by the high school experience. You'll learn ways to gain knowledge and understanding of yourself and the world through volunteering, studying abroad, internships, and more.

Your First Resume: For Students and Anyone Preparing to Enter Today's Tough Job Market by Ron Fry (Franklin Lakes, NJ: Career Press, 2001). Featuring advice, easy-to-use forms, and sample resumes and cover letters, this book gives all the help novice job hunters will need to construct a powerful resume and get the jobs they desire.

Council on International Education Exchange
633 Third Avenue, 20th Floor • New York, NY 10017 • 1-800-407-8839
www.ciee.org
This organization aims to help people acquire knowledge and understanding of the world and develop skills for living in a globally interdependent and cultural diverse atmosphere. It can help anyone find the international journey that's right for them.

National Mentoring Partnership
1600 Duke Street, Suite 300 • Alexandria, VA 22314 • (703) 224-2200
www.mentoring.org
This organization brings mentoring into the lives of people nationwide, helping adults and youth connect. Find tips at the Web site for finding and being a mentor, state and community mentoring resources, and helpful advice on the mentoring process.

Index

About the Authors

Tina Schwager, a Certified Athletic Trainer since 1987, has worked at the clinical, Olympic, professional, high school, and University levels helping people reach their goals of improved health, fitness, and sports performance. She specializes in developing training programs for professional and amateur baseball players. Tina has been active her whole life, running competitively in high school, teaching exercise classes for over 15 years, and working out regularly for fun and fitness.

Michele Schuerger has used her degree in Communication Studies to build a successful career in the entertainment industry. She is currently a Vice President at an advertising agency. Michele believes her involvement in sports— she was a competitive figure skater for eight years and continues to exercise regularly—helped give her the courage and determination to pursue her dream of writing books.

Tina and Michele are the coauthors of *The Right Moves: A Girls' Guide to Getting Fit and Feeling Good* and *Gutsy Girls: Young Women Who Dare,* both published by Free Spirit Publishing. They also have written numerous articles on fitness, conditioning, and goal setting for major magazines, journals, and newsletters. Their desire to inspire young girls to greatness, combined with their love of writing, has helped them create their dream job—becoming published authors!

More Great Books from Free Spirit

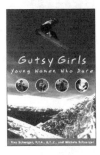

Visit us on the Web!
www.freespirit.com

Stop by anytime to find our Parents' Choice Approved catalog with fast, easy, secure 24-hour online ordering; "Ask Our Authors," where visitors ask questions—and authors give answers—on topics important to children, teens, parents, teachers, and others who care about kids; links to other Web sites we know and recommend; fun stuff for everyone, including quick tips and strategies from our books; and much more! Plus our site is completely searchable so you can find what you need in a hurry. Stop in and let us know what you think!

Just point and click!

new! Get the first look at our books, catch the latest news from Free Spirit, and check out our site's newest features.

contact Do you have a question for us or for one of our authors? Send us an email. Whenever possible, you'll receive a response within 48 hours.

order! Order in confidence! Our secure server uses the most sophisticated online ordering technology available. And ordering online is just one of the ways to purchase our books: you can also order by phone, fax, or regular mail. No matter which method you choose, excellent service is our ultimate goal.

1.800.735.7323 • fax 612.337.5050 • help4kids@freespirit.com

If you liked **COOL WOMEN, HOT JOBS,** you'll also like **BOY V. GIRL?** and **MORE THAN A LABEL.**

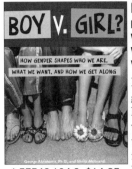

1-57542-104-6, $14.95

BOY V. GIRL?
How Gender Shapes Who We Are, What We Want, and How We Get Along

Is it *really* a boy v. girl world? Does it have to be? Find out what teens *really* think about the differences between boys and girls!

1-57542-110-0, $13.95

MORE THAN A LABEL
Why What You Wear or Who You're With Doesn't Define Who You Are

Freak. Prep. Goth. Loser. Teens share the truth behind the label: what hurts, what helps, and what anyone can do to make a difference.

Call 1-800-735-7323 to order or mail this card for a FREE catalog!

Send me a Free Spirit catalog! (I am a ❑ teen ❑ teacher ❑ parent)

name (please print) _____

street _____

city/state/zip _____

email _____

Visit *www.freespirit.com* to download excerpts, quizzes, and more!

Want to know more about **MAKING POSITIVE CHOICES, COPING WITH CHALLENGES, KEEPING IT TOGETHER, and MAKING A DIFFERENCE?**

Free Spirit can help! We're the award-winning source of Self-Help for Kids® and Self-Help for Teens®. We know the issues young people face, and we have the information and tips you need to succeed. Mail this card for a FREE catalog. (And have one sent to a friend!)

Send me a Free Spirit catalog! (I am a ❑ teen ❑ teacher ❑ parent)

name (please print) _____

street _____

city/state/zip _____

email _____

and send one to: (He/She is a ❑ teen ❑ teacher ❑ parent)

name (please print) _____

street _____

city/state/zip _____

email _____

Visit *www.freespirit.com* to download excerpts, quizzes, and more!

Is it *really* a boy v. girl world?

BUSINESS REPLY MAIL

FIRST-CLASS MAIL   PERMIT NO. 26589   MINNEAPOLIS MN

POSTAGE WILL BE PAID BY ADDRESSEE

free spirit PUBLiSHiNG®
217 Fifth Avenue North, Suite 200
Minneapolis, MN 55401-9776

Free Spirit Publishing
Your SELF-HELP FOR TEENS®
source for over 19 years.

BUSINESS REPLY MAIL

FIRST-CLASS MAIL   PERMIT NO. 26589   MINNEAPOLIS MN

POSTAGE WILL BE PAID BY ADDRESSEE

free spirit PUBLiSHiNG®
217 Fifth Avenue North, Suite 200
Minneapolis, MN 55401-9776